# Great Cooks

## and Their Recipes

## From Taillevent to Escoffier

# McGraw-Hill Book Company

New York   San Francisco   St. Louis   Kuala Lumpur
Montreal   São Paulo   Toronto

# Great Cooks

## and Their Recipes
### From Taillevent to Escoffier

## by Anne Willan

Library of Congress Cataloging in
Publication Data

Willan, Anne.
    Great cooks and their recipes.

    Bibliography
    Includes indexes.
    1. Cookery, International—History.
    2. Cooks.
I. Title.
TX725.A1W46    641.5′9    77–4372
ISBN 0–07–070269–1


A McGraw-Hill Co-Publication
Printed in Switzerland

Composition by:
JOLLY & BARBER LTD.
England

Photolithography by:
FOTO-LITHO HEGO AG, LITTAU
Switzerland

Printed by:
HERTIG & CO. AG, BIEL
Switzerland

Bound by:
GROLLIMUND AG, REINACH
Switzerland

# A MASTER COOK

A master-cook! why, he's the man of men,
For a professor! he designs, he draws,
He paints, he carves, he builds, he fortifies,
Makes citadels of curious fowl and fish,
Some he dry-dishes, some motes round with broths;
Mounts marrow bones, cuts fifty-angled custards,
Rears bulwark pies, and for his outer works,
He raiseth ramparts of immortal crust;
And teacheth all the tactics, at one dinner:
What ranks, what files, to put his dishes in;
The whole art military. Then he knows
The influence of the stars upon his meats,
And all their seasons, tempers, qualities,
And so to fit his relishes and sauces.
He has nature in a pot, 'bove all the chymists,
Or airy brethren of the Rosie-cross.
He is an architect, an engineer,
A soldier, a physician, a philosopher,
A general mathematician.

Lickfinger in Ben Jonson's
"The Staple of News" (1631)

# CONTENTS

*For Mark*

who fathered the idea and brought it to fruition. For the three chapters on the Italian cooks, I owe a special debt to Elisabeth Evans, who skillfully researched the source materials and guided me through unfamiliar territory. I am most grateful to Margo Miller for helping me with the two chapters on the American cooks, and to John Bowle for his comments on the manuscript. I have had equally generous and professional support from Jenny Turtle, who did the picture research, and from Sheryl Julian and Jenie Wright, who tested the recipes. To you all, many thanks.

In the long history of cooking, the first professional whose name is still remembered is Taillevent, master chef in medieval times to an imposing roll of French royal households. Many before him had extolled the pleasures of good eating, but Taillevent's book *Le Viandier* marks the beginning of cooking as we know it; from his time on a succession of cooks and cookbooks records the development of the art.

Taillevent—his real name was Guillaume Tirel, but many apprentices in those days picked up nicknames that they never outgrew—must have been quite a character, for a remarkable amount is known about him in an age when most craftsmen, like the builders of the Gothic cathedrals, passed forgotten into history. In 1326, when he was about fourteen, he was a *happelapin* (kitchen boy) to Queen Jeanne

*Like all kitchen boys, Taillevent began his career as turnspit.*

of France and was charged with the unenviable task of turning the great roasting spits before the open fire. By 1346 Taillevent had risen to *keu* (cook) to King Philip VI, and in 1349 he was granted a house "in consideration of the good and pleasant service the king has received." Soon after, he was raised to the rank of *écuyer*, or squire, and passed from household to household within the Valois family until, in 1381, he was at the top of his profession as master cook to King Charles VI. He probably compiled *Le Viandier* a few years earlier with the encouragement of King Charles V, known as Charles the Wise for his fine judgment and cultivated tastes.

Today, the style of cooking described by Taillevent in *Le Viandier* seems strange. Where we try to develop the flavor and texture of ingredients to the full, medieval cooks pounded and puréed them out of all recognition, then spiced them in such profusion that the original taste was lost. There were very good reasons for this. Food was often so stale

Opposite:
*The medieval Duc de Berry dines in royal style in a setting which Taillevent, as cook to the Valois kings, knew well. In front of the duke stands the carver, about to dismember a platter of little birds, while beside him is the server who would taste each dish to guard against poison. At the end of the table the pantler trims the trenchers—the slices of bread used instead of plates—and beside him a tonsured priest prepares to say grace.*

9

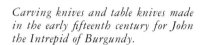

as to be almost rotten; it needed to be pounded and then disguised by strong spices or cheered up with coloring. The golden yellow of saffron was the favorite, but medieval cooks also brightened their drab purées with sandalwood (for red), herbs (for green), and mulberries (for blue).

Also, then as now, there was food snobbery. A pound of saffron cost as much as a horse, but this did not deter Taillevent from using it in more than half his recipes. The caviar of the day were spices like nutmeg, worth seven fat oxen per pound.

Taillevent also used a basic spice, *poudre fin*, resembling curry powder. In fact, modern Indian

*Carving knives and table knives made in the early fifteenth century for John the Intrepid of Burgundy.*

*This dinner for a German nobleman illustrates the medieval convention of placing banquet tables at right angles to*

*The gold cup of the kings of England and France, presented in 1391 by the Duke de Berry to Taillevent's master, Charles VI of France. Like all cups of the time it is covered to guard against poison.*

*the high table, although in order to show the lord's face the artist has seated him with his back to the room. The saltcellar at the lord's left was designed not only to display a valuable commodity, but also to distinguish the host; anyone not seated at the high table was thus "below the salt."*

cookery probably comes closest to medieval, not only in its generous use of spices, but also in its habit of heightening flavor with sweet and acid ingredients. Savory dishes were often seasoned with sugar as well as *vin aigre* (vinegar, literally sour wine) or *verjus*, made from the juice of any tart fruit. Sugar was treated as a seasoning like salt and often sprinkled on a dish at the end of cooking. In fact, there was no distinction between sweet and savory dishes, and regardless of taste they were all placed on the table

Some of Taillevent's recipes are little more than lists of ingredients strung together with a few instructions, but many are more detailed, giving a clear outline of medieval cooking methods and finished dishes. Salt is often lacking from his recipes, partly because it was a valuable commodity usually sprinkled at the table according to individual taste and rank, and partly because so many meats were already salted through preservation in brine. Some of the following recipes may therefore require salt, although to some extent the other medieval flavorings will compensate for its omission.

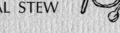

## Civé de veel

Civet, meaning stew, is still a common French dish, though we would call Taillevent's recipe a curry. The sauce is thickened with breadcrumbs or with a purée of peas, in much the same way that legumes are added to give body to curries in southern India. Grain of paradise is a pepper-flavored variety of cardamom, and verjuice is tart fruit juice.

*Roast on the spit or on the grill without cooking the meat too much, cut it in pieces and let it fry in fat in a casserole, and cut onion very finely and fry with it, then take toasted bread softened in wine and beef bouillon or purée of peas and bring to a boil with your meat; then prepare ginger, cinnamon, clove, grain of paradise and saffron to give it color, and dilute with verjuice and vinegar; and let it be well thickened, and plenty of onions, and the bread be browned, and all piquant with vinegar and highly spiced; and it should be yellow.*

## VEAL STEW

FOR THE THICKENING:

3 slices bread
¾ cup (2 dl) red or white wine
1 cup (2.5 dl) beef stock

OR

¼ cup (60g) dried split green peas soaked overnight in water and drained
1½ cups (4 dl) water
pepper

FOR THE STEW:

2 tablespoons lard or oil
2-pound (1 kg) piece boneless shoulder or leg of veal
4 medium onions, finely chopped
2 teaspoons ground ginger
2 teaspoons ground cinnamon
½ teaspoon ground cloves
seeds of 1 cardamom pod
pinch of saffron
salt and pepper
2-3 tablespoons verjuice (see below)
2-3 tablespoons vinegar

The stew was originally served on a thick slice of bread (a trencher), but today most people would probably prefer rice as an accompaniment. This recipe serves 4.

FOR THE THICKENING: If using bread with wine and stock, bake the bread in a low oven (300°F or 150°C) for 30 minutes or until well browned. Let cool, and grind it to fine crumbs a little at a time in a blender, or work it through a grinder. Stir in the wine, let stand 5 minutes until the crumbs are soft, then add the beef stock. If using dried peas, simmer them, covered, in the water for 1½–2 hours or until very soft. Purée the mixture in a blender or work it through a sieve; it should be thick but still pour easily. Season to taste with salt and pepper.

FOR THE STEW: Sear the veal over an open flame, preferably charcoal, so the outside is slightly charred; cut it in 1-inch cubes. In a casserole, heat the lard or oil and fry half the veal until browned on all sides. Take out, fry the remaining veal, and remove it. Add the onions and cook until soft but not brown. Put back the meat, pour over the bread and wine mixture or the pea purée, cover, and bring to a boil. Stir a few spoonsful of the sauce into a mixture of the ginger, cinnamon, cloves, cardamom, and saffron, and stir this mixture back into the meat. Add salt and pepper, cover, and simmer on top of the stove or cook in a moderately low oven (325°F or 163°C) for 1–1½ hours or until the meat is very tender. Stir in the verjuice and vinegar, adding more to taste (the amount needed depends on their tartness).

TO MAKE VERJUICE: Work tart grapes, tart apples, crab apples, or any other tart or unripe fruit through a vegetable mill or strainer, or use a blender to obtain the sour juice; strain if necessary.

*With a little ingenuity, a whole meal can be cooked in a medieval caldron: meat, taking the longest cooking, is immersed in water at the bottom with a plank on top to prevent floating. On the plank is set a crock containing vegetables to be steamed, while a pudding in a cloth is suspended from the handle on a string.*

## Gornault, rouget, grimodin

These are three similar types of mullet. Taillevent suggests poaching and serving them with a favorite medieval spiced sauce called *cameline*, which resembles a relish. Alternatively, he describes how to broil them while basting with verjuice and spices, exactly as fish is barbecued today. Long pepper is a variety of the vine from which peppercorns come, not related to chili peppers which came from the New World about 150 years later.

*Clean the stomach of the fish, and wash them well, then put them in the pan, with salt on top, then water, and cook them; and eat them with cameline sauce; or, if you wish, the shoulders should be split along the back, and then wash them, and put them to roast, plunge them often in verjuice and spice powder.*

### Cameline

*Pound ginger, plenty of cinnamon, clove, cardamom, mace, long pepper if you like, then sieve bread soaked in vinegar and moisten all and salt it to taste.*

## POACHED MULLET WITH CAMELINE SAUCE

4 mullet or other small fish such as red snapper or trout (3/4-1 pound or 400-450g each)

FOR THE SAUCE:

½ cup (1.25 dl) wine or cider vinegar
5 slices bread, crusts discarded
1½ teaspoons ground cinnamon
1 teaspoon ground ginger
seeds of 2 cardamom pods, crushed
½ teaspoon ground cloves
½ teaspoon ground mace
½ teaspoon freshly ground black pepper
salt (to taste)

This recipe serves 4.

Wash the fish thoroughly and dry them on paper towels. Put them in a baking dish, sprinkle them with salt, and add water to almost cover. Cover with foil or a lid and poach in a moderate oven (350°F or 177°C) for 20–25 minutes or until the fish just flakes easily when tested with a fork. Drain them on paper towels and serve with the sauce separately.

*In the Middle Ages to bake bread a fire was lighted in the oven, then when it was hot enough the ashes were removed and the bread was inserted for baking.*

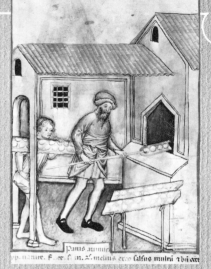

FOR THE SAUCE: Pour the vinegar over the bread and let stand 5 minutes or until soft. Add cinnamon, ginger, cardamom, cloves, mace, and pepper and purée the mixture in a blender; it will be just thick enough to fall from a spoon. Add salt to taste.

## BARBECUED MULLET

2 medium striped bass or pompano (1½-2 pounds or 750-900g each) or 4 mullet or other small fish such as red snapper or trout (3/4-1 pound or 400-450g each)
1 cup (2.5 dl) verjuice (see under Veal Stew)
1 teaspoon ground ginger
1 teaspoon ground cinnamon
½ teaspoon freshly ground black pepper
½ teaspoon ground nutmeg
¼ teaspoon ground cloves
seeds from 1 cardamom pod, crushed
¼ teaspoon salt or to taste

This recipe serves 4.

Split the fish down the back, clean them, and wash well. Pat them dry with paper towels. Mix two tablespoons of the verjuice with the ginger, cinnamon, pepper, nutmeg, cloves, cardamom, and salt. When it is a smooth paste, stir in remaining verjuice. Brush the cut sides of the fish with the mixture, set them cut side down on a barbecue rack, and broil, basting with the verjuice mixture, for 5–10 minutes, depending on the thickness of the fish. Turn over, baste again, and continue cooking until the fish flakes easily when tested with a fork.

at once. Highly flavored meat dishes were served with bland porridges, or with purées of grains and legumes, a custom also evocative of modern Indian cooking.

In Taillevent's time, cooks had to prepare food for a table where there were few implements. It is no wonder that a "gobbet" the size of a finger was the largest permissible morsel or that meats are "hew'd," "smitten," or "grounde to douste" in

Taillevent had a surprisingly wide range of ingredients at his disposal. He mentions over two dozen meats and birds, including stork, heron, and that medieval favorite, the peacock. The bird was skinned with the feathers intact, cooked, and then re-formed "in his hackell [coat]" with the tail erect. Contemporary menus make great play of roast meats, and though Taillevent devotes scant space to them, this is simply a reflection of the shorter direc-

almost every recipe. Forks were unknown and spoons were scarce, so food had to be eaten with the fingers. Meat was tough and teeth were poor, yet the knife—the only common table implement—was regarded as hazardous and its use was discouraged. (Two hundred years after Taillevent, a writer was still warning against the dangers of dipping into the communal pot without wearing a protective gauntlet.) A "trencher" (a thick slice or *tranche* of bread) was used instead of a plate, so gravies had to be thickened with breadcrumbs or egg yolks to stop them from running on the table. Flour was not widely used as a binding agent until at least 200 years later.

tions needed, in the same way that the sections on roasting and boiling in a modern cookbook are disproportionately small compared with their importance. Nonetheless, the popular picture of a medieval feast centered around a whole roast ox is inaccurate. Large animals must have been too tough to be roasted, and Taillevent mentions only young animals—calves, kids, and suckling pigs—in addition to birds. In winter even these were in short supply and almost the only meat available was salted.

Meat of any kind was reserved for the rich, and even they, for over half the days in the year, were restricted to a diet of fish by the fasting laws. Taille-

13

ANISE          PEPPER          PURSLANE

vent lists more than fifty different kinds of salt and freshwater fish. Fast days were strictly observed—the French called them *jours maigres* (i.e., meagre)—and to break them was a serious offence. Vegetables were regarded as the food of the poor (a fact confirmed by the vegetarian diet of the strictest religious sects) who were forced to subsist on milk, cheese, and what they could grow. This included cabbages, leeks, onions, and a multitude of half-forgotten greens like borage, dittany, hyssop, and rue. One of the few medical herbs to have survived the test of time is parsley. This thin fare was supplemented by the occasional fowl, and it was another 200 years before Henry IV could claim that he had brought such prosperity to France that every house had a chicken in its pot (*poule au pot*) on Sundays.

Only a few medieval dishes have survived to the present day. *Hochepot* is very like a modern hot pot and *froumentée* is still known in England as frumenty, a wheaten porridge that is traditionally served on Christmas Eve. *Galantine* and *blanc menger* are familiar words, but their modern equivalents are different. Taillevent's galantine was any dish flavored with the aromatic galingale root, while his blancmange was a white purée, usually of poultry or fish, thickened with rice and ground almonds so it held a shape. Huge quantities of almonds were consumed in medieval times. They were ground for desserts, they were steeped in boiling water to make almond "milk," and they were pounded and used to bind sauces in much the same way as nuts and seeds are used for thickening in Mexican cooking.

Taillevent did a great deal more than simply supervise the cooking. As master chef he was also in charge of provisions, much like a modern quartermaster (*viandier* in fact means victualler). Toward the end of his life (he died in 1395, probably an octogenarian) he headed the half-dozen kitchens of the queen and the various royal dukes as well as those of the king. Whenever he left Paris in search of supplies he was given a travel allowance of "hay and oats for two horses," and with the poor communications and general lawlessness of the late Middle Ages, finding food day after day for the court must have been a Herculean task. According

*Every large household had its garden for herbs, used at least as much for medicine as for cooking.*

ROSEMARY          SUNFLOWER          GINGER

14

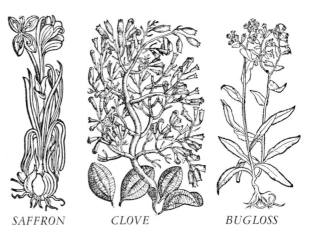

SAFFRON        CLOVE        BUGLOSS

to *Le Ménagier de Paris* (a contemporary household treatise), the requirements each week for all the royal courts included 496 sheep, 70 cattle, 70 calves, 63 hogs, 17 salt hogs, 1,511 goats, 14,900 chickens, 12,390 pigeons, and 1,511 goslings. Such figures reflect the fact that hospitality was considered an important measure of power. Richard II of England is reputed to have entertained 10,000 of his subjects daily, and the French courts were probably organized on a similar scale, although large supplies could never have been kept up regularly and most eating must have followed a pattern of feast and famine. In normal times, the day began with dinner (corrupted from *déjeuner*, to break the fast) taken four hours after sunrise and ended at sundown with a supper consisting of something to sup (i.e., drink) like porridge or soup.

Of the feasts, or banquets, we have ample records. The lord and others of his rank occupied a high table raised on a dais at one end of the hall, set at right angles to the rest of the company, who were seated on long *banquets* or benches. Thus, everyone could observe the rituals of serving a meal—the washing of the hands, the presentation of the finest dishes, and the elaborate precautions taken against poison. All food and drink for the high table was tasted, often by the cook as well as the official taster, and dishes were covered on their journey from taster to table so no poison could be slipped in. The servings depended on rank; the high table was offered platter upon platter in three courses, with as many as twenty dishes in each course. Barons were entitled to only half the quantity given to the high table, knights to a quarter and everyone else to an eighth. The lord was served the meat of the animal, while its entrails were made into *oumble* pie for the lower ranks (hence the expression "to eat humble pie"). The climax of each course came with a "subtletie," a fanciful and often inedible creation several feet high echoing the colorful clothing of the spectators with their tall caps, parti-colored hose, and sweeping coats. The medieval mind was nothing if not literal—an exotic animal or a battle scene was often depicted, and at one wedding feast the cooks made a time-worn joke by sculpting the bride in childbed. More tactfully conceived *pièces montées*, or set

NUTMEG        PARSLEY        THYME

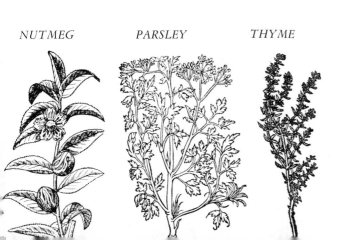

pieces, were still in vogue a hundred years ago and are echoed today in the grandiose ice sculptures that adorn some stately dinners.

Entertainment on this scale called for literally an army of cooks (Richard II employed 2,000 cooks and 300 servitors) deployed with military precision. Taillevent commanded a dozen or more departments, some of whose names still echo a more ordered past. They demonstrate exactly how the catering of a household was organized—there was the pantry (where the *pain* or bread was stored), the cellar, the *bouteillerie* or buttery (where ale and wine were prepared for serving), the spicery, the acatery (the storeroom of the *acheteur* or caterer), the saucery, the larder (for meat, from *lard*, bacon), the pultery (for birds), the confectionery, the pasty

*strainer, the poker for the fire, and the two cleavers wielded simultaneously by the cook (still the quickest method of chopping by hand). Only birds and small animals like suckling pig were tender enough to be roasted* (below).

(for pastry and pies), the scullery (for platters and dishes), and the wafery (where wafers that ended a meal were prepared). The importance of the master cook who ruled this little empire is shown by his rank, which was invariably that of squire with the right to a coat of arms.

Most writers link medieval cooking with the traditions of ancient Rome, and certainly there are parallels between the recipes of *Le Viandier* and those of the only surviving Roman cookbook, attributed to the epicure Apicius. Both medieval and Roman cooks shied away from the tough meat of larger animals, they had a penchant for purées, and they shared the odd (but hygienic) habit of parboiling food before roasting and part-roasting before boil-

*Cooked food is prepared for serving on three-legged tables designed to balance firmly on uneven floors* (below).

16

## Hochepot de poullaille

In medieval times the name *hochepot* meant a pot on a hook, suggesting that the food in it was simmered a long time. An *hochepot* resembles a hot pot; it is also the origin of the expressions "hodgepodge" and "hotch-potch."

*Take your chicken and cut it in pieces and put it to fry in lard in a casserole; then take a little browned bread and the livers of the chicken and soften them with wine and beef stock, and put them to boil with your chicken; then peel ginger, cinnamon and grain of paradise [cardamom] and dissolve them in verjuice; and it should be clear and dark, but not too much.*

### CHICKEN CASSEROLE

2 slices bread
3½-4-pound (1¼-1¾ kg) roasting
  chicken, cut in pieces, with the
  liver
¾ cup (2 dl) red wine
¾ cup (2 dl) beef stock
2 tablespoons lard
salt and pepper
2 tablespoons verjuice (see under
  Veal Stew)
1 teaspoon ground ginger
1 teaspoon ground cinnamon
seeds of 1 cardamom pod,
  crushed

Correctly, the chicken should be served on a trencher (a thick slice of bread), but the *sutil brouet d'Engleterre* (chestnut purée) would be a delicious accompaniment (see next recipe). This recipe serves 4.

Bake the bread in a low oven (300°F or 150°C) for 30 minutes or until thoroughly browned. Let cool, then work it through a grinder or

grind it to fine crumbs a little at a time in a blender. Finely chop the chicken liver and work it through the strainer to remove the membrane. Add the liver to the breadcrumbs, stir in the wine, and let stand 5 minutes until the breadcrumbs are soft. Stir in the beef stock.

In a casserole heat the lard and brown the chicken on all sides. Add the breadcrumb mixture with salt and pepper, cover, and simmer on top of the stove or cook in a moderate oven (350°F or 177°C) for 30 minutes or until the chicken is almost tender. Stir the verjuice into the ginger, cinnamon, and cardamom and stir this mixture into the chicken. Continue cooking 10 minutes or until the chicken is very tender. Take out the chicken and keep warm on a platter. Boil the sauce until it is dark, glossy, and very thick; spoon it over the chicken on the dish.

## Sutil brouet d'Engleterre

A *brouet*, or purée, could contain almost anything—meat, fish, or fowl. This *brouet* made of chestnuts (*purée de marrons*) is still a popular accompaniment to game in Europe.

*Take cooked peeled chestnuts, and cooked egg yolks, and a little pig's liver and pound all together, soften the mixture with a little warm water and sieve it, season with long pepper and saffron and boil all together.*

### CHESTNUT PURÉE FROM ENGLAND

2 pounds (1 kg) chestnuts
3 cups (7.5 dl) water
4 hard-cooked egg yolks
½ pound (250 g) pig's liver, cut in
  pieces and any membrane
  discarded
2 teaspoons freshly ground
  black pepper, or, to taste
pinch of saffron infused in
  2 tablespoons boiling water
salt (to taste)

This recipe serves 6.

Pierce each chestnut with the point of a knife, put them in a saucepan with water to cover and bring to a boil. Drain them a few at a time and peel them, removing both shell and inner skin. If the chestnuts become hard to peel, bring them just back to a boil, but do not let them cook.

Put the chestnuts in a pan with the water, cover, and simmer 30 minutes or until the chestnuts are very tender. Drain them, reserving the liquid. Purée them in a blender a little at a time with the hard-cooked egg yolks and pig's liver, adding just enough of the reserved cooking liquid to make a purée that will drop from the spoon. Or work the chestnuts, egg yolks, and liver through a food mill. Return the purée to the pan, add the pepper and saffron with its liquid, and heat, stirring constantly. Cook the purée 4–5 minutes—it should just hold a shape—but as it dries add more cooking liquid if necessary. Taste it for seasoning—it should be quite peppery.

## *Blanc menger party*

This recipe for *blanc menger* is unusual in that it contains no chicken or fish, but only almonds and rice, exactly like the old-fashioned children's blancmange. *Party* here means "in parts" and the mold is set in gaily striped layers, showing the medieval love of colored foods. Preparing the red, green, blue, and yellow dyes must have been a major task; Taillevent uses bugloss or sunflower for red, azur fin (probably made from mulberries) for blue, parsley or herb-bennet for green, and saffron for orange.

*Take scalded peeled almonds and pound them very well, and soften them with boiled water; then, to make the liaison to bind them, pounded rice or starch are needed. And when the milk has stopped boiling, it must be divided in several parts, in two pots, if only two colors are needed, or whoever wishes can make three or four parts; and it is right that it be very thick, as thick as frumenty, so that it cannot fall when it is set on a plate or in a bowl; then take bugloss or sunflower or mulberries, or parsley, or herb-bennet, or a little saffron sieved with some greenery, so that it keeps its color better when it is boiled; and it is best to have lard and let the bugloss and sunflower soak in it, and the mulberries also. Then throw sugar into the milk when it boils, draw it aside and salt it, and stir vigorously until it is thick and has taken on the color you want.*

## STRIPED BLANCMANGE

6 tablespoons boiling water
1 cup (180 g) whole blanched almonds, finely ground
1 quart (1 l) milk
1 cup (180 g) cream of rice
pinch of saffron
½ cup (120 g) sugar
1 teaspoon salt
2 tablespoons (30 g) lard or shortening
1 teaspoon cinnamon (optional)
½ teaspoon ground cloves (optional)
½ teaspoon ground ginger (optional)
red, blue, and green food coloring

Dessert mold (5-cup or 1¼-liter capacity)

This blancmange is most spectacular when it is set in a tall gelatin mold or in a charlotte mold, so the colored stripes of the mixture show clearly.

Recipe serves 6–8

Lightly oil the mold. Add enough boiling water to the almonds to make a smooth paste. Stir enough cold milk into the cream of rice to make a smooth paste also. Scald the remaining milk, add 2 teaspoons to the saffron, and let stand 20 minutes or more to infuse. Stir the remaining hot milk gradually into the almond mixture, then return to the pan. Add sugar and salt, lard, and spices and bring to a boil; simmer 10 minutes. The mixture will be very thick. Stir this mixture gradually into the cream of rice paste. Return to the pan and simmer 10 minutes longer or until the mixture pulls away from the sides of the pan. Divide it in five parts. Color one part bright red with food coloring and pour it into the lightly oiled mold. Color another part green and add to the mold. Continue adding layers, coloring one blue and leaving the other white. For the final layer, add the saffron and its liquid to the mixture, and add a drop of green coloring. Add to the mold, cover with wax paper, and chill overnight or until firmly set. A short time before serving, run a knife around the edge of the mold and turn it out onto a platter.

## *Tartres de pommes*

Medieval cooks were adept at finding substitutes for sugar, which was an expensive import. Here wine and dried fruits are used to sweeten apples. Purslane, a common herb in medieval times, has large leaves and a sharp taste like sorrel. If you want to use it in this apple pie recipe, add ¼ cup chopped sorrel or spinach to the chopped apple mixture, with the spices.

*Cut up each apple and add figs and put in well-cleaned raisins and mix them together, and put in onion fried in butter or oil, and wine and some pounded apples, soaked in wine, and with the remaining apples, crushed, put saffron and a little of various spices—cinnamon, white ginger, anise and purslane if you have it; and make two large bases of pastry and put all the mixtures in together, and press a thick layer of apple down well with the hand, and the other mixture, and after put on the lid and seal it and gild it with saffron and put it in the oven and cook it.*

## APPLE PIE

FOR THE PASTRY:

2 cups (250 g) flour
½ teaspoon salt
⅓ cup (80 g) butter
2 tablespoons (30 g) shortening or lard
4–5 tablespoons cold water

FOR THE FILLING:

1 onion, chopped
2 tablespoons (30 g) butter or oil

5 dessert apples
3 dried figs, chopped
1/2 cup (100g) raisins
3/4 cup (2 dl) port or sweet
    white wine
1 teaspoon ground cinnamon
1/2 teaspoon ground ginger
1/2 teaspoon crushed aniseed
pinch of saffron infused in
    1 tablespoon boiling water

A deep 9-inch (22-cm) pie pan
This recipe serves 6.

TO MAKE THE PASTRY: Sift the
flour into a bowl with the salt, add
the butter and shortening or lard,
and cut them into small pieces.
Rub with the fingertips until the
mixture resembles crumbs, stir in
enough water to make a pastry that
is soft but not sticky, and knead
lightly until smooth. Wrap and
chill 30 minutes. Set the oven at
moderately hot (375°F or 190°C).

TO MAKE THE FILLING: Fry the
onion in 2 tablespoons butter or
oil until soft but not brown. Peel
the apples, core and chop two of
them, and mix them with the
onion, figs, raisins, and 1/2 cup
(1.25 deciliters) wine. Grate the
remaining apples and mix them at
once with remaining wine so they
do not discolor. Add about a third
of this mixture to the raisin mixture. Stir the cinnamon, ginger,
aniseed, and half the saffron and
liquid into the remaining grated
apples.
Roll out just over half the pastry
dough and line the pie pan. Spread
the raisin mixture in the bottom,
put the spiced apple mixture on
top, and press it down well. Roll
out the remaining pastry to form a
lid, place it on top, and seal the
edges. Brush the top of the pie
with the remaining saffron liquid
and make a hole in the center for
steam to escape. Bake in the
heated oven for 55 minutes or until
the pastry is browned. Serve hot or
cold.

*The tomb of master cook Guillaume Tirel, called Taillevent, is emblazoned with his coat of arms—three little cooking pots.*

ing. Both set high store by songbirds and fowl of fine
plumage, though these were supposed to be inferior
in flavor to less showy birds like hen. For Taillevent
and Apicius it was unthinkable to cook meat without honey and spices on a lavish scale, and they both
loved to transform the appearance and taste of
ingredients "to make of a thousand flavors, one
flavor unique," as the Roman Seneca remarked.
However, the seasonings listed by Apicius were
quite different from those used by Taillevent and it
is highly unlikely that Taillevent ever saw an Api-
cian manuscript since in his day it was an extremely
rare work written for scholars rather than for cooks.
Similarities in the two cuisines therefore have less to
do with the direct influence of Apicius than with
oral traditions going back as far as the Roman occupation of France, combined with the rudimentary
food technology of both eras.
Taillevent's world lacked the national traditions and
frontiers we know today; the cooking described in
*Le Viandier* was common to the court of England as
well as France, and Taillevent's recipes differ little
from those found in other works of the period.
Indeed, there is a suspicion that a recently discovered manuscript, virtually identical to *Le Viandier*,
was written thirty years before Taillevent's birth, in
which case he has the doubtful distinction of being
the first, though not the last, great cook to plagiarize
an earlier work. But deservedly or not, Taillevent
was the most famous and important medieval cook;
*Le Viandier* stands apart from other medieval writings on cookery in having been continuously
recopied and reprinted from Taillevent's death in
1395 until the final edition of 1604. The rich harvest
of French cookbooks did not begin until the 1650s
and until then *Le Viandier* was the most successful
French expression of the art.

19

# Martino

flourished 1450–1475

TEMPLA DOMVM EXPOSITIS:VICOS FORA MOENIA PONTES:
VIRGINEAM TRIVII QVOD REPARARIS AQVAM.
PRISCA LICET NAVTIS STATVAS DARE COMMODA PORTVS:
ET VATICANVM CINGERE SIXTE IVGVM:
PLVS TAMEN VRBS DEBET: NAM QVAE SQVALORE LATEBAT:
CERNITVR IN CELEBRI BIBLIOTHECA LOCO.

Cooking has come to be regarded so much as a
French art that its Italian origins are often over-
looked. But they are there, firmly rooted in the rich
traditions of Italy that Renaissance cooks developed
to such splendid effect. It was the Italians who found
in antiquity new inspirations for their feasts; it was
they who happily blended the sturdy cooking of the
different regions with ideas brought by the Arabs
and crusaders, and founded the sophisticated
cuisine that was later exported, like the other
Renaissance arts, to the rest of Europe. An Italian
cook was also the first to get his recipes in print in a
book called *De honesta voluptate et valetudine* ("Of
Honest Indulgence and Good Health"). The name
of the cook was Martino.

*De honesta voluptate* was printed in Rome in 1474,
the work of a humanist philosopher and man of
letters called Platina, who spent his last years as
Vatican librarian. In the first five chapters he dis-
courses on good food and sober living with the
rational elegance, based on ancient models, that was
the hallmark of humanist writing. Then, abruptly,
the book plunges into five chapters of practical
recipes covering the best of Italian contemporary
cooking, from the cheese tarts so dear to the ancient

*In a cheese shop, a customer
tests the wares for ripeness.*

Romans to Saracen-inspired stews and native pasta.
This curious change of tone in Platina's book
attracted no comment until the 1930s when a
fifteenth-century recipe manuscript was found,
"composed by the respected Maestro Martino,
former cook to the Most Reverend Monsignor the
Chamberlain and Patriarch of Aquileia." The manuscript (now in the Library of Congress) is written in
the Italian of Tuscany, not in the Latin used by
Platina, but the 250 recipes are identical to those in
*De honesta voluptate.*

With this discovery, an acknowledgment tucked

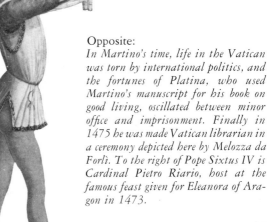

Opposite:
*In Martino's time, life in the Vatican
was torn by international politics, and
the fortunes of Platina, who used
Martino's manuscript for his book on
good living, oscillated between minor
office and imprisonment. Finally in
1475 he was made Vatican librarian in
a ceremony depicted here by Melozza da
Forlì. To the right of Pope Sixtus IV is
Cardinal Pietro Riario, host at the
famous feast given for Eleanora of Aragon in 1473.*

away in Platina's book suddenly assumed new significance – "O ye immortal Gods," he exclaims in a recipe for *bianco mangare*, "which cook could compete with my friend Martino of Como, with whom originates to a large extent that which I am writing here." Whether the particular manuscript in the Library of Congress was actually written before *De honesta voluptate* is uncertain, but Platina's dependence on Martino for his recipes seems beyond dispute. Platina was no cook and he clearly felt some embarrassment about applying his scholarship to so lowly a subject as food, for in the dedication to his book he hastens to explain that he is writing to "assist the well-bred man who desires to be healthy and to eat in a decorous way, rather than he who searches after luxury and extravagance."

damp cloth to prevent it acquiring a smoky taste (one of the persistent problems when cooking over an open fire). His understanding of ingredients is intimate to the point of affection: "Salmon," he remarks, "is a most agreeable fish, most natural boiled, and yet again it is good any way you like to cook it. . . . For whole fish, you need big dishes like my master has, because all fish are much better cooked whole rather than in pieces."

*Crayfish have long been an Italian favorite, and here a fourteenth-century artist lovingly depicts their anatomy. They are served with the time-honored accompaniments of lemon wedges and wine.*

The recipes in *De honesta voluptate* are clearly those of an expert cook – detailed and precise. Martino goes to great pains to explain the reasoning behind his instructions. For example, he advises using a large kettle for boiling meat so it is not packed too tightly, and describes how to cover soup with a

Martino mentions the sausages of Bologna, the rice dishes of Lombardy, the crayfish of Venice and Rome, and the vegetables and fried dishes for which Florence was so famous. His easy familiarity with them all shows that by the fifteenth century a recognizably Italian style of cooking had already de-

Martino is the first cook to give detailed cooking instructions and tips that show he is thoroughly at home with his recipes. Like Taillevent, he rarely calls specifically for salt; often lemon juice, verjuice (sour grape juice), or cheese take its place, but in the following recipes salt and pepper can be added to taste.

## Gambari pieni

Already during the Renaissance Romans were eating a good deal of shellfish, including oysters and the crayfish that came from the water-threaded region along the Po and Piave rivers.

*Boil them [the crayfish] in a little water and vinegar, with as much water as vinegar and plenty of salt, and since the crayfish add liquid do not put too much of this mixture, and boil them hard until the scum rises. And to know when they are cooked note when this scum has boiled two or three times over the caldron; then they should be done, but to be sure you can taste them and you will be content. With the point of a knife open the stomach between the legs, and*

*pound the flesh from the tail and the legs with almonds and a little verjuice; and at times when eggs are permitted you can add the yolk of an egg to this mixture, or more depend-*

*ing on the quantity you want, also a little cheese, a little finely chopped parsley and marjoram. And fill the crayfish with this mixture and fry them in good oil as slowly and gently as possible; and in Lent you will not add egg or cheese.*

## STUFFED CRAYFISH

1½ cups (4 dl) water
1½ cups (4 dl) wine vinegar
2½ pounds (1¼ kg) crayfish
⅔ cup (125 g) whole blanched almonds, ground
2 tablespoons verjuice (see page 11) or lemon juice
4 egg yolks
½ cup (100 g) grated Parmesan or Romano cheese
4 tablespoons chopped parsley
2 teaspoons marjoram
salt and pepper
½ cup (1.25 dl) olive oil (for sautéing)

Large shrimps or prawns (1½ pounds or 750 grams) are an excellent substitute when crayfish are not available. This recipe serves 6.

Bring the water and vinegar to a boil, add the crayfish or shrimps, and boil, allowing 5–7 minutes for the crayfish or 3–5 minutes for the shrimps, depending on their size. Drain them, rinse with cold water, and drain well. If using crayfish, cut through the stomach between the legs to the tail on either side, discarding the soft part of the shell. Lift out the tail meat and the soft part of the stomach, discarding the head sac and intestinal vein. Crack the claws and extract the meat. If using shrimps, cut along the tail on each side of the soft shell and discard it; lift out the meat, discarding the intestinal vein. Clean the hard shells of the crayfish or shrimps and put them aside.

Purée the meat in a blender or chop it very finely. Stir in the ground almonds, verjuice or lemon juice, egg yolks, cheese, parsley, marjoram, and pepper and taste for seasoning. Fill the empty shells with the mixture, pressing it well. A short time before serving, heat the oil and sauté the stuffed shells over medium heat for 4–5 minutes or until lightly browned. Serve them as soon as possible.

## Zucche fritte

These fritters are typically Florentine as the best oil came from that region. The *zucche* used by Martino were most likely the large marrows that are common in Europe (though in his day they were certainly smaller in size). Zucchini were probably brought later from the New World but they must closely resemble Martino's marrows.

*Take marrows and clean them well. And then cut them crosswise in slices as thin as the blade of a knife. And then put them in water and bring to a boil, and then take them out and leave them to dry. Put a very little salt on the slices and cover them with good flour and fry them in oil. Then remove them, and take a little fennel flower, a little garlic and soft bread, and pound well and mix with **agresto** [tart grape juice] to make a good liquid, and put through a sieve and pour this relish on the slices of marrow. They are also good served only with vinegar and fennel flower. And if you desire this relish to be yellow add a little saffron.*

## (continued from previous page)

## ZUCCHINI SALAD

2 pounds (1kg) zucchini, cut in
   ¼-inch (50-mm) slices
½ cup (75g) flour
salt
¾-1 cup (2-2.5 dl) olive oil
   (for frying)

FOR THE DRESSING:

2 tablespoons leaf fennel or
   1 teaspoon fennel seed
1 clove garlic, crushed
2 slices white bread, crusts
   discarded
½ cup (1.25 dl) white wine vinegar
   or cider vinegar
pinch of saffron infused in
   2 tablespoons boiling water
   (optional)
salt (to taste)

If you prefer, a dressing can be made simply of vinegar and fennel with the bread and garlic omitted. This recipe serves 6.

Blanch the zucchini in boiling water for 30 seconds and spread out on paper towels to dry thoroughly. Toss them with the flour and a pinch of salt in a bowl, turning until coated. In a frying pan heat some of the oil and lay in some of the zucchini, separating any slices that stick together. Cook over high heat for ½–1 minute or until just beginning to brown, turn over and brown the other side. Take out and spread them in a shallow serving dish; fry the remaining zucchini in the same way.

FOR THE DRESSING: Purée the fennel, garlic, bread, vinegar, saffron with its liquid (if used), and salt in a blender, or pound the mixture in a mortar with a pestle and work it through a sieve. Spoon the dressing over the zucchini and leave 1–2 hours for the flavors to blend before serving.

## Rape armate

Martino's custom of making a special dish of an ordinary vegetable like turnips was typically Italian; elsewhere in Europe cooks regarded most root vegetables as food for the poor. This particular dish, to be served at the end of a meal, obviously forms what we call a dessert. The combination of sugar with turnips is not as strange as might be expected, for the vegetable is already slightly sweet, and, after all, carrots are commonly used in sweet cakes.

*Cook the turnips in the hot cinders or boil them whole and uncut, and slice them as thickly as the blade of a knife, and have good moist* cacio *[cheese] cut in slices as big as the turnip slices, but thinner, and take sugar, pepper and sweet spices and mix these together, and arrange in a pan in this order starting at the bottom, slices of cheese to make a crust, and on top a layer of turnips with the said spices and much good fresh butter; and so on in this way arrange the turnip, and the cheese until the pan is full, and cook this for a quarter of an hour or more, like a tart. And this dish should be served after the others.*

## TURNIP CAKE

2 pounds (1kg) large white turnips
⅓ cup (80g) sugar
1 teaspoon freshly ground pepper
2 teaspoons ground cinnamon
½ teaspoon ground mace
½ teaspoon ground cloves
1¼ pounds (550g) bel paese cheese
   thinly sliced

A shallow 9-inch (22-cm)
baking dish

By sweet spices in this recipe, Martino was probably referring to non-peppery spices such as cinnamon. Served as a dessert, this quantity is enough for 6. If you prefer to serve the cake with meat or poultry, reduce the sugar to 1 tablespoon; as an accompaniment it serves 8.

Boil the unpeeled turnips in water to cover for 15–30 minutes (depending on their size) or until just tender. Drain them, let cool, and peel off the skins; cut them in ¼-inch slices. Mix the sugar with the pepper, cinnamon, mace, and cloves. Set the oven at moderately hot (375°F or 190°C). Thickly butter the baking dish and arrange a layer of cheese in the bottom. Add a layer of turnip slices overlapping on top and sprinkle them with the sugar mixture. Continue adding layers of cheese, turnip, and sugar until all the ingredients are used, ending with a layer of cheese.
Bake the dish in the heated oven for 30–35 minutes or until the top is browned. Turn out the mold on a platter, like a cake, and cut it in wedges or squares for serving. As a dessert it can be served hot or cold. Serve it hot as an accompaniment.

Martino's master, Ludovico Trevisan (left), was one of the most extravagant characters of his age. A cardinal who advised five popes, he did not hesitate to combine his career as a diplomat with gambling, gourmandise, and the accumulation of vast wealth.

From kitchen to table (below) as shown in a fifteenth-century illuminated manuscript.

veloped. Indeed, there are already signs of common methods and recipes in the few cookery manuscripts that antedate Martino, but none of them is nearly so well organized or complete as his work. Most include, for example, versions of *brodo saracenico* (ground chicken liver blended with bread and spice and often flavored with white wine and dried fruit) and *peverata*, an all-purpose sauce of toasted bread, spices, and liver pounded with wine and vinegar, which Martino uses as a base for his *peperata de salvaticina*, a game stew.

Most of these early Italian cookbooks feature pasta. Its introduction is often credited to Marco Polo, but a chest of macaroni was listed as part of a Genoese inheritance in 1279, a decade or more before he returned to Venice from his travels. Lasagne was the oldest and most common variety, invariably cooked in broth, then baked with layers of cheese; the word comes from the Latin *lasanum* (cooking pot). By the 1350s *lasagnari*, or pasta sellers, were well established. Boccaccio, who wrote the *Decameron* around this time, describes with delight a utopian region called Bengodi where the vines were bound with sausages and a mountain was made of grated Parmesan cheese. People stood on top with nothing to do but make macaroni and ravioli and cook them in capon broth, then roll them down the hill; and as fast as they were eaten, the more there were.

By the time Martino was active, a century after Boccaccio, pasta had become a good deal more sophisticated, although it was still a luxury and in lean years its fabrication was forbidden. Martino describes what he calls *vermicelli*, squares "the size of dice" that were dried in the sun and would keep two years. His *macaroni siciliani*, made by wrapping dough around a stick, were very like modern Neapolitan pasta with the addition of eggs. Nor does he forget the crisp, deep-fried Florentine *crespelli*, usually sprinkled with sugar and spices, that are now called *cenci*. They can be all shapes, he says—rings, buckles, letters; horses or other animals.

The monsignor Martino worked for was almost cer-

Overleaf:

*An elegant Renaissance banquet suddenly interrupted. In this illustration by Botticelli of the* Nastagio degli Onesti III *legend, the guests had apparently reached the last course of their meal before the bizarre intrusion shown in the foreground; the turmoil has caused fruit to be scattered about the floor.*

tainly Ludovico Trevisan, a wealthy, wordly cardinal who became patriarch of Aquileia in 1439 and papal chamberlain a year later. He held both posts through five papacies and by the time he died, in 1465, he wielded so much power that the incumbent pope (Paul II) let both these offices lapse for several years. Ludovico must have been a master to warm any cook's heart. Called the Lucullan cardinal, he spent 20 ducats a day (more than $1,000) on his food, and it was said of him that "forgetting his origins he took on such airs that he was the first of

the cardinals to dare to breed dogs and horses, to introduce licentious parties and banquets more splendid than were suited to his rank, and to restore a more civilized way of life to the Romans, who had declined to such a low state." In fact, he was just the sort of cardinal that later popes tried (with little success) to reform, but fortunately for Ludovico the masters whom he served were anxious to restore

Rome to her former glory and oust the Florentines and Venetians from their pre-eminence.

As the pope's chamberlain, Ludovico headed a household of about 600 and his personal staff probably amounted to half that number. He was responsible for organizing Rome's official banquets and entertainments, which were often held in the open air—today's *corso*, for example, is where races were run. One famous feast of which records survive is that given in 1473 (shortly after Ludovico's time) by Cardinal Pietro Riario for Eleanora of Aragon. It began with little hors d'oeuvres of ten sweet dishes (with gilded oranges and Malvasey wine) and then, after the ceremonial washing of hands, the assembled company tucked into roast chicken and goat's liver, sweetbreads flavored with white wine, capons in white sauce with gilded pomegranate seeds, poultry in purple sauce, and a dozen other delicacies. A pastry figure entitled "Andromeda and the Dragon" rounded off this course, which was followed by two more of equal luxuriance. At least half the entertainment must have been the sight of the lords at table—it was all very good publicity, and as one sarcastic observer remarked, the church treasure had to be used up some way or other.

The riches of the church during the Renaissance were second to none; to cook for a cardinal was the equivalent of cooking for a prince, and Martino must have supervised many an opulent feast. Yet his food is unpretentious, at least by the standards of ancient and medieval tables, and more like the fare of a merchant household. Simplicity was the style in Florence, leader of all the arts until the end of the fifteenth century, and like everyone else Martino was strongly influenced by it. Not all the would-be imitators of Florentine cooking were as skilled as he; a certain Siennese nobleman, stunned by the magnificence of a feast given for Pius II in Florence in 1459, determined to reproduce it at home. Finding no peacocks available, he told the cooks to use ducks instead and dress them in the feathers of an old peacock. A grand molded gelatin, portraying the papal arms in full color, taxed his ingenuity to the full, but he did his best with verdigris, white lead, vermilion, and other paints, never thinking

## Per fare polpette di carne de vitello o de altra bona carne

This recipe for making meat rolls turns up in many old cookbooks. In England they are called veal olives (presumably because of their shape) and in France *oiseaux sans têtes* (birds without heads) because they also resemble little stuffed birds. By Martino's time a trencher (used below for pounding) had developed from the medieval slice of stale bread into a flat plate of wood or metal.

*First cut some lean meat from the leg of the animal and slice it in long thin slices and beat it well on a trencher or table with the flat of a knife, and take salt and pounded fennel and put these on the slices of meat. Then take parsley, marjoram and good lard and beat them together with a little good spice, and spread this well over the slices. Then roll up each slice and put it on the spit to cook; but do not let the heat dry the meat too much.*

### VEAL ROLLS

1½ pounds (750g) thinly sliced veal escalopes
1 teaspoon salt
1 teaspoon fennel seeds, crushed
¾ cup (200g) lard
4 tablespoons chopped parsley
2 teaspoons marjoram
½ teaspoon ground allspice
¼ teaspoon ground cloves or nutmeg

Thread for tying

Any spices can be used instead of allspice and cloves or nutmeg. Butter can be substituted for the lard. This recipe serves 4.

Place the veal escalopes between two sheets of wax paper and pound them with a cutlet bat or mallet until very thin; sprinkle them with the salt and crushed fennel. Cream the lard and add the parsley, marjoram, allspice, and cloves or nutmeg. Spread the mixture over the veal escalopes right to the edges. Bring the edges to the center, then roll into neat bundles. Tie them with thread and spear on a roasting spit. Cook in front of a high heat for 10–15 minutes, depending on the heat, or until lightly browned. Baste the rolls with their juices halfway through cooking. Untie the thread before serving.

## Riso con brodo di carne

This is an ancestor of the famous risotto Milanese, rice cooked in broth colored with saffron and flavored with cheese. In this recipe, cheese is omitted and eggs are added instead; the eggs have a similar thickening effect without adding flavor. The recipe is probably of Arabic origin, since the Arabs brought rice to Europe; Taillevent mentions rice and by 1475 it was being grown in the Po valley, where it is still an important crop.

*For ten servings: First clean and wash the rice very well, and cook it in a good broth made from capon or a large chicken, and it needs to boil quite long. And when it is cooked add good spices, and take three egg yolks and a little of the cooked rice and mix well together. And then add to the rest of the rice and mix together. And it should be colored yellow with saf-*fron. But many people do not like eggs with rice. In this case, follow your master's taste.

### RISOTTO

1 cup (250g) round-grain rice
2½ cups (6 dl) chicken stock
½ teaspoon ground cinnamon
½ teaspoon ground ginger
pinch of saffron, infused in 2 tablespoons boiling water
3 egg yolks
salt (to taste)

Round-grain rice is the type used for risotto in Italy as it absorbs more liquid, making a richer mixture. Martino's favorite spices were ginger and cinnamon, so that is probably what he would have used as "good spices" in this recipe; ginger has an effect similar to pepper, but salt is also needed to suit our tastes unless the chicken stock is very highly seasoned. This recipe serves 4.

Bring the stock to a boil, add the rice, cover, and simmer 20 minutes or until all the liquid has been absorbed. Let the rice stand 10 minutes for the grains to contract slightly, then stir in the cinnamon, ginger, and saffron with its liquid. Stir 2 tablespoons of the rice into the egg yolks and stir this mixture back into the rice; it will thicken slightly. Taste for seasoning.

## Ravioli in tempo di carne

The name ravioli probably comes from *rabiole* meaning "leftovers" in Ligurian dialect. The filling can be made of almost any meat or vegetable and was originally fried like a fritter; Martino seems to be the first cook to enclose it in pasta to make the ravioli we know, and he does not bother to give a recipe for the dough, which would have

*In one of the earliest pictures of pasta, a Boccaccian gastronome is treated to plump gnocchi.*

(continued from previous page)

been a simple flour and water paste. For cheese, he uses the word *cacio*. A cheese called *cacio* or *caccio a cavallo* is still made in Tuscany and Campania.

*To make ten servings: take ½ pound old* **cacio**, *and a little fresh* **cacio** *and 1 pound of fat belly of pork, or a calf's head that has been boiled until it falls apart. Then pound these well and add good well chopped herbs, and pepper, cloves and ginger; and add a pounded chicken breast and it will be even better. And mix all these things well together. Then make a good thin paste and fill it in the normal way with this filling. And these ravioli should not be bigger than a half chestnut, and should be put to cook in broth made from capon or from good meat, and it should be colored with saffron when it boils. And let the ravioli boil for the length of two paternosters. Then serve them and put on them grated* **cacio** *and sweet spices mixed. And these ravioli can be made the same with breast of pheasant, partridge or other birds.*

## RAVIOLI FOR MEAT DAYS

1 pound (450 g) boneless fresh belly of pork, cut in 1-inch (2.5-cm) cubes
1 whole boneless chicken breast, cut in 1-inch (2.5-cm) cubes
2½ quarts (2½ L) chicken stock
2 cups (250 g) grated Parmesan or Romano cheese
¼ pound (125 g) bel paese or mozzarella cheese, chopped
1 tablespoon chopped parsley
1 tablespoon mixed chopped herbs, (thyme, basil, oregano)
½ teaspoon freshly ground black pepper
¼ teaspoon ground cloves
¼ teaspoon ground ginger
salt (to taste)
pasta dough (see below)
pinch of saffron, infused in 2 tablespoons boiling water

FOR SERVING:

1 cup (125 g) grated Parmesan or Romano cheese
½ cup (120 g) granulated sugar mixed with 1 tablespoon ground cinnamon

In the United States fresh pork belly is invariably smoked for bacon or salted for salt pork, so pork shoulder is the nearest substitute; alternatively, any leftover cooked meat can be used instead of the pork and chicken in the recipe. During the early Renaissance, pasta was often sprinkled with cinnamon and sugar, so this is probably what Martino means by serving with sweet spices. It is not known whether the ravioli was usually served drained or with its cooking broth, so either are suggested here. This quantity serves 6–8.

Put the pork in a pan with enough of the stock to cover, add the lid and simmer 1 hour or until just tender. Add the chicken breast and continue simmering 30 minutes or until both the chicken and pork are very tender. Drain them, reserving the stock, and work them in a blender or chop them finely. Add the Parmesan or Romano cheese, bel paese or mozzarella cheese, parsley, herbs, pepper, cloves, and ginger and continue working in the blender with a little cooking liquid to moisten until smooth, or pound them in a mortar and pestle. Taste the filling for seasoning.

Divide the pasta dough in half and roll out as thinly as possible to a large rectangle. Brush the dough with water and put little mounds of the filling (about a teaspoonful) on the dough at regular intervals, about 1½ inches apart. Roll out the remaining dough to a rectangle of the same size, place it on top, and with a small ball of dough dipped in flour, press the top piece down to seal around each little mound of filling. With a fluted ravioli cutter or a knife, cut the ravioli into squares and let dry 2–3 hours.

Bring the remaining chicken stock and the stock from cooking the pork to a boil with the saffron and its liquid. Simmer the ravioli in the mixture for 15–20 minutes or until they are tender but still *al dente* (resistant to the teeth). Either taste the broth for seasoning and serve the ravioli and broth in soup bowls, or drain the pasta before serving. A bowl of grated Parmesan or Romano cheese and a bowl of cinnamon sugar for sprinkling are the authentic accompaniments.

## RAVIOLI DOUGH

4 cups (550 g) semolina or all-purpose flour
1 teaspoon salt
1 tablespoon olive oil
4 eggs, beaten to mix
⅓–½ cup (1-1.25 dl) water

Semolina flour, available in Italian groceries, is especially suitable for pasta as it has a high gluten content which prevents the dough from breaking up during cooking. If all-purpose flour is used in this recipe, 1–1½ tablespoons more water will be needed.

Sift the flour with the salt onto a board or marble slab, make a well in the center, and add the oil, eggs, and half the water. Start mixing the oil, eggs, and water together with the fingertips, gradually drawing in the flour and adding more liquid as it is needed. Knead the dough until it is smooth and very elastic—it should be fairly soft but not sticky. Cover it with a cloth and leave 30 minutes for it to lose its elasticity before rolling.

of edible colors like saffron and herbs. The guests came, admired, ate, and were extremely ill the next morning.

These Renaissance banquets were part of a deliberate evocation of the splendors of ancient Rome. Nostalgia also found a more intellectual outlet, for it was in 1457 that the most famous Roman cookery manuscript, attributed to the epicure Apicius (who lived at the time of Christ), was acquired by the Vatican. Platina undoubtedly was familiar with Apicius since he planned *De honesta voluptate* on the same classical ten-book pattern, and through oral traditions Martino must have had a good idea of what the Roman table was like. Both ancient and Renaissance Italians used a wide variety of vegetables and fruit with great imagination (a taste that was slow to reach the rest of Europe) and both shared a love of the macabre—the flamboyant Ascanio Sforza, for example, invited his fellow cardinals to a banquet where there were bones fashioned in sugar and drinking cups shaped as skulls. The fascination for Roman "flying pies" concealing live birds enjoyed a long life, still lingering in England 200 years after Martino.

However, the actual cooking of Renaissance Italy, as illustrated by Martino's recipes, was far removed from the crudities of ancient Rome and even of the Middle Ages. Martino has little time for outmoded purées and porridges, preferring more substantial dishes containing pieces of meat or whole birds in a sauce—the ancestors of French ragoûts. His vegetables are usually cooked whole, then sliced and served with a sprinkling of cheese or fried as fritters. The old tendency to disguise foods, whether by spicing them heavily or mixing them indiscriminately, is disappearing—no longer would a cook like Martino exclaim triumphantly, as had Apicius, that "no one will recognize this!" On the contrary, Martino tries to bring out the flavor of a single ingredient by careful seasoning and moderate cooking. He pays attention to texture, as in his recipe for veal rolls—thin escalopes of veal which are sprinkled with herbs, rolled, then broiled on a spit. Martino also has several soups based on meat broth, thickened with eggs and breadcrumbs or almonds. Soups were of ever-increasing importance during the Renaissance; often they were substantial dishes, more like our stews, and they were destined to have considerable influence in France, where potages occupied a prominent place in menus until the French Revolution.

Far more important to Martino was the cooking of the Arabs, which had flourished through the Dark Ages (a tenth-century history lists a dozen writers on cookery in Baghdad). Italy, particularly Venice, had long been the gateway through which crusaders and spice merchants passed on their way to the East and Italian scholars had translated several Arab treatises on food and medicine. Martino's habit of sprinkling dishes with sugar and spices is very Arabic and many of his sauces flavored with raisins, prunes, and grapes could have come straight from an Arabic cookbook. The appearance of aniseed, rice, dates, pomegranates, and bitter oranges can be traced to the long Arab occupation of Sicily and Spain, and the sugar cane the Arabs introduced in Cyprus (and later Sicily) allowed them to indulge their sweet tooth—a passion they passed on to the Italians. Martino is one of the first cooks to follow the Arabic habit of using sugar in large quantities to make dishes that are specifically sweet, such as fritters, almond paste cookies, and sugared apples, rather than treating it as a seasoning like salt, in the medieval manner.

It took the Renaissance genius to fuse all these diverse elements into a coherent cuisine, blending the traditional and the exotic with the dishes indigenous to each region. *De honesta voluptate* was the first major step in this direction and its success was well deserved—it ran to over thirty editions in under a hundred years, including many translations into German, French, and Italian. Martino's recipes also led a double life in *Epulario* ("Of Feasting"), an Italian cookbook almost identical to the Library of Congress manuscript. Much translated, *Epulario* appeared in English as well and was still being printed in the mid 1600s, so that Martino's influence stretched throughout Europe for two centuries or more. Yet, by an irony of history, throughout its long life *Epulario* was attributed to one Giovanne de Rosselli and it is almost by accident that Martino's identity and achievement have been rediscovered today.

# Bartolomeo Scappi

flourished 1540–1570

The superb artwork and printing of this 1622 edition of Opera made nothing less than a learned demeanor appropriate for the portrait of its author (right), *Bartolomeo Scappi.*

Bartolomeo Scappi is to cooking as Michelangelo is to the fine arts; in its beauty as a printed work, in its ordered presentation and comprehensiveness, his cookbook *Opera* exemplifies the practical elegance of the High Renaissance. No comparably authoritative work appeared again until the mid-eighteenth century in France, and none has ever matched *Opera* for its series of bold but scrupulously accurate drawings depicting the ideal kitchen furnished with all the equipment of the expert cook. Here is the fish tank full of fish, there the ravioli wheel, the nutmeg grater, and the slotted spoon for draining pasta, and there the kitchen boy manipulating a whisk by rolling the handle between his hands exactly as is done today. The text of *Opera* is as accomplished as the illustrations and the recipes are so thorough in their detail and so clearly indexed that they put many a modern cookbook to shame. Scappi leaves nothing to chance; he even illustrates the perfect traveling saddle with leather bottles and containers, like a modern picnic basket—and stipulates that it needs a strong horse.

Scappi's special saddle, fitted with containers and bottles for a long journey.

*Opera* was printed in 1570, at a time when the arts of good living were studied and enjoyed in Italy with unparalleled ardor; Italian manners were considered models by the ruder gentry of the north, as was the Italian taste in clothes, furnishing, and fine cooking. Gourmet clubs flourished. The members of the *Compagnia del Paiolo* (Caldron Club), to which the painter Andrea del Sarto belonged, competed in preparing the most amusing as well as the most edible feasts. When it was del Sarto's turn to entertain his eleven fellows, he constructed a temple of sausage columns and Parmesan pillars, which housed a songbook of lasagne (the pages inscribed with notes of peppercorns) set on a lectern of sliced veal. Another group, the *Compagnia della Cazzuola* (Casserole Club) dressed up as construction workers and built an edifice of bread bricks and sweet-

Opposite:
*In this painting of "The Marriage in Cana" by Veronese (1593), the jewels of the women, the laden table, the imported silks, and the little black boy all reflect the wealth and cosmopolitan outlook of sixteenth-century Italian society—although the subject is biblical.*

meat stones cemented with lasagne. Leonardo da Vinci put a rather more practical finger in the pie and invented a spit with a propeller that turned in the heat of the fire; his cook Matrina is the only woman ever mentioned in his writings, and he used to sketch the food he wanted so she could do the marketing properly.

Scappi rises easily to the demands of his knowledgeable audience and he was obviously an educated man. From a few scattered allusions in *Opera*, it seems probable that Scappi's first major position was as cook to Cardinal Campeggio, since Scappi describes in detail the banquet which the cardinal organized in 1536 in honor of the Holy Roman Emperor Charles V. (Campeggio was a shrewd lawyer and frequent choice as papal legate for difficult negotiations, as over the divorce of Henry VIII and Catherine of Aragon, so he knew the emperor well.) The fact that it was a fast day made little difference to the spread. No fewer than thirteen courses followed each other in dizzy succession, with soups, fish, pastries, vegetables, and sweet dishes mingled in apparently random combination, though there is a perceptible lightening toward the end of the meal. One representative course offered fried baby squid with lemon, prune pastries, fried lobster tails, fried spinach with vinegar and must (unfermented grape juice), caviar pie, and broccoli cooked in hot oil *alla napolitana* and sprinkled with orange juice.

When Cardinal Campeggio died in 1539, Scappi probably moved on to the household of Cardinal Carpi, member of an immensely wealthy family who possessed one of the greatest Roman palaces. Certainly he was working for another cardinal, since in *Opera* he describes the catering arrangements for the conclave in the winter of 1549–1550 when Julius III was elected. The conclave was unusually long, lasting over two months, and cooking for it must have been quite a strain as arrangements were complex. Each cardinal employed his own servants who cooked his food and in solemn procession brought it to a panel of bishops for inspection. Once approved, the food was put in a revolving hatch so the cardinals were safely isolated from all contact with the outside world, as canonical law required. In such a long drawn-out struggle for election, the wealth and good taste of each cardinal's table must have been an important part of the psychological warfare, and to judge from *Opera*, the conclave was one of the highlights of Scappi's career. Afterward Scappi apparently continued to work for the church,

*The cook to several cardinals and popes, Scappi was familiar with the elaborate ceremonial of serving food during a papal conclave. The procession of servants reaching the table carries scarlet and gold hampers of hot food (cucina), cold food (credenza), and drinks (bottigliaria), each emblazoned with a cardinal's coat of arms. To ensure no messages can reach the conclave, a panel of bishops (right) inspects the food (Scappi says he cannot make pies because the bishops must open them) as well as*

the steward's box and tableware, before passing everything through the revolving hatches behind. The fare of every cardinal in conclave was subject to the same scrutiny. At right the retinue exits down the stairs.

Scappi's pound measure derives from the Roman *libra* and weighed about 12 ounces. This value (called troy weight) is still used for gold and precious stones, but more bulky items come in avoirdupois weight—a term meaning "to have weight" and referring to a 16-ounce pound.

✦✦✦✦✦✦✦✦✦✦✦✦✦✦✦✦✦

## Per fare crostate, cioe pan ghiotto con rognon di vitella arrostito nello spedo

*Crostate* are crisp little morsels often on a base of fried or toasted bread or sometimes pastry; and they are the ancestors of the crisp French *croustades* made of bread or pastry. As *crostini* (*crostate* has come to mean a sweet open pie), they are still a favorite Italian first course, often made with chicken livers or cheese; here Scappi uses veal kidneys in a spicy sauce. Pomegranate juice, with its fruity tartness, was a seasoning the Italians picked up from the Arabs. Burnet is an herb used to flavor butter sauces and cooling drinks, or its slightly bitter leaves can be served in salad.

*Take slices of day-old bread cut knife-thick, and toast them on the grill, and spit-roast veal kidneys with a little of the loin, then let them cool a while, and then chop finely with mint, marjoram, burnet, fresh fennel, or if you have none, use dried fennel, pepper, cloves, cinnamon, nutmeg, sugar, egg yolks, pomegranate juice or clear vinegar, and plenty of salt, and when mixed spread on the toasted slices of bread, and arrange in a pie pan so the slices do not overlap, and cover the dish and heat from above, with a few hot cinders below,*

*(continued from previous page)*

*and leave until the bread has absorbed some of the fat and the mixture is set, and serve hot with pomegranate juice, sugar, and cinnamon. And you can also put fresh butter or melted lard in the pie pan to make the bread richer. The* **crostate** *can also be cooked with a slow fire on the grill.*

## KIDNEY TOAST

2 veal kidneys, if possible wrapped
   in their fat
½-pound piece (250g) lean veal
1 teaspoon mint
1 teaspoon marjoram
1 teaspoon ground fennel
½ teaspoon ground cloves
½ teaspoon ground cinnamon
½ teaspoon ground nutmeg
1 teaspoon sugar
3 tablespoons wine vinegar or
   pomegranate juice
salt and freshly ground
   black pepper
8 egg yolks
8 thick slices white bread

FOR SERVING:

2-3 tablespoons pomegranate juice
1-2 teaspoons cinnamon
1-2 teaspoons sugar

If kidneys wrapped in their own fat are not obtainable, wrap them with the meat in thinly sliced pork fat (barding fat) or fat sliced bacon. To extract the juice from a pomegranate, scoop the seeds into a strainer and press them with the back of a spoon. Lemon juice can be used instead of pomegranate juice but only half the amount will be needed. This recipe serves 8 as a first course or 4 as a main dish.

Cut all but a thin layer of fat from the kidneys, tie some of the discarded fat around the lean piece of veal, and roast kidneys and meat on a spit or in a hot oven (400°F or 205°C) for 30–40 minutes (depending on their size) or until they are browned but still rare in the center. Turn down the oven to moderate (350°F or 177°C). Let the kidneys cool, then coarsely chop them with the fat, discarding the white core. Chop the veal and add it. Add the mint, marjoram, fennel, cloves, cinnamon, nutmeg, sugar, and vinegar and season the mixture highly with salt and pepper. Stir in the egg yolks. Toast the bread and press the kidney mixture on it. Put the pieces of toast on a buttered baking sheet and bake in the heated oven for 15 minutes or until some of the fat from the kidneys has melted into the toast and the mixture holds together. Sprinkle the toast with pomegranate juice (or lemon juice), cinnamon, and sugar and serve at once, allowing one piece as a first course or two as a main dish. The toast can be prepared ahead and baked just before serving.

## *Per friggere, accommodare in agresta le rane*

This is the recipe for the frogs so beloved of Pope Pius IV. They are sautéed with parsley and garlic, or plainly fried and served with *agresto* (tart grape juice) thickened with egg yolks. Frogs are still a speciality of Pius IV's native Lombardy, where they live in the flooded rice fields of the Po valley.

*Remove the head with its big mouth, and cut off the feet up to the first joint, and leave to soak in cold water, changing the water in the course of eight hours, so that the frogs cleanse themselves and plump up, and whiten, and then take them from the water and fry them, either with the legs tucked under the body, or cut off at the joint, removing the bone; sprinkle them with flour and fry them in oil and serve with a little ground salt, and above all do not cover them after frying as they become hard and shrivel and lose their goodness. You can also fry them with cloves of garlic and parsley, and serve them with the garlic and parsley and pepper and ground salt as a sauce, which is the way Pope Pius IV used to eat them in 1564 when I served him. When they have been fried just like this, with flour, you can keep them hot in* **agresto** *sauce made with fresh* **agresto,** *and egg yolks.*

## SAUTÉED FROGS' LEGS

12-14 pairs (about 3 pounds or 1½ kg)
   frogs' legs
⅔ cup (80g) flour with ½ teaspoon
   salt and large pinch of
   pepper
⅓ cup (1dl) olive oil
1-2 cloves garlic, crushed
3 tablespoons chopped parsley
crushed sea salt and
   freshly ground black
   pepper (for serving)

This recipe serves 4 as a main course.

Soak the frogs' legs in cold water for 1–2 hours to plump and whiten them, drain, and dry them on paper towels. Coat them with seasoned flour. Heat the oil in a skillet and fry the frogs' legs over medium heat until lightly browned and tender, allowing 3–4 minutes on each side. Add the garlic halfway through cooking and the parsley just before serving. Serve the frogs' legs as soon as possible with mills of sea salt and black peppercorns for grinding.

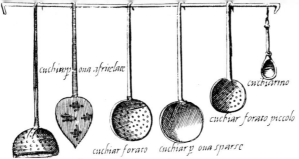

as he makes a casual reference in his book to the "happy year of 1564" when he served the pope. This was Pius IV, a Lombard renowned for his love of puddings and pies as well as, says Scappi, frogs' legs fried in garlic and parsley, for which he gives the recipe. Scappi seems to have spent his last years in the service of Pius V since he reports on the coronation banquet of 1566 and four years later describes himself in *Opera* as *cuoco secreto* or private cook to the pope.

The cooking of *Opera* has progressed far beyond the tentative steps of Martino, writing a hundred years earlier. Opening with a dialogue between himself and his apprentice (a favorite device for explaining the principles of good cooking), Scappi goes on to cover, in six lengthy chapters, meat and poultry, fish, food for meat and fast days, pasta, and diets for the sick. Like all Renaissance cooks, he was interested in the scientific aspects of food, and his experience with elderly popes (Pius IV had trouble with his digestion) must have made him particularly health-conscious. Many of the methods of classical cooking are already developed in Scappi—he is particularly fond of marinating and is also adept at braising and poaching. For example, he soaks chicken in white wine, vinegar, and spices, then bakes it in a sealed *stufatoro* (stewpot), serving the marinade as sauce. The new interest in *stufatori*, which retained the meat juices and blended the flavors by gentle cooking, was typical of a more sophisticated approach to cooking.

Scappi also considers each subject in greater detail than ever before, and he is the first European cook to explore the Arabic art of pastry-making. Martino mentions only a simple flour and water paste, but Scappi details several sophisticated methods for making pastry which he uses in over 200 recipes. One pastry layered with melted lard, then folded and rolled, marks the primitive beginnings of puff pastry. However, it must have been far from today's flaky French delicacy—and equally far from the wafer-thin Arabic pastry that probably served as the model (and is made by a totally different method). A similarly flaky dough was also used for an early type of *vol au vent* (called *crostate*) which was basted with a feather dipped in butter to help it rise during cooking, then filled. Medieval pies with a top crust remained as popular as ever, and often in the filling one meat was wrapped around another (ham around sweetbreads, for instance), making an attractive pattern when the pie was cut—a practice still seen today in French terrines.

Sugar, made from cane cultivated by the Arabs around the Mediterranean basin, was scarce and expensive for centuries. However by Scappi's time plantations in Cyprus and Sicily helped to lower its price, thus bringing sweet cakes and pastries within more general reach. In this sugar factory, cane is chopped (front) and tipped into a crusher (left) from which the juice gushes out. At the back, the cane is pressed again, while the juice is boiled to a concentrated syrup, then poured into conical molds. Cones of sugar were still a familiar sight in the nineteenth century.

The cook dismembers a roast duck, carefully catching the juices, while his kitchen boy extracts the remaining flavor from the bones with a duck press.

*Stufaturo*

Very Italian are Scappi's open pies filled with peas, artichoke hearts, and other vegetables; one crumbly pastry made of equal quantities of flour and butter and flavored with rose water seems to be the ancestor of *pasta frolla*, now used for so many meltingly rich Italian pastries. Also included among Scappi's pastries are waffles (he illustrates the iron), several kinds of fritter, and cakes called *pizze*, bearing but a faint resemblance to the Neapolitan versions of today. Other Italian traits in Scappi's cooking are his love of cheese—he uses ricotta for stuffings and desserts, soft cheese for melting in layered dishes, and Parmesan for sprinkling as a seasoning—and a taste for veal and sausages, including mortadella and salami.

Scappi was well aware of the strong regional influence in Italian cooking. He mentions the fine

oysters and shrimps he saw in Venice; he calls several vegetable and fruit dishes *alla lombarda*; and he has a recipe for *zambaglione*, the fluffy mousse of egg yolks, sugar, and sweet Sicilian wine to which Scappi adds chicken broth. Many dishes are named for gastronomic centers like Rome, Bologna, and Milan because of their traditional patronage of good food. The foreign influence in Scappi is equally strong, reflecting the cosmopolitan position of Rome, which by now had replaced Florence and Venice as the leader in taste. Scappi has a recipe for *succussu all moresca* (Moorish couscous) made in special steamers exactly as today; his trout is *alla tedesca* (German style) and so is his beef marinated with ham and spices. He talks of the plentiful supplies of cod in English waters, reported to him by the cook of an English cardinal, and elsewhere explains that "*crema* is a French word, and it is made from flour, milk and eggs"—today's pastry cream.

As a cook, Scappi was under the nominal direction of the *scalco* or steward who ran the household, though Scappi says the steward must know how to cook, implying that the two offices were not totally

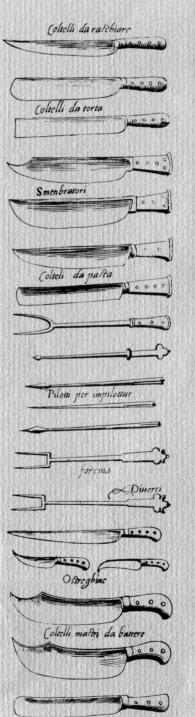

*Coltelli da raschiare*

*Coltelli da torta*

*Smenbratori*

*Coltelli da pasta*

*Pilotti per impilottar*

*forcina*

*Diversi*

*Ostreghine*

*Coltelli mastri da battere*

*Colonna col mortaro*

*nauicella cō piastrelle et quarro piedi*

*nauicella cō piastrelle et 4 piedi*

*nauicella senza piedi*

*Conserua*

*stufator cuato*

*padella p fare oui frittolate*

*stufatoro largo*

*Cucina principale*

*reduto da pani*

*lucerna*

*Camerino per garzoni*

*ordegno*

*murello p pignaite*

*tauola da uola pasta*

*bancho*

*Tauola per imbandire*

The renaissance love of invention was applied to the kitchen with conspicuous success. In this engraving from Scappi's Opera, (left) a chimney hood catches the smoke of the fire, the caldron hangs from a hinged crane and the turnspit is sheltered by a firescreen. On the right stretches a row of ovens with simmering pots, and above them is a hatch for calling orders to the market boys. In the corner knives and spoons are speared in a

*si pana gielo*

*murello*

*lauorano de pasta*

*passano sapori*

bale of straw, and bread rests on a high shelf, safe from animals. On the left stands a sink with running water and the all-important mortar and pestle.

In this detail from a Scappi kitchen scene, (above) cooks are making pasta. One kneads the dough, another folds it, while a third holds the elastic sheet of dough to prevent it from slipping. At hand are a sieve for sifting flour, a ravioli wheel and knife for cutting, a shallow padella pan for baking, and a lemon squeezer.

separate. This is confirmed by the influential cook-book *Banchetti*, written in 1548 by Cristoforo da Messisbugo, a steward who achieved such success that he was ennobled. True to his profession, Messisbugo goes into great detail on the serving as well as the cooking of food, and he is an authority on a new Italian invention, the *credenza*. The *credenza* (now used to describe the side table on which platters to be used are set out) was a course of cold dishes featuring pies, sausages, boiled shellfish, vegetables, salads, and other typical *antipasti*, as well as fruits, sweet cakes, and candies. Display was half the attraction of the *credenza*, and cheek by jowl with sugar statues and gelatin molds there would be fine Venetian glass and precious plate wrought by masters like Benvenuto Cellini. The *credenza* was the forerunner of the French cold buffet—apparently introduced to France by Pierre Buffet, a royal cook who was working in Verona in the early sixteenth century—but in the cooler northern climate cold food never had quite the same appeal as in

Italy, where a *credenza* course alternated with a hot course from the kitchen.

Italian table-settings, a worthy complement to the opulence of the *credenza*, struck Montaigne's fancy during a visit to Rome in 1580: "In front of those to whom they want to do particular honor, who are seated beside or opposite the master, they place big silver squares on which their salt-cellar stands, of the same sort as they put before the great in France. On top of this there is a napkin folded in four and on this napkin the bread, knife, fork, and spoon." Forks were mentioned in an inventory as early as 1360 but Scappi shows one of the first pictures—a stubby, two-pronged implement that no doubt helped circumvent the voluminous ruffs that were in vogue, and also (to judge from an anecdote about a fourteenth-century glutton called Noddo d'Andrea) made the job of eating slippery pasta easier. Protective table napkins, tied around the neck over the ruff and stretching down to cover the lap, were equally indispensable. They were folded

An illustration from the title page of Il Trinciante (the carver) by Vincenzo Cervio shows three pits turning automatically by means of an elaborate mechanism. Notice that small birds requiring quick cooking are closest to the fire, while slower-cooking roasts are set further away so they do not burn.

## Per arrostir nello spedo, e cuocere in piu modi anatre selvaggie

This survey of the kinds of wild duck and how to cook them gives a good idea of Scappi's encyclopedic knowledge. *Brodo lardiero* is a sweet-sour sauce made from toasted breadcrumbs, red wine, tart flavorings, spices like cinnamon and cloves, and a variety of fruits including wild cherries, prunes, and raisins.

*I find that there are different varieties of wild duck—big ones, little ones, ones with variegated feathers and feet, but the best have red feet and bills and they feed in the open countryside, while those that have black bills and feet feed in the valleys and are not so good, but all have the same season from October through to the end of February, and these birds are best during the coldest months, and all like damp and marshy country, and can be spit-roast like cranes, or cooked in brodo lardiero, or cooked in this other way. Pluck and draw the duck and remove the neck and feet and place the duck in a pan with red wine and a little vinegar to cover, and chopped ham, pepper, cinnamon, cloves, nutmeg, ginger, sage leaves and raisins, and close the pan so that the steam does not escape, and cook for 1½ hours, more or less depending on the age and size of the duck, and when cooked serve with this sauce, and you can cook whole large onions with the duck, and prunes and dried wild cherries.*

## WILD DUCK WITH PIQUANT SAUCE

2 wild ducks, with their giblets except the liver
1½ cups (about ½ pound or 250 g) cooked lean ham, finely chopped
3 cups (7.5 dl) red wine
½ cup (1.25 dl) wine vinegar
½ teaspoon freshly ground black pepper
½ teaspoon ground cinnamon
¼ teaspoon ground cloves
¼ teaspoon ground nutmeg
¼ teaspoon ground ginger
2 tablespoons sugar
1 tablespoon sage
¾ cup (125 g) raisins
4 medium onions, halved or ⅓ pound (175 g) pitted prunes (optional)

This recipe is delicious made with squabs, allowing one per person. If adding prunes, reduce the raisins to ½ cup (80 grams); two ducks serve 4.

Put the ducks with their giblets in a casserole and add the chopped ham, wine, vinegar, pepper, cinnamon, cloves, nutmeg, ginger, sugar, sage, raisins, and onions or prunes (if using).
Cover the pan, bring to a boil, and simmer on top of the stove, or cook in a moderate oven for ¾-1¼ hours (the cooking time depends very much on the age and size of the ducks) or until tender. Arrange the ducks on a platter, spoon around the onions or prunes, and keep warm.
Discard the giblets. If necessary boil the sauce to reduce it until fairly thick. Taste it for seasoning and serve it in a separate sauceboat.

## Per fare tortiglione ripieno

Scappi's varied recipes for tortiglioni show how advanced his pastries had become. This particular recipe closely resembles a coffee or tea cake. Scappi's instructions are rather hard to follow, but his aim is obviously to produce a rich, spiced mixture between layers of thin yeast dough.

*Knead together 2 pounds flour, 6 egg yolks, 2 ounces rose water, 1 ounce yeast dissolved in lukewarm water, and 4 ounces fresh butter or lard that does not smell bad, and quite a bit of salt, for half an hour so that the dough is well worked, and then roll it out thinly and cover with melted butter, that is not too hot, or lard, and with the pastry wheel cut all around the edges of the dough that are always thicker than the rest; sprinkle the dough with 4 ounces sugar, and 1 ounce cinnamon, and then have a pound of raisins that have been boiled in wine, and 1 pound of dates also cooked in wine and finely chopped, and 1 pound of seedless raisins boiled in wine, all mixed together with sugar, cinnamon, cloves and nutmeg, and then spread on the dough with pieces of butter, and roll up the dough lengthwise like crêpes, being careful not to break the dough, and this tortiglione must not be rolled up more than three turns so it cooks better, nor handled too much, but then basted with melted butter that is not too hot, then beginning from one end roll it up lightly like a snail or maze; and have a pie pan prepared with a sheet of the same dough, of the same thickness, basted with butter, and put it lightly over the tortiglione without pressing it down, and cook in the oven in a moderate heat, basting with butter from time to time, and when it is cooked sprinkle with sugar, rose water, and serve hot. The pie pan used for the tortiglione should be open and with low sides.*

41

*(continued from previous page)*

## YEAST CAKE STUFFED WITH RAISINS AND DATES

### FOR THE DOUGH:

1 package dry yeast or 1 cake (15g) compressed yeast
½ cup (1.25 dl) lukewarm water
3½ cups (440g) flour
½ teaspoon salt
3 egg yolks
2 tablespoons rose water
¼ cup (60g) sugar
¼ cup (60g) butter or lard, melted

### FOR THE FILLING:

1 cup (200g) raisins
1 cup (200g) currants
1 package (250g) pitted dates chopped
1 cup (2.5 dl) sweet white wine
⅓ cup (80g) melted butter or lard (for brushing)
½ cup (120g) sugar
1 tablespoon ground cinnamon
1 teaspoon ground nutmeg
½ teaspoon ground cloves
¼ cup (60g) butter, cut in pieces

### TO FINISH:

1 egg, beaten with ½ teaspoon salt (for glaze)-optional
1 tablespoon rose water
confectioners' sugar (for sprinkling)

9-inch (22-cm) pie pan; pastry brush

Rose water is available at pharmacies and Middle Eastern stores—a reflection of the Arabic origin of many of Scappi's pastries. Golden raisins can be substituted for the currants. Sugar has been added to the dough to help the yeast grow and hasten rising. This recipe serves 8.

FOR THE DOUGH: Crumble or sprinkle the yeast over the water

and let stand until dissolved. Sift the flour into a bowl with the salt and make a well in the center. Add the egg yolks, rose water, melted butter, sugar, and yeast mixture and stir to form a smooth dough. Turn out onto a lightly floured board and knead for 5 minutes or until the dough is smooth and elastic. Place the dough in a warm greased bowl, turn it over so it is lightly greased all over, cover with a damp cloth, and leave in a warm place to rise for 1½ hours or until doubled in bulk.

Simmer the raisins, currants, and dates in the wine for 8–10 minutes or until they are plump and the wine is absorbed; cool.

When the dough is risen, set the oven at hot (400°F or 205°C). Knead the dough lightly to knock out the air and set aside about a sixth of it. Roll out the remaining dough to the thinnest possible rectangle (about 12 × 18 inches) and trim the edges. Reserve the trimmings. Brush the dough with melted butter and sprinkle with ¼ cup (60 grams) of the sugar mixed with 1 tablespoon of the cinnamon. Mix the cooled raisin mixture with the remaining sugar and cinnamon, the nutmeg and cloves, and spread them on the dough. Dot the filling with the pieces of butter and fold the dough lengthwise to make three layers. Brush the top with melted butter and curl it up loosely in a spiral, with the original folds at the edges, taking care not to break the dough.

Roll out the reserved dough with the trimmings to a very thin round about 12 inches in diameter. Brush the pie pan with melted butter and set the dough spiral in it. Cover it with the dough round, tucking down the edges so the spiral is completely covered. Roll out any scraps to make petals, leaves, and a

stem for a flower decoration on top. Brush the top with melted butter and put in a warm place to rise for 40 minutes or until the dough has almost doubled in bulk. Set the oven at moderately hot (375°F or 190°C). Brush the roll with the egg glaze, if you like.

Bake the roll in the heated oven for ½ hour, turn down the heat to 325°F (165°C) and continue baking ½–1 hour or until well browned, basting from time to time with melted butter. If the cake browns too much during cooking, cover it with foil. When cooked, sprinkle while still hot with rose water, followed by confectioners' sugar, and serve at once.

Forks like these, finely wrought in silver, became status symbols during the Renaissance.

This famous saltcellar sculpted by Benevenuto Cellini for Francis I of France epitomizes the splendor of the

glass, porcelain, enamel, and precious metals that crowded the tables of the rich during the sixteenth century. The figures represent sea and air, sources of salt and pepper.

Scappi's basic knife, spoon, and fork (above) have a simple elegance that rivals the sumptuous silver forks used by the wealthy (right).

into fantastic shapes—waterlilies, melons, the cross of Lorraine, bishop's miters—but as the use of forks spread and eating became more discreet, the importance of napkins declined. Even so, pictures of Louis XIV at table a hundred years later show him wearing one of towel size, draped gracefully from the shoulder as was the custom.

Such complex table-setting and serving arrangements needed the careful supervision of the *trinciante* or carver. He was the third man in the catering triangle, on an equal footing with the cook. His duties have been minutely described by Vincente Cervio in *Il Trinciante*, printed in 1581. As well as dismembering birds and large cuts of meat, the carver was expected to personally serve his master, thus protecting him against the threat of poisoning—more a formality than a necessity by the sixteenth century. Popes and cardinals always took their private cooks on their journeys, and Cervio describes how to set up a special kitchen when a dignitary comes to stay. No doubt the *trinciante* and *scalco* were often at odds with each other, since according to Messisbugo it was the steward's responsibility to welcome guests with due ceremony. He also saw that the servants discharged their duties correctly and supervised journeys to and from the summer villa, not forgetting the fishing rods, playing cards, and dice. Another steward, Domenico Romoli, writing in 1560, warns against the danger of admitting the public to a banquet, as had been the custom. They get drunk, interfere with the service of food, and gobble up the leftovers; much better, he says, to admit onlookers only when the dancing begins and the tables have been cleared of food and precious silver and glass.

In a similar mood of austerity at his coronation in 1566, Pius V (a prudish pope who even had Michelangelo's nudes veiled) gave up the habit of throwing money to the Roman crowd and canceled altogether the usual anniversary banquet the following year. This reaction against the medieval tradition of free-for-all feasting ultimately spread throughout Europe. No longer was it considered the ruler's obligation to dine under the inquisitive gaze of his subjects. In England, this segregation of the classes had relatively little effect on the daily fare of the nobility, but in France it encouraged the development of two separate cooking styles— the *haute cuisine* of the court and nobility, and the *cuisine bourgeoise* that varied from region to region and was based on local ingredients.

Scanning *Opera*, with its more than 1,000 recipes

Scappi's kitchen boy twirls a whisk between both hands to smooth a sauce, exactly like the apprentices of today.

## TO MAKE NOODLES

4 cups (500g) all-purpose flour
3 eggs, beaten to mix
¼-½ cup (7-12.5 cl) lukewarm water
3 quarts (3l) meat or chicken stock, or 2½ quarts (2½l) milk and ⅔ cup (160g) butter

### FOR SERVING:

1 cup (125g) grated Parmesan or Romano cheese
½ cup (120g) granulated sugar mixed with 1 tablespoon ground cinnamon

Scappi's pasta dough is not seasoned but we would probably prefer it with ¾ teaspoon salt added. This recipe serves 6.

Sift the flour (with salt) onto a board or marble slab, make a well in the center, and add the eggs and most of the water. Start to draw the flour into the center, working the mixture with the fingers of one hand; if necessary add more water to make a smooth dough that is soft but not sticky. Knead the dough thoroughly for 5 minutes until it is very smooth and elastic, cover and let it stand 1 hour to lose some of its elasticity.

Roll out the dough as thinly as possible on a floured board, trim the edges and leave for about 15 minutes or until slightly dry but still pliable. Sprinkle the top with flour, roll up the dough loosely, and cut it crosswise into ½-inch strips. Alternatively, roll and cut the noodles with a pasta machine. Spread out the strips on wax paper or paper towels and leave to dry at least 3 hours.

Bring the stock or milk and butter to a boil, add the noodles, and simmer 10–12 minutes or until the noodles are tender but still firm (al dente). Drain them, rinse with hot water, and reheat in the pan with a little butter. Serve with bowls of grated cheese and cinnamon sugar for sprinkling.

## Per far minestra di tagliatelli

Scappi's pasta dough is exactly the same as that made today, both in ingredients and method. After rolling the dough, he wraps it around the rolling pin so it can be cut across easily at narrow intervals (for noodles) or more widely spaced (for broad pasta such as lasagne). Like Martino, Scappi serves his pasta with sugar, cinnamon, and cheese for sprinkling and he gives no indication whether the pasta should be drained or served in its cooking broth. Nor does he mention draining meat or vegetables, where appropriate, so perhaps he simply assumed the cook knew all about it.

*Knead together 2 pounds of fine white flour, 3 eggs and some luke-warm water, mixing them well on a table for the space of a quarter of an hour, and then roll out thinly and leave the pasta to dry for a while, trimming untidy bits at the edge, and when dry, but not too dry as then it would crumble, sprinkle with flour from the sieve to prevent the pasta sticking, and then take the pasta roller [rolling pin] and take one end of the pasta and roll it lightly around the pasta roller, and then slice the rolled up pasta with a broad sharp knife, and when the **tagliatelli** are cut stretch them out and leave them to dry a while, and when dry cook them in fat broth or with milk and butter, and when cooked serve hot with cheese, sugar, cinnamon, and if you wish to have lasagne, when the pasta is on the pasta roller, divide it across in two pieces, and then cut these into squares, and cook them in hare or crane broth, or any meat broth, and serve hot with cheese, sugar, and cinnamon.*

The Italian climate lends itself to eating
outdoors. In this late sixteenth-century
painting, guests in a leafy arbor are
served from the credenza, or buffet
table, laden with fruit and sweet pastries. Renaissance cooks developed flat
gâteaux, little cakes, and waffles to an
art which Scappi is the first to describe
in detail.

and dazzling display of a master cook's equipment
(so much of it still in use today), it might seem that in
1570 Renaissance Italians were irrevocably established as the leaders of European cooking. Yet
within fifty years the initiative had passed to Paris
which, as the focal point of French culture, offered a
more propitious setting for the development of
cooking than the factious cities of Italy. With the
end of the unifying spirit of the Renaissance, the
destiny of Italian cooking lay in the regions rather
than in a single town; Scappi's broad perspective on
cooking fell from favor and by the 1650s *Opera* was
out of print. Nonetheless, in its encyclopedic learning *Opera* marks the high point among Italian

cookbooks. Its design, accuracy, and detail reflect,
in its own sphere, an even more important
influence—that of the scientific method, which
made the seventeenth century a period of such outstanding European genius, more original and important, perhaps, than even the essentially conservative
humanism of the Renaissance itself.

45

# La Varenne

about 1615–1678

François Pierre de la Varenne is the founder of French classical cooking. Ever since it appeared in 1651 critics have both acclaimed and belittled his book *Le Cuisinier françois*, but no one has questioned its importance. It was the first French cookbook of any substance since *Le Viandier* almost 300 years before; it ran to thirty editions in seventy-five years, and as André Simon says, it became "the treasured possession of most French households of any distinction for close on a century." The reason for its success is simple: *Le Cuisinier françois* was the first book to record the immense advance which French cooking had made under the influence of Italy.

News of the Renaissance revolution in cooking began to reach France toward the end of the fifteenth century when King Charles VIII is said to have introduced his subjects to Parmesan cheese and macaroni. In 1505, the first French edition of *De honesta voluptate* appeared in Lyons where there was a thriving Italian community. Italy was powerful in politics as well as in the arts and it was natural that Francis I should have chosen an Italian princess, Catherine de Médicis, to marry his son, the future Henry II. Catherine brought with her a truly royal

A LA HAYE,
Chez ADRIAN VLAC. *1656*

*Title page of* Le Cuisinier françois.

*Catherine de Médicis (1519–1589), the wife of one French king and the mother of three, was renowned for her strength of mind and gourmandise.*

retinue of courtiers and cooks, and for over fifty years she dominated France with her Medici love of magnificence. Her greed was proverbial and on one occasion she overate so grossly of her favorite ragout of cockscombs, kidneys, and artichoke hearts that she almost burst; her son, Charles IX, narrowly avoided a similar fate because of his partiality for *salemigondis*, an Italian stew which inspired the French *salmis*.

By La Varenne's time—he was born around 1615—cooking at the French court had been further enhanced by a fresh influx of Italian chefs who arrived in 1600 with the marriage of yet

Opposite:
*In 1687, a few years after La Varenne's death, the city of Paris entertained Louis XIV at a lavish banquet. As at his ceremonial dinners at Versailles, only a few honored guests sat down with him at the table. Note the modest tableware; the outsize napkins of the ladies and the king suggest that, despite the forks, most food was still eaten with the fingers.*

another Medici, Marie, to Henri IV. Montaigne vividly portrays this new breed of artists in his account of a meeting with the master cook of Cardinal Caraffa: "With magisterial gravity, he delivered me a discourse on this science of food—first about the general composition of the sauces, and then describing in detail the nature of their ingredients and their effects; then about differences in salads according to the season: what should be heated and what should be served cold, and the way to garnish and embellish them to please the eye. After that he came to describing the order of service, full of fine and important considerations; the whole overlaid with rich and high-sounding words that are generally used to report upon the government of an empire."

Unwittingly, Montaigne had summed up the essence of the new cuisine. It was precisely such attention to detail, balance, and harmony that made the Renaissance arts so great. As applied to cooking, it meant the demise of the inflated banquets of medieval times, with their great displays of meat and fowl and their feckless use of costly spices. *Le Cuisinier françois* belongs to another world. Gone are the exotic birds and multi-flavored purées. Cuts of meat are easily identifiable and they are treated as now, with the best reserved for roasting and the rest cooked more slowly in liquid to break down the tough fibers. Both meat and fowl are simmered in subtly blended ragoûts, and La Varenne recognizes the importance of reducing cooking juice to concentrate the flavor. His very first recipe is for the all-important bouillon which is often called *fonds* (base) in French. He has several interesting liaisons flavored with mushrooms, almonds, or truffles, and La Varenne is the first French cook to add the classic thickening *roux* (of fat and flour) to bouillon to make velouté sauce. An astonishing number of modern dishes are mentioned in *Le Cuisinier françois*, including *boeuf à la mode, oeufs à la neige*, omelettes, beignets, and even pumpkin pie. He gives special attention to the preparation of vegetables, he uses a bouquet garni to flavor stocks and sauces, and he introduces such techniques as using egg whites to clarify a *gelée*.

La Varenne also introduced the French to new ways of cooking tail, feet, tongue, and other variety meats that had long been popular in Italy. Sea fish (especially lobsters and oysters) begin to rival freshwater fish in his repertoire, showing how communications with Paris, 100 miles from the sea, had improved. Not that this prevented the greatest drama in the

*A seventeenth-century* bourgeoise *does the marketing, taking her choice of peaches, apricots, grapes, plums, raspberries, apples, melons, and a number of vegetables. Inspired by the Italian example, the French improved the variety and quality of their produce enormously at this time.*

annals of cooking, the suicide of the Prince de Condé's cook, Vatel, in 1671. Madame de Sévigné describes how Vatel went unhappily to bed after the roast meat had run short at a dinner for the king. Determined that all should go well the next day, he rose early to take stock of his provisions. Only two carts of fish had arrived instead of the dozen he had ordered. The missing fish turned up fifteen minutes later, but Vatel knew nothing of it; in despair, unable to face the disgrace, he had run upon his sword. The court was overwhelmed by the news: "people said it was because his honor had meant so much to him; his courage was both praised and condemned."

At the court of Louis XIV it was a point of pride to be interested in cooking, and in the years that followed the publication of *Le Cuisinier françois* many nobles gaily turned their hands to the stove. The

Brilliant cook though he was, La Varenne's ability to express his ideas in writing leaves a good deal to be desired. He gives few quantities in his recipes and his instructions are much less detailed than those of his Italian predecessors. His use of spices is restrained and the omission of salt much more noticeable than it was earlier, when food tended to be saturated with spices. Salt and pepper have therefore been added to the following recipes.

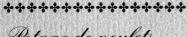

## *Potage de poulets aux pois verts*

Fresh green peas were new to France in the time of La Varenne, but he had already developed the classic combination of peas with lettuce found today in *petits pois à la française*. His potages are not soups but substantial stews.

*When your chickens are well cleaned and trussed, put them in a pot with good stock, and skim them well, then put your peas into a frying pan with butter or lard, and cook them gently with lettuces, that you have blanched (that is, put in cold water); also simmer your bread, and then garnish it with your chickens, peas and lettuces, then serve it.*

## CHICKEN CASSEROLE WITH GREEN PEAS

3½-4-pound (1¼-1¾-kg) roasting chicken, trussed
3 cups (7.5 dl) well-flavored chicken stock
1 large romaine lettuce, cut in 2-inch (5-cm) pieces
2 tablespoons (30g) butter
3-4 cups (350-450g) shelled fresh green peas
½ cup (1.25 dl) water
1 teaspoon sugar
salt and pepper
4 slices bread, crusts discarded

This recipe serves 4.

Put the chicken, breast up, in a large deep saucepan, pour 2 cups (5 deciliters) of the stock over it and bring slowly to a boil. The breast will cook in steam while the tougher thighs simmer in stock. Skim well, cover, and simmer ¾–1 hour or until the chicken is tender and no pink juice runs out when the thigh is pierced with a skewer. Take out the chicken and keep warm. Boil the stock until it is reduced to 1 cup (2.5 deciliters). Wash the lettuce thoroughly in cold water and drain it. In a casserole heat the butter and sauté the peas gently for 1–2 minutes without allowing them to brown. Add the water with the sugar, salt, and pepper and lay the lettuce on top. Cover and simmer for 15 minutes, stirring occasionally, or until the peas are just tender.

Work the bread, a little at a time, in a blender or rub it through a strainer to form crumbs. Bring the remaining 1 cup (2.5 deciliters) stock to a boil, add the breadcrumbs, and simmer gently until the mixture is the consistency of cooked cereal.

When the chicken is cooked, discard the trussing strings and set it on top of the peas and lettuce. Stir the reduced chicken stock into the breadcrumb mixture, bring this sauce to a boil, and taste it for seasoning. Spoon it over the chicken and serve.

## *Pasté d'anguilles*

This eel pâté is remarkably like *coulibiac*, a Russian dish which is popular in France today. *Coulibiac* consists of layers of salmon, hard-cooked eggs, chopped mushrooms, and rice, all enclosed in pastry. Even the accompanying sauces are similar; modern chefs would serve both melted butter (La Varenne puts butter inside the pâté) and hollandaise, which closely resembles La Varenne's sauce of egg yolks and verjuice (tart grape juice).

*Dress the eels, cut them in rounds and season them; prepare your pastry, and fill it with eel, hard-cooked egg yolks, mushrooms, truffles, if you have them, artichoke bottoms, and good fresh butter. Serve the pâté uncovered, with a white sauce made of egg yolks thinned with verjuice; in case it collapses, fasten it together with buttered paper and string; when cooked, discard the paper.*

## EEL PÂTÉ EN CROÛTE

FOR THE PASTRY:

3 cups (375g) flour
½ teaspoon salt
⅔ cup (160g) butter, at room temperature
⅓ cup (80g) lard or shortening
6-7 tablespoons (about 1 dl) cold water

FOR THE FILLING:

1½-pound (750g) fresh eel, skinned
yolks of 6 hard-cooked eggs, crumbled
½ pound (250g) small mushrooms, stems trimmed level with caps
small can truffles, drained and thinly sliced (optional)
4 cooked artichoke bottoms
⅔ cup (160g) butter
salt and pepper
1 egg, beaten to mix with ½ teaspoon salt (for glaze)

FOR THE SAUCE:

3 egg yolks
¼ cup (7 cl) verjuice
¼ cup (7 cl) water

*(continued from previous page)*

Salmon is an excellent alternative to eel. Verjuice is made of the strained juice of sour grapes or any unripe fruit; lemon juice is the best substitute. La Varenne refers to his sauce as "white"—it is possible that he whisked the egg yolks and verjuice together over very low heat to form a pale, mousselike sauce, as described below. For fish pâtés like this one, La Varenne suggests a "garnish from the garden, such as mushrooms, truffles, asparagus, hard-cooked egg yolks, artichoke bottoms, capers, chard [a white beet], pistachios," but a simple bunch of watercress is acceptable. This recipe serves 6.

TO MAKE THE PASTRY: Sift the flour with the salt onto a marble slab or board and make a well in the center. Add the butter and lard or shortening and work with the fingertips until the mixture resembles crumbs. Add a few tablespoons of cold water and continue working, adding more water as necessary, until the crumbs begin to stick together. Knead the dough lightly to form a ball, then work it with the heel of the hand for about 1 minute, pushing it away and bringing it together until it is as pliable as putty. Cover and chill.

TO FILL: Cut the eel into fillets, discarding the bone; cut each artichoke bottom into 3 rounds. Set the oven at hot (400°F or 205°C). Roll out the pastry dough on a floured board to a 15 × 10 inch rectangle. Arrange half the eel fillets in a 10 × 3½-inch strip in the center and sprinkle with salt and pepper. Add the crumbled hard-cooked egg yolks, mushroom caps, truffles if used, artichoke bottoms, and remaining eel fillets in layers, sprinkling each layer with salt and pepper, and dotting all but the top layer with butter. The rectangle should be as tall and as neat as possible.

Cut a square of excess dough from each corner and brush the edges of the dough rectangle with egg glaze. Lift one long edge of the dough on top of the filling and fold over the opposite edge to enclose it. Press gently to seal the dough and fold over the ends to make a neat package. Roll the package over onto a baking sheet so that the joined ends of dough are underneath. Brush pâté with glaze. Roll out the excess dough into a long strip, cut it into narrow bands, and lay the bands over the pâté to decorate it. Press one long band around the base to finish the edge. Brush the pâté again with glaze. Make a "collar" of doubled foil about 2 inches high, butter it, and tie it around the pâté with string or secure the ends with a pin. Make two small holes in the top of the pâté for steam to escape and insert two "chimneys" of foil to keep the holes open. Bake the pâté in the heated oven for 15 minutes or until the pastry is firm at the sides. Remove the foil collar, brush again with egg glaze, and continue baking 10 minutes or until the pastry is lightly browned. Turn down the oven to moderate (350°F or 177°C), cover the pâté loosely with foil, and continue baking 1–1¼ hours or until a skewer inserted in the center for ½ minute is hot to the touch when withdrawn.

FOR THE SAUCE: Put the egg yolks, verjuice, and water in a small heavy-based pan or in the top of a double boiler and heat gently, whisking constantly, for 5–7 minutes or until the mixture is light and mousselike and the consistency of hollandaise sauce. Add salt and pepper to taste. Do not cook it too quickly or allow it to become too hot or it will curdle.

TO SERVE: La Varenne suggests cutting around the top of the pâté and lifting off a lid of pastry to reveal the contents. A modern chef might cut the pâté like a loaf, so the layers can be seen. Either way the pâté should be served hot, with the sauce separately.

## *Lapereaux en ragoût*

Game birds, and young animals like the rabbit called for here, were favorites on the tables of the rich in the seventeenth century. However, the poor were not so lucky; game was reserved for the *seigneur* and in certain periods the penalty for poaching was death. La Varenne seasons this dish with a bouquet garni—one of the first mentions of the term.

*You can fricassée rabbits in the same way as chickens or sauté them in a frying pan with a little flour mixed with butter, put them to cook gently with good stock and season them with capers, orange or lemon juice, and a bouquet garni or scallions, then serve.*

## RAGOÛT OF RABBIT

4 tablespoons (30g) flour
salt and pepper
4 tablespoons (60g) butter
8 pieces (about 3 pounds or 1½ kg) rabbit
1½ cups (4 dl) stock
2 tablespoons capers
juice of 1 orange or 1 lemon
bouquet garni or 4 spring onions chopped

Chicken pieces can be used instead of rabbit in this recipe, which serves 4.

Add salt and pepper to the flour and use it to coat the pieces of rabbit. In a large skillet or shallow casserole melt the butter and brown the rabbit pieces on all sides over medium heat. Add the stock, the capers, orange or lemon juice, bouquet garni or spring onions, and bring to a boil. Cover and simmer on top of the stove or cook in a moderate oven (350°F or 177°C) for ¾–1 hour or until the rabbit is very tender. Taste the sauce for seasoning, discard the bouquet garni if using, and serve.

Duchess of Burgundy invented a sweet-sour sauce of vinegar and sugar for meat, and the indolent Duke of Nevers nonetheless bestirred himself to do his own marketing. The queen, Maria Theresa of Spain, tried to introduce the dishes of her homeland, but the French did not take to them kindly and only drinking chocolate and *olla podrida* (the catchall stew of beef, game, poultry, and vegetables that is served with its cooking broth) survived beyond her reign. To the king's mistress, Madame de Maintenon, goes the credit for *cotelettes à la Maintenon*, which were pared of their fat and baked in paper for the days when the royal digestion was in a delicate state.

This was not often; Louis XIV was a voracious eater, more glutton than gourmet. He liked his food floating in gravy with double the usual quantity of spice and was accustomed to consume "four plates of different potages, a whole pheasant, a partridge, a big plate of salad, lamb cut up in its gravy and seasoned with garlic, two good pieces of ham, a plateful of pastries, fruit, preserves, and hard cooked eggs" at a regular meal. Potages (which then meant anything cooked in a pot) are featured prominently by La Varenne. Some resemble a stew of meat and vegetables (including such classics as partridge with cabbage and duck with turnips) served with the reduced cooking liquid as gravy. Others are a purée of vegetables, sometimes thickened with bread, resembling a modern soup.

During the seventeenth century the range of fruit and vegetables in France was transformed, not only by imports from the Far East and the Americas, but also by more extensive cultivation of plants that had hitherto been ignored. Henri IV had planted the first orangery at the Tuileries Palace at the turn of the century, and fifty years later La Varenne could take the availability of oranges and lemons for granted, not to mention plums, apricots, peaches, and cultivated strawberries. Among vegetables, leeks and onions lost their monopoly to cucumbers, kale, carrots, and cauliflower. Spinach was well established, having become fashionable at the time of Catherine de Médicis (hence *florentine* for a spinach garnish), and the variety of salad greens was much greater—chicory dates from this time, as does romaine lettuce, the seeds of which were reputedly sent from Rome by Rabelais in 1537. Globe artichokes, credited with aphrodisiac properties, were unfailingly popular.

From the New World came potatoes and tomatoes, though the former were not widely grown until the

In this illustration from Le Jardinier françois *by* Nicholas de Bonnefons (1651), *cooks are peeling fruit (left), boiling preserves, and skimming jam (foreground). At the back a cook rolls fruit cheese, a confection of fruit and sugar worked until candied. Behind her hang molds and a jelly bag.*

1750s, and tomatoes were long suspected of being poisonous. However, Jerusalem artichokes were adopted more quickly and La Varenne suggests braising them, then sautéing them with onions and a grate of nutmeg. They came from North America, but the French named them *taupinambours* because their introduction coincided with the arrival in Paris of some Brazilian Indians of the Topinambour tribe. Their English name is equally misleading; the early American colonists called them artichokes because they tasted like the globe variety, while the Italians realized that they belonged to the sunflower family or *girasole*, a word which became anglicized to Jerusalem.

The inspiration these new ingredients offered to an inventive cook can be imagined. La Varenne eagerly proposes such recipes as asparagus or cauliflower soup, fricassee of cucumber and artichokes *à la poivrade*. He delights in green peas, a new arrival from Italy, putting them in soups and serving them with chicken. Later, green peas became a craze at court, and Madame de Sévigné noted in 1696: "There is no end to this interest in peas. . . . Some ladies sup with the king, and sup well at that, only to return home to eat peas before retiring, without any care for their digestion."

La Varenne was scarcely thirty-five when *Le Cuisinier françois* first appeared. At that point he had already been master cook for ten years to the Marquis d'Uxelles, for whom he named his most famous creation, the duxelles of mushrooms seasoned with herbs and shallots, which is still a favorite flavoring for fish and vegetables. Beyond that, little is known about La Varenne himself, except that his name was a pseudonym, taken for some reason from a disreputable cook of an earlier generation who did a little pimping business for his master, Henri IV, and "gained more by carrying the *poulets* (love letters) of the king than by larding them in the kitchen." La Varenne died in 1678 in relative obscurity, having benefited little from his success as a bestselling author.

La Varenne is also credited with the authorship of *Le Pastissier françois*, the first comprehensive French work on pastry-making and one of the most remarkable cookbooks of all time. Although a comparatively large printing was made by the illustrious Elzevir Press in 1655 (two years after the book first appeared), few copies survive, no doubt because of "the sticky fingers of the loyal craftsmen who have used it" over the years. And no wonder; many modern cookbooks could take a lesson from *Le*

*During the seventeenth century, the medieval art of carving meat was extended to cutting artistic designs in pears, oranges, and other fruit.*

*Pastissier*, with its step-by-step directions, accurate measurements, and instructions for temperature control. The book is clearly inspired by Italian works such as Scappi's *Opera* that were most detailed and sophisticated in their treatment of pastry. The methods in *Le Pastissier* for making pie pastry, puff pastry, macaroons, and waffles, for instance, are precisely the same today, and it is the first book to mention the small baking ovens known as *petits fours*, now the name for the little cakes and cookies often served with coffee.

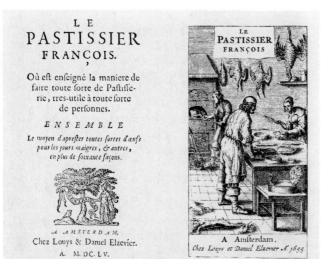

*The title page of the 1655 edition of* Le Pastissier françois *from the celebrated Elzevir Press. A pastry cook was responsible for savory pâtés and pies as well as sweet pastries, hence the game hanging in the kitchen. On the stool is a finished peacock pie decorated with the head and tail feathers.*

La Varenne's name, however, did not appear on any of the early editions of *Le Pastissier françois*, and there is some reason to doubt that he wrote it. The profession of *pâtissier* was completely separate from that of *cuisinier*, and it is hard to believe that two years after writing *Le Cuisinier françois*, the same author could turn out a second book so different in style and content. Several of the same recipes appear in both books, but *Le Pastissier* is much more

detailed; its author gives precise instructions, while La Varenne writes in a shorthand that assumes a thorough knowledge of cooking. If La Varenne did write the book, he must have worked closely with an Italian pastry cook.

French cooking developed so rapidly in the wake of *Le Cuisinier françois* that even before his death, La Varenne was criticized as old-fashioned. In 1674, for example, an unidentified Sieur Roland upbraided La Varenne for "such a prodigious superfluity of dishes, such a quantity of stew and hotchpotch, such a singular compilation of viands. . . ." It is certainly true that some medieval traits linger in *Le Cuisinier françois*. La Varenne has a tendency to use archaic flavorings like musk and ambergris (believed to be an aphrodisiac) and he recommends some very medieval pies and hashes containing, to modern tastes, an inordinate number of ingredients. Some of his garnishes are lavish in the extreme, like *béatilles* made of cockscombs, chicken wingtips, and livers sautéed and served in a sauce thickened with egg yolk. French writers have also accused La Varenne of the reactionary habit of sweetening savory dishes with sugar, but here they may be mistaken. His intention was probably to achieve with delicate meats like chicken the same kind of sweet-sour effect that we still enjoy with cheesecake. Such combinations have all but disappeared from the French repertoire but are still very much alive in the cooking of northern Europe, particularly Germany and Scandinavia.

*Le Cuisinier françois* is a seminal work; it marks the end of medieval cooking and the beginning of *haute cuisine* and as such it contains elements of both. When it was written, France was entering a period of prosperity as the memory of the bitter religious wars of the previous century receded and the reign of Louis XIV, the Sun King, assumed all its glory. La Varenne opened the way to this new era, sharing the limelight with only one other cook, Massialot, who wrote *Le Cuisinier royal et bourgeois* in 1691. Fifty years later both books had been superseded by an outpouring of new works; La Varenne was disparaged and then forgotten. Yet he was the first cook to bring order to an undisciplined art that had been developing in France, virtually undocumented for three centuries. Without him French cooking might never have reached its full flower.

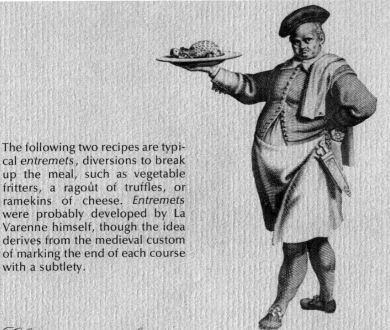

The following two recipes are typical *entremets*, diversions to break up the meal, such as vegetable fritters, a ragoût of truffles, or ramekins of cheese. *Entremets* were probably developed by La Varenne himself, though the idea derives from the medieval custom of marking the end of each course with a subtlety.

## Champignons farcis

Fairy ring mushrooms, morels, truffles, and fungi of all kinds were enormously popular in the seventeenth century. Louis XIII loved them so much that as he lay on his deathbed he insisted on stringing morels to dry for the summer. A *bard* is a thin sheet of pork fat.

*Choose the largest mushrooms to hold the stuffing, which you will make of several meats or good herbs, so that it is delicate, and bind it with egg yolks, then your mushrooms being stuffed and seasoned, set them on a bard or on a little butter; cook them and serve with lemon juice.*

## STUFFED MUSHROOMS

½ pound (250g) uncooked veal or breast of chicken
2 tablespoons chopped chives
salt and pepper
2 egg yolks
1 pound (500g) large mushroom caps
3 tablespoons (45g) butter
a squeeze of lemon juice

This recipe serves 4 as a first course or an accompaniment to a main dish.

Set the oven at moderate (350°F or 177°C). Work the veal or chicken meat twice through the fine plate of a grinder. Add the chives with plenty of salt and pepper and stir in the egg yolks to bind the mixture. Remove the stems from the mushrooms and spoon the mixture into the mushroom caps, mounding it well. Spread the butter in a heatproof baking dish, set the mushrooms on top, and bake them in the heated oven, basting often, for 25–30 minutes or until the mushrooms are tender and the stuffing is browned. Sprinkle with lemon juice and serve hot.

## Asperges à la sauce blanche

This "white sauce" made with butter and egg yolks, but not a trace of flour, illustrates how the art of making sauces was still in its infancy at the time of La Varenne. It is an early version of hollandaise, which had not yet received its name.

*Take stalks of asparagus, scrape them, then cut them equally, cook them with water and some salt and take them out as lightly cooked as possible, it is the best, and let them drain, then make a sauce with fresh butter, a yolk of egg, salt, nutmeg, a trickle of vinegar, and when all is well stirred and the sauce subtly thickened, serve it.*

## ASPARAGUS WITH CREAM SAUCE

1–1½ pounds (500-700g) fresh asparagus
salt

FOR THE SAUCE:

1 egg yolk
1½ teaspoons white wine vinegar
pinch of salt
pinch of nutmeg
¼ cup (60g) butter

This recipe serves 2.

Trim the white part from the asparagus so the stalks are the same length. Rinse them in cold water and with a vegetable peeler remove the tough skin from the lower ends of the stems. Tie the stalks in two bundles and stand them, stems down, in 1–2 inches boiling salted water in an asparagus cooker or a tall pan such as the bottom of a double boiler. Cover and simmer 8–10 minutes or until the green tips are just tender. Lift the asparagus carefully from the pan, drain on paper towels, discard the strings, and keep in a warm place.

FOR THE SAUCE: Put the egg yolk, vinegar, salt, nutmeg, and a nut of the butter in a heavy-based pan or in the top of a double boiler and heat gently, whisking lightly. Whisk in the remaining butter piece by piece so the sauce thickens creamily. Do not allow it to become too hot or it will curdle. Taste the sauce for seasoning and pour into a bowl to serve with the asparagus.

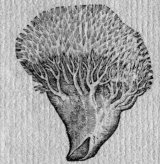

Noix pour jouër, faire de l'hui-le, ou manger, ainsi que les POIDS VERT, ou POIDS MANGE-TOUT.

*Capiuntur Homo pisces.*
On prend des Poissons à l'Hameçon.

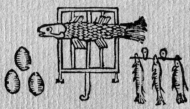

## Oeufs frais ,

POISSON Roti & HARANGS Salés, font pour le Carême & autres jours de l'année, soit maigres ou gras, & selon l'apétit ou le bon marché.

*"Walnuts are for playing, for making oil and for eating, and so are green peas," says a seventeenth-century child's primer.*

## To make another soft Cake or Tart without Cheese, which Cake the Flemmings do call Bread dipped in Eggs

The following recipe comes from *The Perfect Cook*, a translation of *Le Pastissier françois* that was published in London in 1656, making it one of the very first French cookbooks to appear in England. The detailed instructions illustrate clearly the difference in style between *Le Pastissier* and *Le Cuisinier françois*—such precision was not to be equaled until the time of Carême, writing 150 years later.

*Put into a Bason, or upon a Table, two pints of fine flower, break and beat two eggs into it, adde thereunto half a pound of fresh butter which you shall have caused to be melted over the fire, with a quarter of a pint of milk, put also into this mixture a spoonful of good beer yeast which is somewhat thick, and rather more than less, as also salt at discretion. You must well mixe and work all these things together with your hands, till you reduce them into a well knitted paste, and in the kneading of this*

*your paste you must now and then powder it with a little flower.*
*Your paste being thus well powdered will be firm, after which make it up into the form of a Loaf, and placing it upon a sheet of Paper, you must cover it with a hot Napkin.*
*You must also observe to set your said paste neer unto the fire, but not too high, lest that side which should bee too nigh the fire might become hard. You shall leave this said paste in the said indifferent hot place untill it be sufficiently risen, and it will require at least five quarters of an hours time to rise in and when it shall be sufficiently risen, which you may know by its splitting, and separating it self, you must make it up into the form of a Cake, or Tart, which you must garnish over, and then put it into the Oven to bee baked.*
*The Ovens hearth must be as hot almost as when you intend to bake indifferent great household Bread. This Tart or Cake will require almost three quarters of an hours baking, or at least a great half hour; and when it is drawn forth of the Oven, you may powder it with some sugar, and sprinkle it with some rose-water before you do serve it up to the Table, which depends of your will.*

## RICH EGG BREAD

1 cup (250g) butter, cut in pieces
1¼ cups (3dl) milk
2 packages dry yeast or 2 cakes (30g) compressed yeast
5½-6 cups (700-800g) flour
1½ teaspoons salt
2 eggs, beaten to mix
1 egg, beaten to mix with ½ teaspoon salt (for glaze)

TO FINISH (OPTIONAL):

confectioners' sugar (for sprinkling)
1 teaspoon rose water

This recipe makes 1 large round of bread.

Heat the butter with the milk until melted and let cool to tepid. Sprinkle or crumble the yeast over it and leave 5 minutes or until dissolved. Sift 5½ cups (700 grams) of the flour with the salt into a bowl or onto a board, make a well in the center, and add the eggs with the yeast mixture. Stir with the hand, gradually drawing in the flour to make a dough that is soft but not sticky, adding more flour if necessary. Knead the dough on a floured board until smooth and elastic. Shape the dough into a ball, set it on a floured tray, and sprinkle the top with flour. Cover it with a warm cloth and set in a warm place for 1–1½ hours or until the surface begins to crack.
Knead the dough to knock out the air, shape it into a round loaf, and set it on a baking sheet. Cover it and leave again to rise for 1 hour or until almost doubled in bulk. Set the oven at hot (400°F or 205°C). When the dough is risen, brush it with egg glaze and bake in the heated oven for 30 minutes; turn the oven down to moderate (350°F or 177°C) and continue baking for 55 minutes or until the loaf is browned and sounds hollow when tapped on the bottom. Transfer it to a rack to cool. If you like, while the bread is still hot sprinkle the top with sugar and spoon over the rose water.

Opposite:
*This French feast of 1707 with its horseshoe table and great pièces montées, or subtleties, shows how medieval banqueting habits still lingered among the fruits, rich gâteaux, and pastries of a more sophisticated age.*

Combite que dio tres noches seguidas en ___ Paris el ex.<sup>mo</sup> Señor Duque de Alva ~
en celebracion del nacimiento del Seren.<sup>mo</sup> ___ Señor Principe de Asturias año 1707

# Robert May

1588–about 1665

To turn from French to English cooking in 1600 is
to step back in many ways a hundred years. The
refinements of the Renaissance, spreading northward
through France, were slow to cross the Channel and
the influence of Scappi and the other great Italian
chefs was so remote as to be almost imperceptible.
Memories of great medieval banquets, with their
indiscriminate display of flesh, fish, and fowl, were
still very much alive. It was with small success that
Henrietta Maria of Spain, who married Charles I in
1625, tried to introduce the dishes of her homeland
to the court.

However, the proud independence of the English
table was soon to be subverted by far more lasting
influences, resulting from the political upheavals of
Charles I's reign and the Civil War. For years
refugees scuttled to and fro across the Channel and
the future King Charles II made France his home for
a decade. By the end of the interregnum, when the
king was restored in 1660, English cooks finally
struck out in new directions, determined at least to
try the fancy foreign foods that seemed to be so much
enjoyed elsewhere.

A cautious interest in the new cooking of conti-
nental Europe, tempered by a truly British determination to stick to tradition, characterize *The Accomplisht Cook* by Robert May, first published in 1660.
May opens his book with four pages on the Spanish
stew of *olla podrida*, known to the English as olio.
Later he describes how to make *stoffado* (pot roast)
and *quelque shose* (fancy French dishes which the
English mockingly called "kickshaws") and cheer-
fully labels some very English ways of cooking meat
as *à la mode*. A poetic tribute at the front of the book
notes:

> *He is so universal, he'l not miss,*
> *The Pudding nor Bolonian Sausages.*
> *Italian, Spaniard, French, he all*
>     *out-goes,*
> *Refines their Kickshaws and Their*
>     *olios.*

But behind this chic façade, May turns with relief to
those quintessentially English dishes: puddings,
pies, and roasts. As William Forrest, an Elizabethan
chronicler, remarked: "Our English nature cannot
live by roots, by water, herbs, or such beggary bag-
gage, that may well serve for vile outlandish quarters; give Englishmen meat after their old usage,
beef, mutton, veal, to cheer their courage." By
May's time roasting had really come into its own,
and large cuts of meat like leg of mutton, loin of

THE

# Accomplisht Cook,

### OR THE

## ART & MYSTERY

OF

# COOKERY.

Wherein the whole A R T is revealed in a
more easie and perfect Method, than hath
been publisht in any language.

Expert and ready Ways for the Dressing of all Sorts
of FLESH, FOWL, and FISH, with variety of
SAUCES proper for each of them; and how to
raise all manner of *Pastes*; the best Directions for
all sorts of *Kickshaws*, also the *Terms* of CAR-
VING and SEWING.

An exact account of all *Dishes* for all *Seasons* of the
Year, with other *A-la-mode Curiosities*

The Fifth Edition, with large Additions throughout
the whole work: besides two hundred Figures of
several Forms for all manner of bak'd Meats,
(either Flesh, or Fish) as, Pyes Tarts, Custards,
Cheesecakes, and Florentines, placed in Tables,
and directed to the Pages they appertain to.

Approved by the fifty five Years Experience and In-
dustry of *ROBERT MAY*, in his Atten-
dance on several Persons of great Honour.

*London*, Printed for *Obadiah Blagrave* at the *Bear* and
*Star* in St. *Pauls Church-Yard*, 1685.

Opposite:
*On 18 November 1623, King James I of
England and his son Charles (left)
entertained the Spanish ambassador at
an intimate dinner, in striking contrast
to the public feasts of medieval times.
The square table is typical of the Stuart
period.*

*Carving was one of the many medieval rituals that survived to Robert May's time. The figures below of a leg, quarter, and shoulder of lamb and a beef tongue are typical of those in carving manuals of the time.*

pork, chine of beef, and whole lamb added variety to the smaller roasts of the medieval table. For accompaniment May suggests a series of "sauces" that might well have come from a modern English menu. "Mustard," he writes, "is good with brawn, beef, chine of bacon and mutton; verjuyce [tart fruit juice] good to boiled chicken and capons." He also recommends "swan with chaldrons," an essence of entrails probably rather like meat glaze, and "ribs of beef with garlick, mustard, pepper, verjuyce, and ginger."

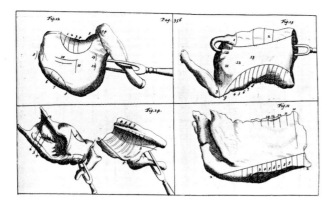

Large roasts demanded considerable skill in carving, an art graphically summed up in an early sixteenth-century book from which Robert May quotes at length. "Break that deer," he urges, "leach [slice] that brawn," "rear that goose," "lift that swan," and so on through more than three dozen different birds and fishes. Such instructions were of ancient origin, but they were by no means superfluous in a time when meat was cut up before serving because everyone ate with their fingers and a spoon. The fork had been brought to England from Italy in 1608 by Thomas Coryat, but it remained an object of curiosity and earned its importer the nickname of *Furcifer*—literally fork-bearer, but also meaning a villain who deserves the gallows. It was not until the 1650s that the use of forks became widespread, and one ingenious rogue made a small fortune under Parliament by selling knives and forks as souvenirs supposedly made from a bronze statue of Charles I, who had lately been beheaded.

French and Italian influence also acquainted the English with new vegetables. *The Accomplisht Cook* contains recipes for "spinage" tart, buttered "sparagus" and pickled "cowcumbers." In their

Robert May, like his French contemporary La Varenne, specifies few quantities in his recipes, but he does take care with seasoning, invariably adding salt where appropriate.

✦✦✦✦✦✦✦✦✦✦✦✦✦✦✦✦

## *To Stew Crabs*

With no inland point further than sixty miles from the coast, the English have always consumed a good deal of shellfish.

*Being boil'd take the meat out of the shells, and put it in a pipkin with some claret wine, and wine vinegar, minced tyme, pepper, grated bread, salt, the yolks of two or three hard eggs strained or minced very small, some sweet butter, capers, and some large mace; stew it finely, rub the shells with a clove or two of garlick, then dish the shells, the claws and little legs round about them, put the meat into the shells, and so serve them.*

## PIQUANT CRABMEAT

⅔ cup (160g) butter
2 cups (1 pound or 500g) crab meat
1 cup (2.5 dl) red wine
1½ tablespoons wine vinegar
1 teaspoon thyme
1⅓ cups (100g) fresh white breadcrumbs
2 hard-cooked egg yolks, sieved
1 tablespoon capers
¼ teaspoon ground mace
salt and pepper
1 clove garlic, cut

### FOR GARNISH:

2 tablespoons (30g) butter
½ pound (250g) crab claws

4 large or 8 small crab shells or individual serving dishes

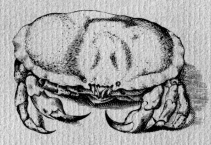

This recipe serves 4 as a main dish or 8 as a first course.

Melt the ⅔ cup (160 grams) butter in a pan and add the crab meat, wine, vinegar, thyme, bread-crumbs, egg yolks, capers, mace, salt, and pepper. Cook gently, stirring occasionally, for 8 minutes or until most of the liquid has evaporated. Rub the crab shells or serving dishes with the cut garlic clove.

FOR THE GARNISH: Melt the butter, add the crab claws with a little salt and pepper, and heat gently. When the crab meat mixture is cooked, taste it for seasoning, pile it in the crab shells or dishes, and top with the crab claws.

## To Bake Turkey for to be eaten cold

Turkeys, brought from the Americas in the sixteenth century, had become commonplace in England a century later. Pies like this, containing a whole boned bird with stuffing, were still served at Christmas 100 years ago and less elaborate pies of veal, ham, or pork are an English institution. Interestingly, Robert May was well aware that cold food needed more seasoning than hot. The lard used in this recipe as a stuffing was almost certainly bacon (*lard* in French); skirret is a root resembling parsnip.

*Take a turkey-chicken, bone it, and lard it with pretty big lard, a pound and half will serve, then season it with an ounce of pepper, an ounce of nutmegs, and two ounces of salt, lay some butter in the bottom of the pye, then lay on the fowl, and put in it six or eight whole cloves, then put on all the seasoning with good store of but-ter, close it up, and baste it over with eggs, bake it, and being baked fill it up with clarified butter.*

*Thus you may bake them for to be eaten hot, giving them but half the seasoning, and liquor it with gravy and juyce of orange.*

*Bake this pye in fine paste; for more variety you may make a stuffing for it as followeth; mince some beef-suet and a little veal very fine, some sweet herbs, grated nutmeg, pepper, salt, two or three raw yolks of eggs, some boil'd skirrets or pieces of artichocks, grapes, or gooseberries, etc.*

## TURKEY PIE

puff pastry made with 1½ cups (375g) butter, 3 cups (400g) flour, ½ teaspoon salt, and 1-1¼ cups (2.5-3 dl) cold water
9-10-pound (4½-5kg) whole turkey, boned with bones reserved (see below)
1 teaspoon ground white pepper
1 teaspoon ground nutmeg
1½ teaspoons salt
¼ cup (60g) butter
3-4 whole cloves
1 egg, beaten to mix with ½ teaspoon salt (for glaze)

### FOR THE STUFFING:

½ pound (250g) beef suet, ground
½ pound (250g) ground veal
1 tablespoon chopped parsley
1 tablespoon mixed chopped herbs (chives, thyme, marjoram, and oregano)
1 teaspoon ground nutmeg
salt and pepper
3 egg yolks
½ pound (250 g) cooked parsnips cut in walnut-sized pieces or 4 cooked artichoke bottoms, cut in eighths
½ pound (about 1 cup or 250g) seedless green grapes

### FOR SERVING HOT:

turkey bones and giblets
1 tablespoon orange juice

### FOR SERVING COLD:

¼ cup (60g) melted butter

A deep 14-inch (35-cm) oval or round pie dish or shallow baking dish

Instructions for boning the turkey and making puff pastry can be found in any classic cookbook. Beef suet is obtainable at most butchers—the best comes from around the kidneys. This recipe serves 12.

Make the puff pastry and chill thoroughly.

FOR THE STUFFING: Mix the suet, veal, herbs, nutmeg, and salt and pepper, adding plenty of seasoning if the pie is to be served cold. Stir in the egg yolks. Spread out the boned turkey, skin side down, and sprinkle it with white pepper, nutmeg, and salt. Spread the veal stuffing on top and scatter over it the pieces of parsnip or artichoke and grapes. Fold the edges of the turkey skin to the center, overlapping them to make a round or oval that will fit the pie dish. Spread the ¼ cup (60 grams) butter in the pie dish and lay the dish upside-down on the folded turkey. Turn over turkey and dish and set right side up; tuck the cloves under the turkey. Set the oven at hot (425°F or 218°C).

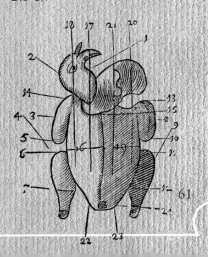

61

*(continued from previous page)*

Roll out the pastry 1 inch larger than the dish and cover the top of the pie, tucking the pastry down into the edges to allow for shrinkage. Cut a small hole in the center for steam to escape. Make a 1-inch chimney from aluminum foil and place it in the hole. Brush the pie with egg glaze. Decorate the top with leaves and flowers made from pastry trimmings and brush these also with glaze.

Bake the pie in the heated oven for 20–25 minutes or until the pastry is puffed and lightly browned. Set a pan on the rack underneath to catch any drippings. Cover the pie with foil, tucking it under the edges. Turn down the oven to moderate (350°F or 177°C) and continue baking for 2 hours or until a skewer inserted in the center of the pie for half a minute is very hot to the touch when withdrawn.

IF SERVING HOT: Simmer the turkey giblets and bones in water to cover with a very little salt for 1–1½ hours. Strain this stock and boil it until reduced to ¼ cup (7 centiliters); add the orange juice. When the pie is cooked, heat the orange juice mixture until very hot, but not boiling, and pour it into the pie through the steam hole.

IF SERVING COLD: Let the pie cool to tepid. Pour in the melted butter and let the pie cool completely.

### To Roast a Shoulder of Mutton with Onions and Parsley, and Baste it with Oranges

England was famous for wool as early as the second century and by the Middle Ages the mutton from her sheep had become the staple meat. Oranges appear in many of May's recipes—they had been common in England since Elizabethan times, when cheerful crowds were in the habit of throwing oranges and eggs at each other on May Day. Anchovy is excellent with lamb, giving a piquant flavor with no trace of fish.

*Stuff [the mutton] with parsley and onions, or sweet herbs, nutmeg, and salt, and in the roasting of it, baste it with the juyce of oranges, save the gravy and clear away the fat; then stew it up with a slice or two of orange and an anchovie, without any fat on the gravy, etc.*

## ROAST SHOULDER OF LAMB WITH ORANGE

4-5-pound (2-2½-kg) shoulder of lamb, blade bone removed to make a pocket
2 tablespoons (30g) butter
1½ cups (3.5 dl) orange juice
1 cup (2.5 dl) boiling water
1-2 slices of orange
2 anchovy fillets, finely chopped

FOR THE STUFFING:

¼ cup (60g) butter
5 medium onions, sliced
medium bunch of parsley, chopped, with stems discarded
¼ teaspoon ground nutmeg
salt

Trussing needle or poultry pins and string

This recipe serves 4–6.

Set the oven at moderately hot (375°F or 190°C).

FOR THE STUFFING: In a saucepan melt the ¼ cup (60 grams) butter, add the onions, and press a piece of foil on top. Cover with the lid and cook very gently, stirring occasionally, for 15—20 minutes until the onions are very soft; do not brown them. Remove the foil, let cool, and stir in the parsley and nutmeg with salt to taste. Put the stuffing into the pocket in the lamb and sew it up or fasten it with poultry pins and string. Spread the 2 tablespoons (30 grams) butter over the meat, set it in a roasting pan, and spoon over a little of the orange juice. Roast the lamb in the heated oven, allowing 18 minutes a pound plus 18 minutes more for medium-done meat, or until a meat thermometer registers 160°F (71°C). Baste the meat often during cooking with the orange juice, reserving ½ cup (1.25 deciliters). Transfer the lamb to a platter, removing the string, and keep warm. Discard all the fat from the pan, add the boiling water, remaining orange juice, orance slices, and anchovy and bring the gravy to a boil, stirring to dissolve the pan juices and crushing the orange slices and anchovy. Simmer 5 minutes and taste for seasoning. Strain and serve separately with the lamb.

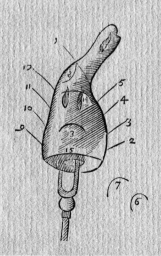

appreciation of potatoes and salads, the English were a step ahead of the French; La Varenne has scarcely a salad recipe, but Robert May devotes a whole section to salads of all kinds. According to John Evelyn, who wrote a book on salads in 1699 called *Acetaria*, "sallets are a composition of edule [edible] plants and roots of several kinds, to be eaten raw or green, blanch'd or candied [i.e., pickled]." Robert May's idea of a salad is much wider—he adds almost anything and arranges the ingredients lovingly in patterns on the platter. The common bond is a dressing made of "oyl and vinegar beaten together, the best oyl you can get."

These innovations did not dislodge pies from their supremacy on the English table. Cooks vied with each other in baking outsize pies like one from the diocesan kitchens of Durham cathedral which contained a hundred turkeys. Pies were also a favorite vehicle for practical jokes. *Antiquitates Culinariae*, one of the earliest histories of food dating from 1791, relates how in earlier times dwarfs would be hidden in giant pies, undergoing such "temporary incrustation for the cruel amusement of their owners." On other occasions clowns interrupted banquets by plunging into custard pies "to the unspeakable amusement of those who were far enough from the tumbler not to be bespattered by this active gambol." One famous party trick lives on, at least in the nursery:

> Sing a song of sixpence,
> A pocketful of rye,
> Four and twenty blackbirds
> Baked in a pie.
> When the pie was opened,
> The birds began to sing.
> Oh! wasn't that a dainty dish
> To set before a king.

Robert May himself is famous for a truly monstrous "trophy" to which he gives pride of place at the front of his book. "The likeness of a ship of war in pasteboard" is drawn into the dining room on a cart to confront a cardboard and pastry castle with battlements, portcullis, and guns of pasteboard armed

THE QUEENE-LIKE CLOSET Or RICH CABINET

Printed for Rich: Chiswell And Tho: Sawbridge 1681.

2 *Cucumis Anguinus.*
Adders Cucumber.

1 *Lactuca sativa.*
Garden Lettuce.

with real gunpowder. In between stands a giant pastry stag (full of wine) and to its right and left two great pies, one containing live blackbirds, the other live frogs (inserted in the baked pie shells through a hole in the crust). A lady then sets off the frolic by pulling an arrow from the stag. Out gushes its "blood" and while the guns of the ship and the castle fire away, the ladies throw eggshells of sweet water at each other to "sweeten the stinck of powder." Finally, when the fun begins to pall, the lid of a pie is lifted and "out skip some frogs, which make the ladies to skip and shreek." Next come the blackbirds, whose flight extinguishes the candles "so that what with the flying birds and skipping frogs, the one above, the other beneath, will cause much delight and pleasure to the whole company."

Such amusements had been common at the court of Queen Elizabeth, under whose reign May was born in 1588. His life spanned four reigns as well as the intervening rule of Parliament—some of the most turbulent years of English history—and at the end of his career in the 1660s May looked back wistfully on the peace and prosperity of Elizabeth's age. "Hospitality," he lamented, "which was once a relique of the gentry and a known cognizance to all ancient houses, hath lost her title through the unhappy and cruel disturbances of these times."

Nonetheless May's career shows that England was more affluent than ever before. By his own account his training began in Paris, where he spent five years as a youth, followed by apprenticeship in London and appointments in thirteen different households. All his employers were gentry or minor members of the nobility, an unheard-of possibility a hundred years earlier, before commerce had enriched the merchant oligarchy and when only royalty or the church could have afforded a cook of May's education. Needless to say, the staff he commanded was more modest; in place of the hundreds supervised by a master cook in Taillevent's times, Robert May probably headed a team of twenty to twenty-five. Most would have worked in the kitchen itself. According to an account of an earl's household in 1617, the kitchen staff included several undercooks (May's father, himself a cook, had four), three pastrycooks, three kitchen boys, a buyer, purveyor (supplier), a part-time butcher, and three errand boys. The rest of the staff were assigned to the cellar, pantry, buttery, ewery, and scullery, showing that medieval household organization had survived more or less intact.

Tarts Royal these first three.

Strawberry Tart, *fig.* 246.

Closed Tarts of several Fruits, according to the season of the year, in the middle commonly called a Trotter Pye, *p.* 242.

Laid Tart.　　Laid Tart of three colours.　　Laid Tarts.　　Laid Tarts.

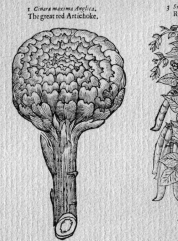

3 *Smilax hortenfis rubra.*
Red Kidney Beane.

2 *Phaseolus niger.*
Blacke Kidney Beane.

Overleaf:
*The coronation feast of James II was given in Westminster Hall in 1685, twenty years after Robert May died, but formal dining would have changed little. The custom of covering every inch of space on the table with dishes arranged in a geometric pattern shows clearly; little space is left for serving plates and none for glasses, which are passed by the servers.*

*Wine, women, and song add to the pleasures of good food; note the pies decorated with plumaged birds. Pies are all-important to Robert May—whether baked in a pie dish or enclosed like a medieval pasty with a top and bottom crust, he gives at least a hundred recipes for them. For raised pies the lid and sides of crust were often used instead of a dish and were not eaten. Some of his suggestions for decorating the lids are shown below.*

All manner of Cut-Laid Tarts, either in puff pafte, or any ftrained ftuff, or of preferved ftone-fruit or Curuel'd fruit.

Difhes of minced Pies for all manner of Flefh or Fowl, according to thefe Forms, *Page* 232, 233.

Set Tarts for any kind of Plumbs or Cherries, *pa.* 246, 247.

Quince pies, *pa.* 240, 241.

Double bordered Cuftards.

Spinage Tarts of three colours, *Pag.* 247.

A ftanding Tart of puff-pafte.

Goofeberry Tart.

Rice Florentine.

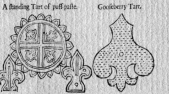

65

E.Moore fecit

"When a feast is made ready, the table is covered with a carpet and a table-cloth by the waiters, who besides lay the trenchers, spoons, knives, with little forks, table-napkins, bread, with salt-celler."
—from instructions for a banquet in Stuart England.

Nor had medieval recipes totally disappeared. Scattered throughout May's book are dishes that belong to an earlier age: *furmety, blamanger,* and *umble pies*, as well as sparrows spiced with cinnamon and bustard served with the same sweet-sour *cameline* sauce used by Taillevent. This is no coincidence, for 300 years earlier there had been little to distinguish English cooking from French. There could be no closer parallel to Taillevent's *Le Viandier* than the contemporary *Forme of Cury* compiled by the cooks of the English king Richard II in the 1380s. Here one finds the same emphasis on spices, with sugar used as a seasoning, like salt; there is the same tendency to mash all food to a purée, and even the language of the two books is alike.

A hundred years later, however, the French struck out in new directions as the nobility eagerly studied Apicius, Taillevent, and Platina and adopted their ideas. In England, on the other hand, cooking as an art was largely ignored and *Forme of Cury* lay forgotten until an eighteenth-century antiquary rescued it as a curiosity. Until Robert May, in fact, English recipe books almost always formed part of general treatises on household management and good husbandry. The most famous was *The English Housewife*, written by Gervase Markham in 1615, with a cookery section that digresses in happy inconsequence from how to recover tainted venison to preserving quinces and making pies. Cooking, like medicine, was considered to be something of a mystery, and as late as May's time book after book appeared revealing the secrets of "the closet." Cookery spilled over into quackery and herbal lore flourished in the still room. Here *eau-de-vie* (then regarded exclusively as a medicine) was distilled and remedies brewed with dried herbs. The technique of distilling had been known since the thirteenth century, but it was only around May's time that it was turned to good account by farmers in the Cognac region of France.

May meddles with none of this domestic pharmacopoeia; he was a professional writing for professionals. "Fellow cooks," he declares in a forthright manner, "that I might give a testimony to my country of the laudableness of our profession, that I might encourage young undertakers to make a progress in the practice of this art, I have laid open these experiences." Nobody was more qualified to do so; with "above 55 years of service" behind him when he wrote his book, May had a unique sense of what was expected of an English cook. This was not a succession of kickshaws and olios, nor pies filled with blackbirds, though such fantasies were important to the prestige of a chef and his master. Rather, in *The Accomplisht Cook* May is addressing thrifty, middle-class households, assuring them that "in the contrivance of these my labors, I have so managed them for the general good, that those whose purses cannot reach to the cost of rich dishes, I have descended to their meaner expense." Such emphasis on economy is not to be found in French cookbooks for another two centuries, and by no means all Englishmen were in sympathy with it. Anthony Wood, a contemporary historian, complained of the "cold meat, cold entertainment, cold reception and cold clownish woman" to be found at his brother's house.

In the works of Robert May and La Varenne, the distinction between English and French cooking is already discernible. The English took a strictly functional approach in contrast to the French, who were happy to spend hours perfecting the smallest detail and developed a special cooking vocabulary to describe their new art. Then as now, the French and English ranked the creature comforts differently, the French giving high priority to the pleasures of the table, and the English to the amenities of the home. The French were always in hot pursuit of new ideas, whereas the Englishman's curiosity was limited to a little dabbling in olios. The foreign ways with food that so interested May never moved the body of English cooking, and Pepys's dinner of 1659 of "a dish of marrow-bones; a leg of mutton; a loin of veal; a dish of fowl, three pullets, and a dozen of larks all in a dish; a great tart, a neat's tongue, a dish of anchovies, a dish of prawns, and cheese," would scarcely have been out of place on the table described 200 years later by Mrs. Beeton.

## To make a grand Sallet of divers compounds

The neats tongue mentioned in this recipe is ox or calf's tongue, and samphire is an aromatic salty plant that was used for pickling; the identity of caperons and crucifix pease is uncertain.

*Take a cold roast capon and cut it into thin slices square and small (or any other roast meat as chicken, mutton, veal, or neats tongue) mingle with it a little minced taragon and an onion, then mince lettice as small as the capon, mingle all together, and lay it in the middle of a clean scoured dish. Then lay capers by themselves, olives by themselves, samphire by itself, broom buds, pickled mushrooms, pickled oysters, lemon, orange, raisins, almonds, blue-figs, Virginia Potato, caperons, crucifix pease, and the like, more or less, as occasion serves, lay them by themselves in the dish round the meat in partitions. Then garnish the dish sides with quarters of oranges, or lemons, or in slices, oyl and vinegar beaten together, and poured on it over all.*
*On fish days, a roast, broil'd, or boil'd pike boned, and being cold, slice it as abovesaid.*

### MIXED SALAD FOR AN ENTRÉE

3 cups (400g) diced cooked capon, chicken, lamb, veal, or tongue
1 teaspoon tarragon
1 onion, very finely chopped
1 head Boston or romaine lettuce, coarsely chopped
1 orange or 1 lemon (for decoration)

FOR THE GARNISH:

3-4 tablespoons capers, drained
½ cup (100g) green olives
½ cup (100g) black olives
small bunch watercress, stems discarded
¾ cup (100g) bean sprouts
½ cup (100g) marinated mushrooms
½ cup (100g) marinated oysters
2 lemons, peeled and cut in segments
¼ cup (100g) raisins
¼ cup (50g) blanched toasted almonds
3-4 fresh figs, sliced, or 3-4 dried figs chopped
1 large cooked potato, diced

FOR THE DRESSING:

3 tablespoons wine or cider vinegar
½ teaspoon salt
½ teaspoon pepper
½ cup (1.25 dl) olive or salad oil

The garnishes for this salad are chosen to follow the original recipe as closely as possible, but many other ingredients could be used, such as small tomatoes, hard-cooked eggs, artichoke hearts, and pickles. This recipe serves 4–5.

Mix the cooked capon or meat with the tarragon and chopped onion and toss with the lettuce. Pile this mixture in the center of a large platter or deep tray and arrange the garnishes around the edge in neat individual piles, putting ingredients of contrasting colors next to each other.

FOR THE DRESSING: Whisk the vinegar with salt and pepper until the salt dissolves. Whisk in the oil until the dressing emulsifies, then taste for seasoning. Spoon the dressing over the salad and garnishes.

FOR DECORATION: Cut "teeth" in the orange or lemon with a lemon zester, cut the fruit in half lengthwise, then slice each half crosswise to show the teeth. Arrange the slices on the border of the platter.

## Minced Pies of Beef

Originally mincemeat was made literally of minced (ground) meat, which was mixed with dried fruit and spices to preserve it through the winter. Today the meat is usually omitted, leaving the familiar sweet combination of dried fruits, but the genuine mincemeat made by Robert May has much more body and flavor.

*Take of the buttock of beef, cleanse it from the skins, and cut it into small pieces, then take half as much more beef-suet as the beef, mince them together very small, and season them with pepper, cloves, mace, nutmeg, and salt; then have half as much fruit as meat, three pound of raisins, four pound of currans, two pound of prunes, etc. or plain without fruit, but only seasoned with the same spices.*

### MINCEMEAT

2 pounds (1kg) cooked lean beef, ground
3½ pounds (1¾ kg) beef suet, ground
2 teaspoons ground black pepper
1 tablespoon ground cloves
2 teaspoons ground mace
2 teaspoons ground nutmeg
1 tablespoon salt
2 cups (400g) raisins
3 cups (600g) currants
½ pound (250g) pitted prunes, coarsely chopped

(continued from previous page)

The flavor of mincemeat matures if it is packed in a crock and kept covered in a cool place for a month or more—it need not be sealed. Today most cooks would add a cup or two (250–500 grams) of sugar to Robert May's recipe and moisten the mixture with 1–2 cups (2.5–5 deciliters) sherry or white wine. This quantity makes about 7 pounds (3 kilograms) of mincemeat.

Mix the ground beef and suet thoroughly with the spices. Add the fruit, with sugar and sherry or wine to taste, and mix well again. Pack in a crock or bowl (not aluminum), cover, and store.

## Quelque shose

As its name suggests, quelque shose was a light little dish—this particular recipe resembles a pancake flavored with currants. A manchet was a loaf made of the finest quality flour from which most of the bran had been sifted. Coarser loaves were called "cheats" or "cockets," and "trete"—the roughest of all—was almost black and usually made of rye flour. The tansie referred to in the recipe was a cross between an omelet and a baked custard, flavored with the herb tansy. Until the nineteenth century, sugar was sold in blocks which had to be grated or "scraped" before using.

*Take ten eggs, and beat them in a dish with a penny manchet grated, a pint of cream, some beaten cloves, mace, boil'd currans, some rose-water, salt, and sugar; beat all together, and fry it either in a whole form of a tansie, or by spoonfuls in little cakes, being finely fried, serve them on a plate with juyce of orange and scraping sugar.*

## SPICED PANCAKES

1 cup (200g) currants or raisins
2 cups (200g) fresh white breadcrumbs
¼ teaspoon ground cloves
½ teaspoon ground mace
pinch of salt
¼ cup (60g) sugar
1¼ cups (3dl) heavy cream
5 eggs, beaten to mix
2 teaspoons rose water
4-6 tablespoons (60-90g) butter (for frying)

FOR SERVING:

2 oranges, cut in segments
granulated sugar (for sprinkling)

Rose water is sold in Middle Eastern groceries and some pharmacies. This recipe makes about ten 3-inch pancakes or one large one serving 6.

Pour boiling water over the currants or raisins, let stand 15 minutes or until plump, and drain them. Mix the breadcrumbs in a bowl with the cloves, mace, salt, and sugar and stir in the cream. Gradually beat in the eggs and continue beating 2 minutes. Let the batter stand 15 minutes for the breadcrumbs to soften, then stir in the rose water and drained raisins. In a skillet heat about 2 tablespoons (30 grams) butter and pour in the batter with a pitcher to form 3-inch pancakes. Cook them over medium heat until browned, turn, and brown the other side. Keep them warm while frying the remaining batter, adding more butter as necessary. Alternatively, heat 4 tablespoons butter in a 10 or 11-inch skillet. Add all the batter and cook over medium heat until browned on the bottom and still soft on top. Slide the skillet under the broiler and cook until the top is set and browned. Slide the cake out onto a heated platter. Cut it in wedges and serve the cake or the pancake with orange segments and sugar for sprinkling.

## To make a Posset simple

Nourishing pick-me-ups like this posset were once a part of every cook's repertoire. Sack is the old word for sherry.

*Boil your milk in a clean scowred skillet, and when it boils take it off, and warm in the pot, bowl, or bason some sack, claret, beer, ale, or juyce of orange; pour it into the drink, but let not your milk be too hot, for it will make the curd hard, then sugar it.*

## SIMPLE POSSET

FOR EACH PERSON:

¾ cup (2dl) milk
3 tablespoons sherry, red Bordeaux wine, beer, or orange juice
2 teaspoons sugar

A posset can be served in individual glasses or in a large punch bowl.

Scald the milk and heat the sherry, red wine, beer, or orange juice in a separate pan until very hot—do not allow it to boil as the posset curdles easily. Heat heavy glasses, mugs, or a punch bowl by filling with very hot water, then discarding it. Pour in the milk and gradually stir in the hot sherry, wine, beer, or juice, stirring constantly; the milk will thicken slightly. Stir in the sugar and serve at once while still very hot.

# Menon

flourished 1740–1755

The age of Louis XV marks a high point in the
cultural life of France. Cooking was no exception,
acquiring all the pomp of a national movement as it
came to be valued as a peculiarly French art. Between 1735 and 1755 more great cooks wrote more
great cookbooks than in any comparable period
before or since and they enjoyed unprecedented
recognition. The most successful member of this
prolific generation was Menon, whose many books
include the last of the great manuals of court cookery and the first of many cookbooks written for the
bourgeoisie.

Almost 100 years separate Menon from La Varenne
and during this period French cooking had
developed dramatically. In the time of La Varenne,
it was still clearly rooted in the traditions of Renaissance Italy and medieval France. By the eighteenth
century, this inheritance had been left far behind
and it was to the genius of French cooks, working
under the patronage of a cultivated aristocracy, that
France owed its unquestionable supremacy in the
kitchen. Part science, part art, cooking was now a

LA
CUISINIERE
BOURGEOISE.
SUIVIE DE L'OFFICE
*A L'USAGE*
De tous ceux qui se mêlent de dé-
penses de Maisons.

Nouvelle Edition corrigée & considerablement
augmentée, à laquelle l'on a joint la maniere
de disséquer, connoître & servir toutes sortes de
Viandes.

A PARIS,
Chez GUILLYN, Quay des Augustins, entre
les rues Pavée & Gît-le cœur, au Lys d'or.

M. DCC. XLVIII.
Avec Approbation & Privilége du Roy.

*Louis XV, great-grandson
of the Sun King, reigned
from 1715–1774.*

fashionable subject of debate in the self-conscious
Parisian salons. Stupefying banquets which dulled
the intellect fell into disfavor and the preferred
setting for the exercise of wit and gallantry was the
supper. The change was less in the number of dishes
(which remained copious) than in the number of
guests; ideally not more than twenty people
gathered round the table. When Louis XIV's sixty-
eight-year reign came to an end in 1715, even age-
old court habits had to change. The new king dis-

Opposite:
*In the eighteenth century no art was left
to chance. At this "Delectable Supper"
by Moreau-Le-Jeune, every aspect has
been studied from the menu to the
cuisine, the table appointments, the
furnishings, the clothing, and even
the gestures of the participants.*

73

Opposite:
*Under Louis XV, French tables were enriched with dishes of a luxury not seen since Renaissance Italy. These pieces painted by Alexandre Desportes were from the royal collection.*

dained his great-grandfather's habit of admitting the public to watch the royal meals, preferring to enjoy the company of the queen or of one of his mistresses in private—so much so that he installed a table which sank through the floor to the kitchen, where it was invisibly replenished for the next course.

Naturally Louis XV's hostesses vied for royal approval of their cuisine. Madame du Barry gave her name to a cauliflower soup and Madame de Pompadour, good bourgeoise that she was, was famed for her table where simple country dishes offset the flights of fancy of more aristocratic temperaments. For relaxation, the king himself would

Although the aristocracy took the applause, most culinary invention must have been the work of their chefs, who were in great demand. "It will not be long now before cooks assume the title of artists in cookery," wrote Mercier in 1780 in his fascinating account of life in Paris, *Le Tableau de Paris*. "They are pampered and spoiled, their tantrums are soothed, and it is normal to sacrifice all other servants for their sake. To entice away the cook from a household is a terrible and unforgiveable trick." Madame du Barry went so far as to employ a woman cook. The story goes that after a superb supper, Louis XV asked to talk to the chef. When a woman

1 *Madame du Barry*

2 *Madame de Pompadour*

3 *Duc de Richelieu*

4 *Prince de Dombes*

5 *Prince de Soubise*

6 *Queen Marie Antoinette epitomized the extravagance of the late-eighteenth-century French nobility and the isolation of the court from the common people.*

often work in the kitchens under the supervision of his friend, the Prince de Dombes, who was the secret author of an attractive little recipe book *Le Cuisinier gascon*. The Duc de Richelieu is said to have brought mayonnaise to France, naming it after his victory at the siege of Mahon in Spain, although some writers have argued that it is of ancient French lineage, descended from *moyeu* meaning egg yolk. It was Bertrand, cook to the Prince de Soubise, who launched the soubise (onion) purée that is still an important basic preparation. The two were a colorful pair; the prince is said to have made his omelettes from pheasant and partridge eggs (an extravagance that can hardly have been justified by the results), while Bertrand once shocked his master by ordering fifty hams to make a single sauce. "I will, if you choose, put all the fifty hams into a glass vial no bigger than my thumb," he boasted.

74

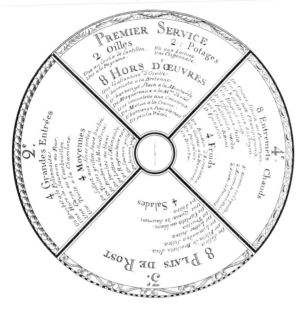

*The supper menu served to Louis XV and Madame de Pompadour on Friday, 4 November 1757, shows clearly the four services in which a dozen dishes or more were set on the table at once in a geometric pattern.*

catalogue of recipes and menus, embracing many of today's classic garnishes (some created by Marin) and almost 100 sauces, few of which would be strange to today's chefs.

For some reason Marin's polished work did not enjoy a lasting success and it was a similar three-volume book written by Menon in 1755, *Les Soupers de la cour*, which held the stage until the French Revolution swept away all demand for such lavish productions. To modern tastes the profusion of dishes Menon describes is overwhelming—a typical menu for thirty lists well over a hundred dishes, served in five courses. After the first and third courses, the whole table was cleared and a completely fresh set of dishes laid out in an established geometric design. The second and fourth courses were smaller, complementing the twenty to thirty dishes already on the table. The appointments of the table were just as elaborate as the food. Centerpieces such as china soup tureens, branched candelabra, and bonbonnières proliferated and instead of the single glass or goblet and knife and spoon used a century before, there was an array of cutlery and crystal for each place setting. Plates were changed between each course—even, remarked a bewildered observer, when they were not dirty.

In *Soupers de la cour* the sauces which have made French cuisine famous are highly developed, and Menon adds them to everything, from hors d'oeuvres through dessert. Most savory sauces were based on a *coulis* (cullis) of meat and ham which was sliced and cooked very gently in a little fat so the juices were extracted and browned lightly on the bottom of the pan. Then flour was added and the cullis was completed with stock, wine, vegetables, and seasonings in much the same way a sauce is

*The example set by Louis XIV's gardener, La Quintinie, led to the development of the superb fruits and vegetables of Menon's time.*

was presented, the king was so impressed that he awarded her one of the highest decorations in France, the Order of the Holy Ghost, known familiarly as the Cordon Bleu, from the blue sash worn by the members. Whether or not this tale is true, to this day the term cordon bleu is correctly applied only to a woman.

Menon was almost certainly one of the most sought after master cooks, but nothing is known about him, not even his first name. He had the luck to be the last in the line of heirs to the traditions of La Varenne, and by the time his first book *Le nouveau traité de la cuisine* appeared in 1739, Menon had a head start of which he took full advantage. This did not pass unnoticed; Marin, another master cook whose *Dons de Comus* had appeared in the same year, complained in a later edition that "more than one reader has noticed . . . the fruit that assiduous study of *Dons de Comus* has produced." He was probably referring to the supplementary volume entitled *La nouvelle Cuisine* which Menon had boldly added to his *Traité* in 1742, continuing the movement toward a simpler style of cooking first launched by Marin in *Dons de Comus*.

Marin's book begins with a pedantic essay criticizing *la cuisine ancienne* for its "extraordinary complexity and detail" and promises that in *la cuisine moderne* cooks will find "less trouble, fewer mixtures yet as much variety; a simpler, cleaner, and more knowledgeable kind of chemistry." From today's vantage point of instant cookery it is a little difficult to credit Marin with simplifying the art. But he certainly did organize it. *Dons de Comus* is a logically planned

In the hundred years since La Varenne, the advances made in drafting recipes were considerable. Menon's instructions are detailed and he has a wide variety of technical terms such as *braiser* and *blanchir* at his command.

❖❖❖❖❖❖❖❖❖❖❖❖❖❖❖❖

## *Petits pâtés de poisson*

The continuous refinement of French cooking during the eighteenth century is clearly seen by comparing this recipe from *Soupers de la cour* with La Varenne's eel pâté (page 49), written a hundred years earlier. An *écu* was a French coin.

*Chop the flesh of whatever fish you like and mix it with dried breadcrumbs, cream, salt, pepper, nutmeg, shallots, parsley, chopped spring onion, two egg yolks and a piece of good butter; pound all together. Take puff pastry and roll it out a little thicker than an écu, and cut it with a pastry cutter according to the size of the molds; line a mold; put stuffing in the middle and cover with another piece of pastry; press your finger lightly all around just to give it shape; glaze the pastries and cook half an hour; serve them fresh from the oven.*

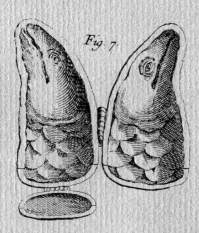

Fig. 7

## LITTLE FISH PASTRIES

4 slices white bread, crusts discarded
1 pound (500g) salmon, whiting, pike, haddock or other well flavored fish
1 cup (2.5 dl) heavy cream
2 teaspoons salt
½ teaspoon freshly ground black pepper
¼ teaspoon grated nutmeg
2 shallots finely chopped
3 tablespoons chopped parsley
2 spring onions finely chopped
2 egg yolks
2 tablespoons (30g) butter, creamed
puff pastry made with 2 cups (250g) flour, 1 cup (250g) butter, pinch of salt, 1 teaspoon lemon juice, and ½-¾ cup (1.25-2 dl) ice water
egg glaze made with 1 egg, beaten to mix with ½ teaspoon salt

18 small pie (tart) pans (2½ inches or 8 cm diameter); 3 and 3½-inch (8 and 9 cm) round cookie cutters

As a main course, the pastries can be made in larger pans, or for cocktail hors d'oeuvres the filling can be baked in small puff pastry turnovers. The method for making puff pastry is given in any classic French cookbook. This quantity makes 18 medium-sized pastries suitable for a first course.

Bake the bread in a very low oven until dry but not browned. Work it to crumbs, a slice at a time, in the blender or rub through a wire strainer. Chop the fish, discarding all skin and bones. Mix the fish with the breadcrumbs, cream, salt, pepper, nutmeg, shallots, parsley, and spring onions. Purée the mixture in a blender a little at a time until smooth and transfer it to a bowl. Alternatively, pound the fish, breadcrumbs, and seasonings

in a mortar with a pestle and gradually work in the cream. Taste the mixture—it should be highly seasoned. Beat in the egg yolks and butter. Set the oven at hot (400°F or 205°C).
Roll out the pastry to ¼-inch thickness and stamp out twelve 3-inch rounds and twelve 3½-inch rounds. Lay the pastry trimmings carefully one on top of the other, roll out again, and stamp out 6 more rounds of each size. Line the small pie pans with the large rounds, fill them with fish mixture, and moisten the inside edges with egg glaze. Cover with the smaller rounds and press the edges gently together. Brush the tops with glaze and chill 15 minutes. Set pie pans on a baking sheet and bake in the heated oven 30 minutes or until a skewer inserted in the center of the pastries for ½ minute is hot to the touch when withdrawn. Serve the pastries as soon as possible.

## *Filet de boeuf à l'italienne*

Fillet of beef, simply roasted without a marinade, is one of Menon's favorite dishes, showing how much the quality of meat had improved by the mid-eighteenth century. To lard means to thread the meat with strips of pork fat to make it more tender.

*Lard the upper surface of a fillet of beef, after trimming it well; make cuts in the other side and insert a mixture of parsley, scallion, mushrooms and half a clove of garlic, all finely chopped, basil and powdered bay leaf, kneaded together with grated bacon and seasoned with salt and pepper; wrap the fillet in paper and cook it on a spit; when cooked, coat the side that was not larded with breadcrumbs; brown it in front of the fire and serve a* **sauce italienne** *on top.*

*(continued from previous page)*

## Sauce petite italienne

Like most of Menon's sauces, this is thickened with a cullis—a purée that could be based on concentrated meat essences thickened with a roux of fat and flour, or on vegetables like dried peas or lentils. *Sauce italienne* foreshadows today's classic brown sauces, based on espagnole sauce instead of a cullis.

*In a casserole put a slice of ham, three or four mushrooms, two or three shallots, half a clove of garlic, a quarter of a bay leaf, and a good tablespoon of oil; cook the mixture over medium heat, moisten it with consommé, a little cullis and half a glass of champagne and simmer it over low heat half an hour; skim off any fat and strain.*

## FILLET OF BEEF ITALIENNE

4-5 pounds (2-2½ kg) fillet
  of beef
⅛ pound (60g) fat bacon,
  cut in ¼-inch (60-mm) strips
  (for larding)
½ cup (40g) fresh white
  breadcrumbs (to finish)

### FOR THE STUFFING:

2 tablespoons chopped parsley
1 spring onion, finely chopped
3 large mushrooms, finely
  chopped
½ clove garlic, crushed
1 teaspoon basil
½ teaspoon crushed bay leaf
⅛ pound (60g) fat bacon,
  very finely chopped
salt and pepper

Larding needle

By wrapping his fillet in paper, Menon ensured that it cooked evenly, but with today's less fierce fires the meat would not brown. This recipe serves 6–8.

FOR THE STUFFING: Mix the parsley, spring onion, mushrooms, garlic, basil, bay leaf, and bacon with salt and pepper (add no extra salt if the bacon is salty) and work the mixture on a board with a metal spatula until the bacon fat softens and binds the stuffing together.

If roasting in the oven, set the oven at hot (400°F or 205°C). Lard the underside of the meat with the bacon; slash the top of the meat lengthwise with a series of cuts about ¾ inch deep and press the stuffing into them; spread any remaining stuffing on top. Tie the meat with string in a firm roll and set it, larded side down, on a rack in a roasting pan. Roast it in the heated oven, allowing 15 minutes per pound or until a meat thermometer inserted in the center registers 140°F (60°C), for rare beef; baste the meat often during cooking.

If roasting on a spit, light the fire or broiler. Slash the meat lengthwise about ½ inch deep on all sides and insert the stuffing; lard the meat, tie it firmly in a roll with string, and spear on the spit. Roast the beef fairly close to the heat, allowing 15 minutes per pound or until a meat thermometer registers 140°F (60°C)—cooking time varies very much with the heat of the fire; baste during cooking.

When the beef is done, sprinkle the top with the breadcrumbs, baste well with drippings and brown under the broiler. Serve *sauce italienne* separately, or spoon a little over the meat.

### SAUCE ITALIENNE

½-pound slice (250g) country
  ham
¼ pound (125g) mushrooms,
  sliced
2-3 shallots, sliced
½ clove garlic, crushed
small piece bay leaf
1½ tablespoons oil
pepper
2 cups (5 dl) brown stock
⅓ cup (1 dl) dry white wine
salt (optional)

### FOR THE CULLIS:

3 tablespoons (45g) butter
3 tablespoons (30g) flour
3 cups (7.5 dl) brown stock

Menon's meat cullis is not only extraordinarily extravagant, but it takes hours to make. However, an acceptable substitute can be made by reducing good brown stock. This recipe makes about 2 cups (5 deciliters) sauce.

TO MAKE THE CULLIS: Boil the stock until it is reduced by half. In a saucepan melt the butter, stir in the flour, and cook, stirring, until the flour is golden brown. At once pour in the reduced stock and cook over low heat for 2–3 minutes.

Place the ham, mushrooms, and shallots in a heavy-based pan and add the garlic and bay leaf; sprinkle with oil and pepper. Cook over low heat so that the juices are drawn out of the ham and continue cooking until the juices brown. Add the 2 cups (5 deciliters) stock, wine, and cullis and bring to a boil. Simmer 50–60 minutes or until the sauce is glossy and the consistency of cream. Taste it for seasoning—if the ham was salty, more salt will not be needed. Skim off any fat and strain.

made now. The ham was a vital ingredient; those from Montánchez in central Spain (from pigs said to be fattened on a diet of vipers and acorns) had the highest reputation, as evidenced by *sauce espagnole*, the modest present-day descendant of the original cullis. A cullis was thick, concentrated, and very extravagant. According to Vincent La Chapelle, another of the great eighteenth-century master cooks, "if you treat about ten or twelve persons, you can take no less than a whole leg of veal to make your cullis with, and the nut of a ham to make it good." White sauce was supposed to be the creation of the chef to the Marquis de Béchamel, private secretary to Louis XIV and a noted food connoisseur, but this was disputed by the Duc d'Escars who exclaimed, "That fellow Béchamel has all the luck. I was serving breast of chicken *à la crème* twenty years before he was born, yet, as you can see, I have never had the chance of giving my name to the most insignificant of sauces."

The French court went to almost any lengths for the sake of novelty. Menon's imagination stretched on occasion to 100-dish dinners in a single color (white was considered the most elegant) or based on a single meat. For the latest in fruits and vegetables, the court turned to the kitchen garden planted at Versailles by Louis XIV. In this venture the king had been aided by a gardener of genius, La Quintinie, who laid out the prototype *potager* (a name that nicely anticipates the destination of its contents) with neat rows of vegetables and fruit trees espaliered against a high wall for protection against the wind. Louis XIV had taken a personal interest in the propagation of new stock and from Versailles originated many of France's superlative fruit and vegetable varieties. Louis XV maintained the tradition by importing the latest plants from Holland and England, and by establishing state nurseries in every province, from which cuttings were distributed free. However, no amount of coaxing would per-

suade the French to change their attitude to the potato, which although common in England by the 1750s was still regarded in France as pig food. Not until prodded by a fanatical doctor named Parmentier, who once cooked a whole dinner—soup, entrée, entremet, salad, cake, cookies, and even

*Antoine-Augustin Parmentier was a crusading scientist who finally persuaded the French to eat potatoes, and who gave his name to potato soup. Appropriately, he is holding emblems of three staple foods—ears of wheat, a cob of corn, and potato flowers.*

*By Menon's time* confiserie *was, and has remained, a separate branch of French cuisine. Like most authors of the time, Menon wrote a book on it*—La Science du maître d'hôtel confiseur. *Here preserved and candied fruits are displayed on a side table.*

79

bread—using potatoes, did the French begin to appreciate the cheap nourishment they offered. (Parmentier, appropriately, has given his name to potato soup.)

*Soupers de la cour,* successful though it was, presented little that was new to the readers of Marin and La Chapelle. The reason Menon's renown outlived theirs was the lasting success of his earlier book *La Cuisinière bourgeoise,* which struck quite a different note, claiming to "reduce expenses, simplify methods, and go some way towards bringing what has seemed the preserve of opulent kitchens within the range of the bourgeoisie." Addressed, significantly, to the female cook, the hearty country recipes it contains such as *andouilles,* calf's feet *à la Sainte Menehoulde,* and leg of lamb *à la persillade* are still the backbone of much household cooking in France.

Written in 1746, *La Cuisinière bourgeoise* was reprinted more often than any other French cook-

*"Petits pâtés tout chauds," proclaims this seller of hot pies. He is a realistic representative of the surrealist figures of French tradesmen depicted (below) by Nicholas de Larmassin.*

*Habit de Cuisinier.*

*Habit de Rôtisseur.*

*Habit de Fruitiere.*

*Habit de Poissonniere.*

## Saumon en hatelet

This is a good example of the newly developed hors d'oeuvres (literally, "outside of the work")—simple little side dishes served between the soup and the roast.

*Cut the salmon in squares the thickness of a thumb, marinate them with a little oil, two raw egg yolks, salt, pepper, parsley, scallion, shallots, all chopped, coat them with breadcrumbs, broil and serve with remoulade in a sauceboat.*

## Sauce à la remoulade

Remoulade is just one of the many classic sauces created in the eighteenth century. Menon's remoulade is regarded today as a household version, the more common one being based on mayonnaise highly spiced with mustard.

*In a pan put a shallot, parsley, scallion, a touch of garlic, an anchovy and some capers, all chopped very finely, salt and pepper; beat with a little mustard, some oil and vinegar.*

## SALMON KEBABS

2 pounds (1kg) salmon steaks, cut ¾ inch (2 cm) thick
1½ cups (125g) dry white breadcrumbs

FOR THE MARINADE:

6 tablespoons (1 dl) oil
2 egg yolks
1 teaspoon salt
½ teaspoon pepper
2 tablespoons chopped parsley
2 spring onions, finely chopped

4-8 kebab skewers

This recipe serves 4 as a main dish or 8 as a first course.

Cut the salmon into ¾-inch cubes, discarding skin and bones.

FOR THE MARINADE: In a large bowl beat the oil into the egg yolks and stir in the salt, pepper, parsley, and spring onions. Add the salmon, toss well, cover, and let marinate 1-2 hours.

Thread the salmon cubes on skewers and roll them in breadcrumbs. Broil them 4–5 inches from the heat until browned on both sides, allowing 4 minutes each side. Serve with remoulade sauce.

## REMOULADE SAUCE

2 shallots, finely chopped
2 tablespoons chopped parsley
1 spring onion, finely chopped
1 small clove garlic, crushed
2 anchovy fillets, chopped
1½ tablespoons capers
1 tablespoon Dijon-type mustard
5 tablespoons wine vinegar
¾ cup (2 dl) oil
salt and pepper to taste

This recipe makes 1¼ cups (3 deciliters) sauce.

Put the shallots, parsley, spring onion, garlic, anchovy fillets, and capers in a bowl and stir in the mustard. Stir in the vinegar, then beat in the oil a little at a time so the sauce emulsifies and thickens slightly. Add salt and pepper to taste.

## Ouille de différent façons

*Ouille* is none other than the Spanish national dish *olla podrida*—a huge stew of many meats and vegetables. The Spanish term translates into English as,

*Habit de Patricier.*

*Habit de Caffetier.*

*Habit de Vinaigrie.*

*Habit de Jardinier.*

Opposite:
*At the end of the seventeenth century, three new drinks took Paris by storm— coffee, tea, and chocolate—and were dispensed in the new coffeehouses. Café Procope, the first Paris café, opened in 1686 and became a literary and political rendezvous in the following century. Patrons depicted here include Rousseau, Diderot, and Voltaire.*

*(continued from previous page)*

literally, "rotten pot" and into French as *pot pourri*. The ancestor of *pot au feu*, *pot pourri* is mentioned in France as early as 1587 and during the seventeenth and eighteenth centuries its popularity never flagged, possibly because it was such an easy and spectacular dish to serve for large numbers. Here, Menon stays with the Spanish: *olla* has become *ouille* and is used to mean a stew or mixture in the same way as, in English, *olla* became "olio." But in Spanish, *olla* refers to the earthenware pot in which the stew is made.

*In a casserole put a partridge, a leg of lamb, five or six pounds of beef round and a shank of beef; brown the meat on the stove, turning it from time to time in the casserole until it is about to stick on the bottom; moisten it with simmering broth or with hot water; boil over a low heat for six or seven hours; after an hour of cooking, add all kinds of blanched vegetables, such as parsley roots, carrots, parsnips, onions, turnips, celery, leeks and a mignonette made by putting in a piece of cloth some pepper, ginger, cinnamon, whole cloves, coriander, mace, a clove of garlic and a little savory. Add only a little salt: this broth should be slightly colored, clear and well flavored; the recipe will do for all kinds of clear ouilles, which are distinguished only by the name of the vegetables which are served on top; it will also serve for crayfish and rice ouilles and others; simmer the soup a long time with sliced bread or croûtes [pieces of toasted bread]; serve in a ouille pot and arrange whatever vegetables you would like on top.*

## POT POURRI

2-3 tablespoons oil
1 partridge or pheasant, trussed
3-4 pounds (1¼-1¾ kg) leg of lamb, on the bone
3-4 pounds (1¼-1¾ kg) round of beef, preferably on the bone
3-4 pounds (1¼-1¾kg) beef shanks, cut in 2-inch (5cm) slices
3-4 quarts (3-4 l) beef or chicken stock
bunch of parsley
1 pound (500g) carrots, quartered
1 pound (500g) baby onions, peeled, or 3-4 medium (500g) onions, peeled and quartered
4-5 (400g) baby turnips, peeled and halved
¾-1 pound (400g) parsnips, peeled and halved lengthwise
1 head celery, cut in 2-inch (5-cm) lengths
4-5 medium leeks, halved lengthwise
salt
large loaf of French bread, sliced diagonally

FOR THE MIGNONETTE:

2 teaspoons black peppercorns
2-3 pieces dried ginger root
3-inch (7.5-cm) stick of cinnamon
1 teaspoon whole cloves
1 teaspoon coriander seeds
2 blades mace
1 clove garlic
2 teaspoons savory

Menon's recipe is ambiguous in that he does not explain whether the vegetables cooked with the meat are served with it, or whether they are thrown out and other vegetables are prepared separately. He probably discarded the vegetables cooked with the meat, because after 5-6 hours of cooking they would be tasteless. Today the usual method is to add vegetables near the end of preparation, timing their cooking carefully so they are all tender at the same moment (this is the tricky part of any boiled meat dish).

If boiling water instead of stock is used for this recipe, a few onions and carrots should be added at the beginning of cooking, then discarded before the accompanying vegetables are added. A fowl can be substituted for the partridge or pheasant, and vegetables that are unobtainable can be omitted, though as wide a selection as possible should be included. This recipe serves 12.

In a very large pot such as a ham kettle or casserole heat the oil and brown the partridge or pheasant on all sides. Take it out and brown, in turn, the leg of lamb, the round of beef, and the beef shanks. Replace the lamb and beef round in the pot with the shanks and pour over the stock—it should cover the meat.
Tie the spices and herbs for the mignonette in cheesecloth and add to the pot. Cover it, bring it slowly to a boil, and skim well. Simmer it, skimming from time to time, for 2–2½ hours, depending on the weight and thickness of the meat—it should be almost tender. Taste the broth for seasoning and add a little salt if needed.
If using pheasant, add it now, and continue simmering 15 minutes. Add the partridge, if using, and the parsley and carrots and simmer 10 minutes more. Add the onions, turnips, parsnips, celery, and leeks and continue simmering 15–20 minutes or until all the meats and vegetables are tender. If you like, toast the bread slices.
Transfer the meats to serving platters, arrange the vegetables around them, and keep warm. Add the bread or toast to the soup and boil 10–15 minutes to reduce until well flavored and thick; discard the bunch of parsley and the mignonette, and taste the broth for seasoning. Menon would have served meats, vegetables, and broth together in one great pot, but today the broth is usually served first, followed by the meat and vegetables.

book until modern times. It became the bible of a new class of cook, the restaurateur (the name comes from the restorative bouillon they invariably served).

The first restaurant (as we would understand the term) opened in 1765 and was an instant success. During the troubled years following the revolution, restaurants became a way of life for town dwellers, and by the close of the century there were estimated to be 500 of them in Paris alone. Hitherto, no one had eaten out except of necessity (when traveling, for example) though for centuries prepared food had been sold "to go" by the different guilds—the *pâtissiers* (with their savory pies, cakes, and pastries), the *chaircuitiers* (cooked meat sellers specializing in pork), the *oubliers* (waffles and wafers) and the *rôtisseurs* (offering roast meat and fowl). The senior of these guilds, *the boulangers*, originally made their loaves round in *boules*, but the French soon realized that by making them elongated they could enjoy more crust.

For liquid refreshment in Paris there was little but taverns to choose from until 1686, when an enterprising Sicilian called Procopio opened the first café. Parisians found a new way of life; in its heyday, the Café Procope was the literary and political meeting place of Paris (it still exists as a restaurant) and imitations quickly followed, each with its own coterie. As well as coffee, Procopio dispensed his native ices—the first to be commonly available in France. By our standards they were primitive con-

coctions of frozen fruit juice, with a coarse texture more like granité than sherbet, but they were immensely popular. In Menon's time the Orangerie at the Tuileries was surrounded by icehouses for the use of court officials, and he devotes a whole chapter of *Soupers de la cour* to sherbets and ice creams.

Menon wrote for both the old order and the new, and therein lies his distinction. *Soupers de la cour*, with its casual assumption of unlimited time and ingredients, places Menon firmly in the Old World where (in the words of Carême) "everything was done in the grand manner; within the households of the King, and of the Princes de Condé, d'Orléans, and de Soubise, the maîtres d'hotel were famous for the excellence of their tables; the men who ran these noble households were truly outstanding both as great chefs and as great administrators; their undercooks benefited from their teaching, and with the added encouragement they received from the honor and benevolence extended to them by great princes, French cooking was daily enriched and enhanced by their renown." Yet in *La Cuisinière bourgeoise* Menon was writing for the new order—for a world in which the great households had surrendered the initiative to restaurateurs who were forced to work within economic limits, but who enjoyed an independence unknown to their predecessors. In catering to such an audience, Menon began a cookbook tradition that is still flourishing today.

La Boulanger.
*Paris Chez I. Cobart rue St Jacques à la Reine &c.*     *Avec Privil du Roy.*

## *Bignets de fraises*

Few dishes are simpler or more delicious than fritters—a fact reflected by their constant popularity since the time of Taillevent.

*In a casserole put two handsful of flour with a little oil, a little salt, and three whipped egg whites; moisten with a little white wine, to thin the batter without making it too liquid; take hulled large strawberries, dip them in, fry them and serve glazed with sugar and a hot iron [i.e., a salamander].*

## STRAWBERRY FRITTERS

1 quart (500g) large
    strawberries, hulled
deep fat (for frying)
granulated sugar (for
    sprinkling)

FOR THE BATTER:

1 cup (125g) flour
pinch of salt
1 tablespoon oil
3 egg whites
¾ cup (2 dl) sweet white wine

Many fresh fruits can be substituted for the strawberries—fresh pineapple cubes, peach slices, and apple rings are particularly suitable. This recipe serves 6.

FOR THE BATTER: Sift the flour into a bowl with the salt. Make a well in the center and add the oil. Beat the egg whites until stiff. Add to the well with the wine. Stir, gradually drawing in the flour to make a smooth batter.
Heat the deep fat to very hot (375°F or 190°C on a fat thermometer); light the broiler. With a skewer or two-pronged fork, dip the strawberries one by one in the batter and drop them into the fat. Fry them, a few at a time, for 2 minutes

or until lightly browned. Drain them on paper towels and keep hot in a warm oven with the door open while frying the remaining fritters. Sprinkle with granulated sugar and broil ½–1 minute or until the sugar is caramelized. Serve at once.

## *Gâteau de Savoie*

In the time of Menon, most *gâteaux* were flat round cakes, like shortbread, or the *gâteau des rois* of puff pastry that is still made in France for Twelfth Night. However a few cakes were baked in deep casseroles, often with indented lids so hot coals could be placed on top to distribute the heat more evenly. With such primitive methods, of course, baking was still very much a hit-and-miss affair as is shown by Menon's advice on how to disguise a scorched cake with icing. Menon starts off his recipe by weighing his ingredients against eggs—a popular method that led to old-fashioned terms like "three-egg cake." Pound cake was originally made by weighing a

pound of eggs against butter, sugar, and flour.

*Put fourteen eggs in a scale and on the other side add equal weight of fine sugar, remove the sugar and put in its place flour of the weight of seven eggs, remove the flour, put it aside, break the eggs, put the yolks in a pot, the whites in another; put the sugar you have weighed with the yolks and a little grated lemon and some toasted chopped orange flowers, beat all together for half an hour; then add the egg whites, stiffly whipped, and the weighted flour, adding it little by little and stirring the mixture at the same time with the whisk.*
*Take a deep casserole of average size, or a mold that should first be rubbed with fine butter, wipe it well with a cloth and spread it all over with fine butter; put in your mixture and cook it in a moderate oven for a good hour and a half; when done, turn it out carefully on a plate; if it is an attractive golden brown, serve it as it is; if it has too much color, it must be iced with a white icing, made with very fine sugar, an egg white and the juice of half a lemon; beat them all well together in a crockery plate with a wooden spoon until the icing is very white and use it to cover the whole cake; do not serve it until the icing is set.*

## SAVOY CAKE

4 eggs, separated
¾ cup (180g) sugar
grated rind of 1 lemon
1 teaspoon orange flower
    water
½ cup (60g) flour
½ cup (100g) potato starch

FOR THE ICING:

1 egg white, lightly beaten
juice of ½ lemon
1½ cups (180g) confectioners'
    sugar, sifted

8-inch (20-cm) springform pan

A light sponge cake, very like Menon's and known as *biscuit de Savoie*, is still made today.

Orange flower water, obtainable at specialty grocery stores and pharmacies, is the closest modern equivalent to toasted orange flowers. The cake is best eaten fresh.

Set the oven at moderate (350°F or 177°C) and lightly grease the pan. In a bowl beat the egg yolks with an electric beater or large whisk until slightly thickened. Gradually add the sugar, lemon rind, and orange flower water. Continue beating until the mixture is very thick and light in color.

Combine and sift the flour and the potato starch; whip the egg whites until stiff. As lightly as possible, fold the egg whites into the mixture alternately with the sifted flour. Spoon the mixture into the prepared pan and bake in the heated oven for 50 minutes or until the cake draws away from the sides of the pan and the top has formed a firm crust. Loosen the sides of the cake with a flat knife. Let cool in the pan, then turn out onto a rack.

FOR THE ICING: Put the egg white into a bowl with the lemon juice. Add half the confectioners' sugar, a little at a time, and stir well to mix. Set the bowl over a pan of hot water and add remaining sugar, a little at a time, to make an icing that just coats the back of a spoon. When the icing is smooth, pour it over the cake, letting it drip down the sides; leave until set.

*L'Art de bien faire les Glaces*

The Italian art of making ices was adopted enthusiastically by the French. In this eighteenth-century engraving, cherubs are stirring ice cream, putting it to freeze in a churn, pounding ice (right), and filling pots for serving.

# Hannah Glasse

1708–1770

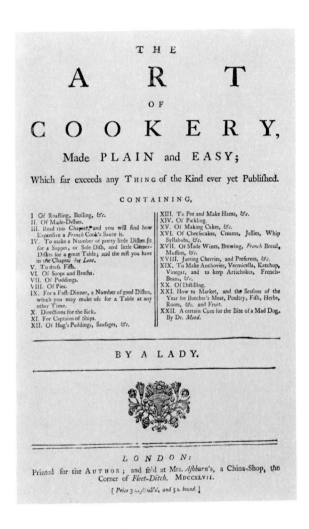

Hannah Glasse wrote the most successful English cookbook of the eighteenth century, but her fame owes more to chance than good cooking. Mrs. Glasse was a mystery. When *The Art of Cookery Made Plain and Easy* first appeared anonymously in 1747, the modest "By a Lady" on the flyleaf tickled the public fancy; the signature "H. Glasse" which was scrawled in the fourth edition of 1751 only added to the enigma for no one knew whom this could be. The matter became sufficiently intriguing to interest no less a figure than Dr. Johnson, who apropos of the book's origins remarked drily that "women can spin very well, but they cannot make a good book of cookery."

Mrs. Glasse remained a mystery until the twentieth century when she was tracked down by methods worthy of the most tortuous detective novel. The sleuth was local historian Madeleine Hope Dodds, and the plot turned on the list of subscribers printed in the first edition of *The Art of Cookery*. Several of these subscribers came from Northumberland and were connected with a family called Allgood. It then emerged that the head of the family, Sir Lancelot Allgood, had had a sister called Hannah who was born in 1708 and had married one John Glasse. Ingenious proof of Miss Dodds' discovery was provided by a curious contemporary work called *Professed Cookery*, written by a certain Ann Cook. The third edition of 1760 opens with a seemingly unprovoked attack on "A Lady," expressed in painful doggerel:

> *She steals from ev'ry Author to her Book,*
> *Infamously branding the pillag'd Cook,*
> *With Trick, Booby, Juggler, Legerdemain. . . .*

and later:

> *Yet Criticisers Sentiments may pass,*
> *What title can be due to broken Glass. . . .*

What did Ann Cook have against Hannah Glasse? Since *The Art of Cookery* was the older of the two books, Hannah could hardly have stolen her recipes. No, the wound went much deeper than that and was apparently inflicted by Hannah's brother Lancelot. The Cooks kept an inn at Hexham near the Allgood family seat and blamed their misfortunes (and ultimate ruin) on Sir Lancelot, who had had occasion to publicly impugn their honesty.

It was presumably the signature in the 1751 edition of *The Art of Cookery* that alerted Ann Cook to its authorship. From other unflattering allusions in

Opposite:
*Covent Garden in 1737. Ten years later, when* The Art of Cookery *was published, Hannah Glasse moved to nearby Tavistock Street.*

89

*Professed Cookery*, it seems likely that Ann Cook knew more about her rival than was comfortable for the Allgoods, for recent research in family papers reveals that Hannah was only the half-sister of Lancelot, being the child of a liaison between her father and a local woman. Her father was already married when Hannah was born, and she was taken into his household as part of the family—she later told Lancelot (the only legitimate child) that her real mother was "a wicked witch."

Hannah was obviously an impulsive girl; in 1724, when only sixteen, she eloped from her grandmother's house in London with a penniless adventurer, John Glasse. A spate of family letters followed: "I am sorry at what I have done, but only at the manner of doing it," she maintained stoutly. After the accusations and recriminations usual on such occasions had died down, Hannah was left married to a thirty-year-old widower, a subaltern officer on half pay whose precarious financial situation was scarcely improved by the annuity of £30 left to Hannah when her father died the following

The BRITISH-BUTCHER,
*Supplying JOHN-BULL with a Substitute for BREAD. Vide. Message to Lord-Mayor.*

BILLY the BUTCHER'S advice to JOHN BULL.
Since Bread is so dear, (and you say you must Eat,)
For to save the Expence, you must live upon Meat;
And as Twelve Pence the Quartern you can't pay for Bread,
Get a Crown's worth of Meat...it will serve in its stead.

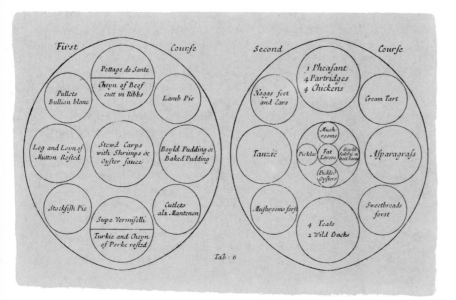

*Despite the British reputation for eating beef, in Hannah Glasse's time meat was not within the reach of all pockets. "A crown, take it or leave it!" sniffs a supercilious butcher to an impecunious customer.*

*Large numbers of different dishes were arranged together on the eighteenth-century table, constituting a single course. In France a dinner might consist of four or even five courses, but the English generally limited themselves to two, like these designed by Patrick Lamb, who wrote* Royal Cookery *in 1710. "Tanzie" is a cream dessert flavored with the herb tansy, and "forst" means farced (stuffed).*

year. However John Glasse seems to have done well enough; for the next twenty years he and Hannah lived a not unprosperous life, partly at Broomfield in Essex (where John Glasse was buried) and partly in London. Eight children were born but Hannah outlived most of them and her family line petered out in obscurity.

In a letter of November 1744, Hannah shows the first signs of independent enterprise, suggesting she may market Dr. Lower's tincture—a patent medicine which later had great success as Daffy's Elixir. No more was heard of this project but a year later comes her first mention of *The Art of Cookery*. By January 1746 she could report, "My book goes on very well and everybody is pleased with it, it is now in the press."

In her recipes, Hannah Glasse takes a more practical line than her French contemporaries; she concentrates on specific instructions for each recipe and usually ignores the more general principles that may lie behind them. Already she takes some of her cooking terms from the French, and this richness of Gallic cooking vocabulary still continues.

## To Pot Salmon

Potted salmon has nothing to do with liquor; to pot means to pack thoroughly cooked meat or fish so as to exclude all the air, then to seal the top with butter. When properly done, the mixture can be kept for several months—a necessity in the days before refrigeration. Jamaica pepper is allspice, one of the only spices native to the Western Hemisphere. Salprunella is a type of saltpeter.

*Take a Piece of fresh Salmon, scale it, and wipe it clean (let your Piece, or Pieces, be as big as will lye cleverly in your Pot) season it with Jamaica Pepper, black Pepper, Mace and Cloves beat fine, mixed with Salt, a little Salprunella beat fine, and rub the Bone with; season with a little of the Spice, pour clarified Butter over it, and bake it well; then take it out carefully, and lay it to drain; when cold, season it well, lay it in your Pot close, and cover it with clarified Butter as above.*
*Thus you may do Carp, Tench, Trout, and several Sorts of Fish.*

## POTTED SALMON

2½ cups (600g) butter
2 pounds (1kg) salmon steaks or 2-pound (1-kg) piece of salmon
2 teaspoons ground allspice
2 teaspoons ground black pepper
1 teaspoon ground mace
½ teaspoon ground cloves
2½ teaspoons salt
1 teaspoon saltpeter (optional)

1 soufflé dish or crock (1-quart or 1-liter capacity) or 6 ramekins

Potted salmon makes an excellent first course served with hot toast. It can be served in one large pot or individual ramekins. Saltpeter (available at pharmacies) is needed only if the salmon is to be kept more than two weeks. This quantity serves 6.

For potted dishes, butter must be clarified, for the milky liquid in regular butter makes food spoil more quickly. Heat the butter gently until melted, then chill it until set; discard the milky liquid at the bottom of the cake of butter. Set the oven at moderate (350°F or 177°C). Wash the salmon and pat it dry with paper towels. If using a whole piece of salmon, cut it in half horizontally through the backbone. Mix the allspice, pepper, mace, cloves, salt, and saltpeter (if used) and rub them into the cut

surfaces of the salmon. Lay the salmon in a baking dish so the pieces are tightly packed together. Melt about a quarter of the clarified butter, pour it over the salmon, and cover tightly. Bake the salmon in the heated oven for 20–45 minutes, depending on the thickness of the fish, or until no transparent section is left in the center. Transfer the salmon to a plate to drain and cool. Divide it into pieces, discarding skin and bone, and pack it tightly in a soufflé dish or crock, or in individual ramekins, taking care to exclude all air. Melt the remaining clarified butter and pour it over the salmon to seal it. It can be kept for up to two weeks in the refrigerator or for a month if saltpeter was added.

## A Ragoût of Oysters

Mrs. Glasse might rail against Frenchified cooking, but like all her contemporaries, she did not go so far as to exclude fricassées, ragoûts, and other French-inspired recipes from her book. She was not familiar with a French roux and invariably thickens her sauces by a more laborious method such as the one below. Raspings are crumbs rasped or grated from a dry loaf of bread.

*Open twenty large Oysters, take them out of their Liquor, save the Liquor, and dip the Oysters in a Batter made thus: Take two Eggs, beat them well, a little Lemon-peel grated, a little Nutmeg grated, a Blade of Mace pounded fine, a little Parsley chopped fine; beat all together with a little Flour, have ready some Butter or Dripping in a Stew-pan, when it boils, dip in your Oysters, one by one, into the Batter, and fry them of a fine brown; then with an Egg-slice take them out, and lay them in a Dish before the Fire. Pour the Fat out of*

(continued from previous page)

*the Pan, and shake a little Flour over the Bottom of the Pan, then rub a little Piece of Butter, as big as a small Walnut, all over with your Knife, whilst it is over the Fire; then pour in three Spoonfuls of the Oyster-liquor strained, one Spoonful of White Wine, and a Quarter of a Pint of Gravy; grate a little Nutmeg, stir all together, throw in the Oysters, give the Pan a Toss round, and when the Sauce is of a good Thickness, pour all into the Dish, and garnish with Raspings.*

## To Make Gravy

Hannah Glasse's gravy may not be as concentrated as French cullis but by our standards it is certainly a rich basic sauce.

*If you live in the Country, where you can't always have Gravy Meat, when your Meat comes from the Butcher take a Piece of Beef, a Piece of Veal, and a Piece of Mutton; cut them into as small Pieces as you can, and take a large deep Sauce-pan with a Cover, lay your Beef at Bottom, then your Mutton, then a very little Piece of Bacon, a Slice or two of Carrot, some Mace, Cloves, Whole Pepper Black and White, a large Onion cut in Slices, a Bundle of Sweet Herbs, and then lay in your Veal. Cover it close over a very slow Fire for six or seven Minutes, shaking the Sauce-pan now and then; then shake some Flour in, and have ready some boiling Water, pour it in till you cover the Meat and something more: Cover it close, and let it stew till it is quite rich and good; then season it to your Taste with Salt, and strain it off. This will do for most Things.*

## RAGOÛT OF OYSTERS

FOR THE BATTER:

½ cup (60g) flour
3 eggs
grated rind of ½ lemon
¼ teaspoon ground nutmeg
¼ teaspoon grated mace
1 tablespoon chopped parsley

FOR THE RAGOÛT:

½ cup (125g) butter (for frying)
1 quart (about 2 dozen) select oysters, with their liquor
1 teaspoon flour
½ tablespoon butter
1 tablespoon white wine
¾ cup (2dl) gravy (see below)
pinch of nutmeg
salt and pepper (optional)
2-3 tablespoons browned breadcrumbs (for garnish)

Any homemade meat gravy can be substituted for the gravy below. This recipe serves 4 as a first course.

FOR THE BATTER: Sift the flour into a bowl, make a well in the center, and add 2 eggs. Beat to make a smooth paste, add the remaining egg with the lemon rind, nutmeg, mace, and parsley and beat 1 minute. Drain the oysters, reserving the liquor.
In a frying pan, melt a little of the butter, dip several of the oysters into the batter, drain them slightly, and fry them over brisk heat until brown on both sides; remove and

keep warm. Fry the remaining oysters in the same way, using more butter as necessary.
Sprinkle the teaspoon of flour into the pan, set it over low heat, and rub over the ½ tablespoon of butter until melted. Stir in the oyster liquor with the wine, gravy, and nutmeg and bring to a boil. Add the oysters and heat gently, shaking the pan to mix them with the sauce, until very hot. Taste for seasoning, transfer to a serving dish, sprinkle with browned breadcrumbs, and serve at once.

GRAVY

½ pound (250g) stew beef, diced
½ pound (250g) boned shoulder or breast of lamb, diced
3-4 slices (60g) bacon
1 carrot, sliced
blade of mace
4-5 whole cloves
½ teaspoon black peppercorns
½ teaspoon white peppercorns
1 large onion, sliced
bouquet garni
½ pound (250g) stew veal, diced
2 tablespoons flour
2½ cups (6dl) boiling water
salt

Makes about 2 cups (5 deciliters) gravy).

In a heavy-based pan spread the beef and lamb and top with the bacon, carrot, mace, cloves, peppercorns, onion, bouquet garni, and lastly the veal. Cover and cook over low heat, shaking the pan from time to time, for 5-7 minutes or until the juices run from the meat. Sprinkle over the flour, stir to mix, and pour in the boiling water.
Bring to a boil, stirring; cover and simmer over low heat 1-1½ hours or until the gravy is rich and well flavored. At the end of cooking it should be the consistency of thin cream. Season it to taste with salt, and strain.

*The Art of Cookery* finally appeared the following year and (no doubt to Hannah's surprise) ran to over twenty editions in fifty years. Just why the book was so popular is hard to understand. Its contents are unimpressive, differing little from half a dozen other household recipe books that were published before and after it. Lacking an alphabetical index, its organization also leaves a good deal to be desired—no fewer than nine repetitive recipes for gravy are scattered through four different chapters. The section on fish has only five entries, while the rest of the three score fish recipes are included in the chapter on fast days, sandwiched between a pretty almond pudding and endive ragoo. Worse still, whole sections of the book are not original; the chapter on creams in the first edition is taken word for word from the first (1727) edition of *The Compleat Housewife* by Eliza Smith. Later editions of

both books borrowed material from each other, so that by the time Hannah Glasse died, *The Art of Cookery* was about twice as long as the slim folio volume she had originally written. However, it is unlikely that she was entirely to blame for this plagiarism; without a whisper of permission, publishers regularly expanded successful cookbooks by picking up passages from more recent works.

Whatever the limitations of *The Art of Cookery* as a book, the typical English fare that Hannah somewhat confusedly describes has much to recommend it. The pies, particularly the savory ones of veal, ham, chicken, and the like are outstanding; they come in all varieties—Hannah's savory veal pie is flavored with oysters, sweetbreads, asparagus tips, and wine, while medieval traces linger in the sweet veal pie with raisins, currants, grapes, white wine, and Spanish (sweet) potatoes. When it comes to preserving, great versatility is shown in the bevy of pickles and relishes which the English still love to serve with cold meats; pickled barberries, pickled walnuts, and anchovy catchup would all be viewed with astonishment in France, as would the English wines made of gooseberries, elderflowers, and even turnips, born of necessity in a climate unsuited to grapes.

John Glasse died in 1747, the year *The Art of Cookery* was published. He had never been a reliable earner of money but after his death Hannah's financial problems worsened. She set up as a dressmaker with her daughter Margaret (trained

93

## To make Whipt Syllabubs

Syllabub is an ancient English dessert dating from medieval times. It is made of cream beaten with fruit juice or wine until thick. The origin of the name is obscure; it may come from *sille* (white wine from the Champagne region of France) and *bub*, meaning a bub-bling drink. Mrs. Glasse gives sev-eral recipes; this one has a base of wine or fruit juice tinted green, orange, or pink with the syllabub spooned on top. Another less practical version calls for milking the cow directly into the syllabub mixture. Sack is an old word for sherry and Seville oranges are the bitter oranges used for mar-malade.

*Take a Quart of thick Cream, and half a Pint of Sack, the Juice of two Seville Oranges, or Lemons, grate in the Peel of two Lemons, half a Pound of double-refined Sugar, pour it into a broad earthen Pan, and whisk it well; but first sweeten some Red Wine, or Sack, and fill your Glasses as full as you chuse, then as the Froth rises, take it off with a Spoon, and lay it carefully into your Glasses till they are as full as they will hold. Don't make these long before you use them. You may use Cyder sweetened, or any Wine you please, or Lemon, or Orange-whey made thus; squeeze the Juice of a Lemon or Orange into a quarter of a Pint of Milk, when the Curd is hard, pour the Whey clear off, and sweeten it to your Palate. You may colour some with the Juice of Spinach, some with Saffron, and some with Cochineal, just as you fancy.*

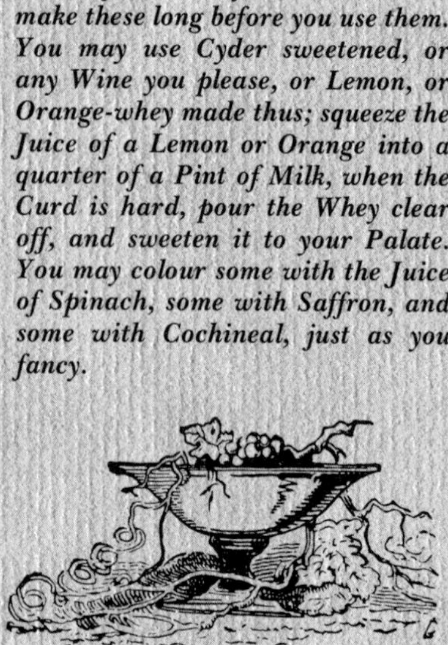

*[Handwritten letter, partial transcription:]*

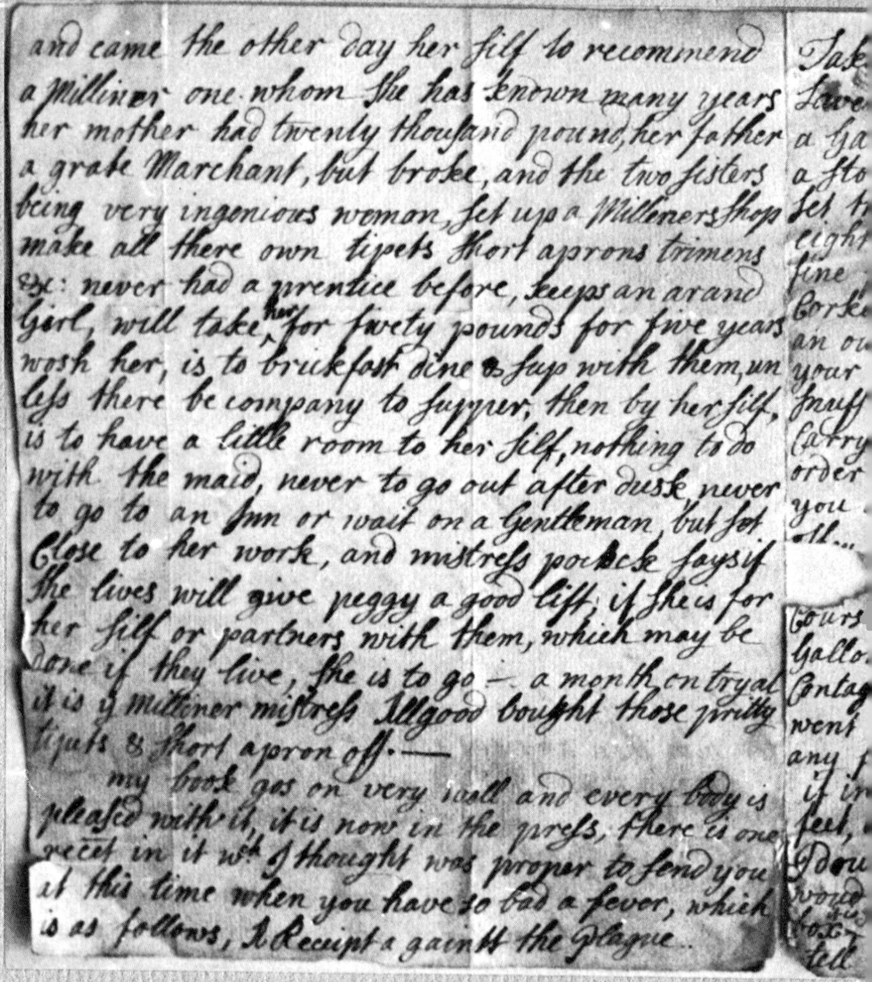

and came the other day her self to recommend a Milliner one whom she has known many years her mother had twenty thousand pound her father a grate Marchant, but broke, and the two sisters being very ingenious woman, set up a Milliners shop make all there own tipets short aprons trimens &c: never had a prentice before, keeps an arand Girl, will take her for forty pounds for five years wash her, is to breakfast dine & sup with them, un less there be company to supper, then by her self, is to have a little room to her self, nothing to do with the maid, never to go out after dusk never to go to an Inn or wait on a Gentleman, but set close to her work, and mistress poincke says if she lives will give peggy a good lift, if she is for her self or partners with them, which may be done if they live, she is to go — a month on tryal it is if milliner mistress Illgood bought those pritty tipets & short apron off.——

my book goes on very well and every body is pleased with it, it is now in the press, there is one recet in it wch I thought was proper to send you at this time when you have so bad a fever, which is as follows, A Receipt against the plague...

*[Right column fragment of handwritten text, partially visible:]*

Tak...
Lave...
a Ga...
a Sto...
Set t...
eight...
fine...
Corke...
an ou...
your...
snuff...
Carry...
order...
you...
...

Yours...
Gallo...
Contag...
went...
any r...
if ir...
feel,...
I dou...
would...
box &...
tell...

## SYLLABUB

### FOR THE COLORED LAYER:

1 cup (2.5 dl) red wine or cider, or ½ cup (1.25 dl) sweet or medium sherry, or whey made of 1½ cups (3.75 dl) milk with the juice of 1½ lemons or 1½ oranges and a few drops of edible food coloring

2-3 tablespoons sugar, or to taste

### FOR THE SYLLABUB:

½ cup (1.25 dl) sweet or medium sherry

grated rind and juice of 1 lemon or 1 orange

½ cup (120 g) sugar

2 cups (5 dl) heavy cream

Red wine, cider, sherry, or colored whey made of milk and fruit juice can be used for the bottom of this two-layered syllabub, to serve 6.

FOR THE COLORED LAYER, IF USING WHEY: Beat the lemon or orange juice into the milk, let stand 30 minutes so the milk curdles thoroughly, and strain the whey through cheesecloth, discarding the curd. Color the whey with green, yellow, or red food color-ing. Sweeten the colored whey, red wine, cider, or sherry with sugar to taste and spoon it into 6 stemmed glasses.

FOR THE SYLLABUB: In a bowl stir the sherry, lemon or orange rind and juice, and the sugar until the sugar is dissolved. Beat in the cream and continue beating until thick froth rises to the surface. Skim off the froth with a metal spoon and spoon carefully into stemmed glasses to form a layer on top of the liquid. Continue beating and skimming off the froth until only a little thin liquid is left in the bowl; the glasses should be full to the brim. Chill and serve within 4 hours.

...ue, sage, mint, Rosemary, wormwood and
a handfull of each, infuse them together in
...of white-wine Vinegar, put the whole in to
...t closely covered up, and pasted over the Cover
...t thus clos'd up, upon warm wood-ashes for
...s: after which draw off (or strain through
...e) the liquid and put it in to bottles well
...s into every quart bottle put a quarter of
...of Camphire. With this preparation wash
...th, and rub your loins & y.r temples every day
...le up your nostrils when you go into y.e air, &
...t you a bit of spunge dipp'd in the same in
...mell to upon all occasions, especially when
...near any place or person that is infected.
...that four Malefactors (who had robb'd
...ouses, and murder'd the people during th..
...he plague own'd when they came to the
...at they had preserv'd themselves from the
...by using the above medicine only, and that they
...whole time from House to House -- without
...l the Distemper.
...r fever lay green sope to y.e bottom of y.e
...e Diet drink will cure y.e worst of fevers
...did not received my last if you had, you
...a bin surpris'd, not finding your quilt in y.e
...ffe: Give to my bro.r & sister, and pray
...m.r Fenton pay'd me my years annuity

as a milliner) and apparently attracted some distinguished customers. Her brother Lancelot, who stayed with her in London in 1749 when he was a member of parliament, wrote that "Hannah has so many coaches at her door that, to judge from appearances, she must succeed in her business. . . . She has grand visitors with her, no less than the Prince and Princess of Wales, to see her masquerade dresses." But Hannah was no businesswoman; her husband had lamented that "she does not calculate well as I could wish in many things," and soon she was cashing in her only reliable source of income, the family annuity. In May 1754 the crash came, and Hannah was declared bankrupt to the tune of £10,000—a huge sum. Luckily she was registered as a trader, otherwise she would have been personally responsible for her debts and liable to be thrown into the notorious debtors' prison. After this debacle, Hannah lost touch with her Northumberland relations, so much so that when the death of "Hannah Glasse" was briefly reported in 1770, no one connected her with the "H. Glasse" of *The Art of Cookery*. So began the mystery of her identity.

Little is known about her last years, but she certainly continued to write books, first *The Servant's Directory* (1760) and then *The Complete Confectioner*,

Below:
*The British taste for tea was firmly established by Hannah Glasse's day, though it was still expensive. Here the mistress of the house (left) measures tea from an unlocked caddy. The table is set with the delicate china especially made for such a luxury.*

probably published in the year of her death. The English had long excelled at cakes and pastries, which became much more common once supplies of cheap sugar were assured from the West Indian colonies. Hannah shows a remarkable grasp of how to boil syrup to different degrees of concentration (the foundation of the art of confectionery), and she gives one of the first English recipes for ice cream. The results must have been unpredictable: her only instructions are to take "cream and mix with what you think proper to give it flavour and colour" and then to freeze it over ice and salt. Here she lags far behind her French counterparts, as ices had been popular in France for close on a century.

As in France, cookery writers flourished in England in the eighteenth century but there was a striking difference between the two schools. In England all the most famous writers were women—a phenomenon virtually unknown to the French until the twentieth century. Women cooks had been

# How to Make Chocolate Cream

Cocoa beans were brought back by Cortes from Mexico in the sixteenth century, and chocolate became so popular as a drink that the Catholic church divided in heated debate on whether drinking chocolate on a fast day constituted mortal sin. However, chocolate flavoring did not catch on until much later and Mrs. Glasse was one of the first English cooks to use it.

*Take a Quart of Cream, a Pint of white Wine, and a little Juice of Lemon; sweeten it very well, lay in a Sprig of Rosemary, grate some Chocolate, and mix all together; stir them over the Fire till it is thick, and pour it into your Cups.*

## CHOCOLATE CREAM

3/4 cup (180g) sugar
1 cup (2.5 dl) sweet white wine
juice of 1/2 lemon
2 cups (5 dl) heavy cream
sprig of fresh rosemary or 1 teaspoon dried rosemary
4 squares (125g) semisweet chocolate, grated

8 mousse pots, stemmed glasses, or custard cups

We are so used to mixing spices like cinnamon with chocolate, that the addition of a herb seems strange; however, chocolate and the aromatic flavor of rosemary blend remarkably well. This quantity serves 8 as the dessert is very rich. Rolled cookies or ladyfingers would be a suitable accompaniment.

In a heavy-based pan stir the sugar into the white wine and lemon juice until dissolved. Stir in the cream—it will thicken slightly and be full of bubbles. Add the rosemary and chocolate and cook over low heat, stirring until the chocolate melts. Bring to a boil and boil, stirring, for about 5 minutes or until the mixture is the consistency of thick cream. Take from the heat, let cool slightly, then strain into mousse pots, glasses, or custard cups. Serve cold.

# To pickle Large Cucumbers in Slices

As any gardener knows, cucumbers have the annoying habit of ripening all at the same time. Eighteenth-century cooks, particularly the English, preserved them as pickles to serve over the winter with cold meats. A race of ginger is a root. A crown was a coin.

*Take the large Cucumbers before they are too ripe, slice them the Thickness of Crown-pieces into a Pewter-dish: To every dozen of Cucumbers, slice two large Onions thin, so on till you have filled your Dish; with a Handful of Salt between every Row; then cover them with another Pewter-dish, and let them stand twenty-four Hours; then put them in a Cullender, let them drain very well, then put them into a Jar, and cover them over with White Wine Vinegar, and let them stand four Hours; then pour the Vinegar from them into a Copper Sauce-pan, and boil it with a little Salt. Put to the Cucumbers a little Mace, a little whole Pepper, a large Race of Ginger sliced, and then pour the boiling Vinegar on. Cover them close, and when they are cold, tye them down; they will be fit to eat in two or three Days.*

## CUCUMBER PICKLES

12 cucumbers, cut in 1/8-inch (30mm) slices
2 large onions thinly sliced
1/2 cup (125g) salt
4 cups (1 l) white wine vinegar
3 blades mace
1 teaspoon black peppercorns
1 1/2-inch (4-cm) piece dried ginger root or 3-inch (8-cm) piece fresh ginger root, peeled and sliced

Heatproof glasses or jars, and paraffin wax

This recipe makes 6 quarts (6 liters) of crisp not-too-sweet pickles.

In a large bowl (not aluminum) layer the cucumbers and onions, sprinkling the layers with all but 1 teaspoon of the salt. Cover and let stand 24 hours. Drain them in a colander, stirring once or twice so they drain thoroughly. Pack them in a crock or jelly glasses, pour over enough white wine vinegar to cover them, and let stand 4 hours. Drain the vinegar into a pan (not aluminum) and bring to a boil. Add a little of the mace, peppercorns, ginger root, and remaining salt to each glass of cucumbers, pour over the boiling vinegar, and seal them at once with a layer of paraffin wax. Despite Mrs. Glasse's advice that the pickles can be eaten within two days, they are much better if kept for at least a month.

accepted in England as far back as the late 1600s (when Hannah Woolley's *Queene-like Closet* ran to several editions) and in the 1700s Elizabeth Moxon, Mrs. Smith, Mrs. Raffald, and (at the close of the century) Mrs. Rundell all shared the bandwagon with Hannah Glasse. These women wrote for families with servants and Mrs. Glasse might be speaking for them all when she observes: "If I have not wrote in the high polite style I hope I shall be forgiven; for my intention is to instruct the lower sort, and therefore must treat them in their own way." The French would have considered few of these manuals as cookbooks, and when *The Art of Cookery* is compared with *Soupers de la cour* the difference is clear—one exemplifies domestic economy and the other *haute cuisine*.

The odd man out on the English scene was Vincent La Chapelle, who worked for Lord Chesterfield and brought out his *Modern Cook* in 1733. He himself was French, a precursor of the chefs who emigrated to England after the revolution. Lord Chesterfield grew melons, grapes, and pineapples in his hothouses—"the growth, the education and the perfection of these vegetable children," he wrote, "engage my care and my attention next to my corporal one"—and he moved among friends whose palates had been educated on the Grand Tour. Hannah Glasse and her fellows had a rooted dislike of such foreign nonsense. "Such is the blind folly of this age," she exclaims, "that they would rather be imposed on by a French booby than give encouragement to a good English cook." The chief target of her wrath is that foundation of French cuisine, the

cullis. "Read this chapter and you will find how expensive a French cook's sauce is," she says, and she suggests a scaled-down version using only a pound of veal and half a pound of bacon instead of the whole leg of veal and whole ham called for in classic French books. Mrs. Raffald even insists that "lemon pickle and browning answers both for beauty and taste (at trifling expense) better than cullis." Such parsimony with ingredients, totally absent from French *haute cuisine*, is at least partly responsible for the depressing reputation of English food. As Voltaire reportedly said, "In England there are sixty different religions, but only one sauce."

The simpler English approach to eating was equally evident in their menus; only two courses were the rule (compared with up to five in France), the first of soup and "made" dishes (often in a sauce) and the second of more substantial roasts with side dishes of vegetables and sweet and savory pies. This lighter English diet was fortified by a cooked breakfast and eternal cups of tea. By Hannah Glasse's time, the Englishman's love of tea was already legendary; Dr. Johnson could scarcely control his bibulous instincts when it was served (once he drank twenty-five cups at a sitting), and a Swiss pastor, Carl Philipp Moritz, when vacationing in England was indelibly impressed by bread and butter "as thin as poppy leaves" and "by another bread and butter, usually eaten with tea, which is toasted by the fire and is incomparably good. This is called toast."

It is no accident that the most memorable feature of English food was the bread and butter. The outstanding characteristic of the cooking described by Hannah Glasse is its wholesome plainness, still found today in English country cooking. Many of her recipes remain in the British repertoire, but it is not for these that she is remembered. Rather her fame rests on the most popular cookery catchphrase of all time, "First catch your hare," which originated in her innocent instruction, "Take your hare when it is cas'd [skinned] . . ." The idea of the cook racing out to catch a hare before putting it in her pot has amused countless generations.

# Francesco Leonardi

flourished 1750–1790

In the middle of the eighteenth century, Europe idled in a halcyon age. Intermittent famines, and the military skirmishes of the great powers as they jockeyed for political dominance, scarcely disturbed the golden prosperity that in England produced the great country houses of the classical revival, and in France the escapist Fragonard paintings of silk-clad shepherdesses gamboling in a fairy tale landscape. This was the age of the Grand Tour, when scions of wealthy families pursued the well trodden cultural path of Paris, Heidelberg, Rome, Naples, and Venice, with a brief glimpse of the Matterhorn and the ruins of Pompeii along the way.

Into this self-assured cosmopolitan world was born the first Italian cook of any importance since the Renaissance—Francesco Leonardi. "In this world it is not your nationality that makes you what you are, but your talent," declares Leonardi with prescience in his most important cookbook, *L'Apicio moderno*. He certainly put his own talents to good use. By his own account, Leonardi's long career stretches from the 1740s to the 1800s, from the elegance of Naples (then at its apogee), through royalist France and the St. Petersburg of Catherine the Great to the French Revolution and the Napoleonic Wars.

*L'Apicio moderno* was first published in 1790, and its title is significant. Apicius compiled the famous cookbook of ancient Rome and Leonardi intended his work to be both Italian and "modern" in the sense of international and scientific. Given the supremacy of French cuisine in the fashionable kitchens of the time, any "international" work on cooking was bound to be based on French techniques and recipes. (Astonishingly, La Varenne's *Le Cuisinier françois* was still being reprinted in Italian as late as 1815.) However, *L'Apicio* is more than a mere imitation of its French counterparts; with its 3,000 recipes culled from half a dozen countries and its sections of general culinary interest describing, for example, the wines of Europe or new methods of preserving food, it is more like an encyclopedia. There is a Russian nettle soup flavored with onion and garnished with pieces of chicken and hard-cooked eggs, and a chicken *alla tartara* marinated in oil, onion, garlic, and lemon, then broiled. From Germany and Poland come soups containing "chenedel," Leonardi's rendering of the German *knoedel* or dumpling. There are recipes for sauerkraut and gnocchi *alla tedesca* containing breadcrumbs, pounded rice, butter, nutmeg, Parmesan, egg yolks, and liver—a dish still to be found in the Dolomites. Leonardi also has a good grasp of

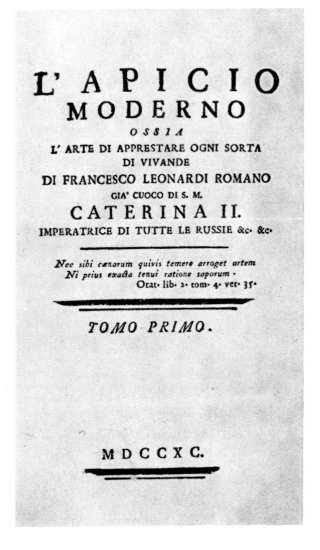

L'APICIO
MODERNO
*OSSIA*
L' ARTE DI APPRESTARE OGNI SORTA
DI VIVANDE
DI FRANCESCO LEONARDI ROMANO
GIA' CUOCO DI S. M.
CATERINA II.
IMPERATRICE DI TUTTE LE RUSSIE &c. &c.

*Nec sibi cænarum quivis temere arroget artem.*
*Ni prius exacta tenui ratione saporum .*
Orat· lib· 2· tom· 4· ver· 35·

*TOMO PRIMO.*

MDCCXC.

Opposite:
*Music and masked balls were a highlight of eighteenth-century Italian society. The Venetian painter, Pietro Longhi, captures the hedonistic spirit of these occasions which Leonardi, when beginning his career in Naples, must have witnessed.*

English cooking as described by Hannah Glasse—he notes their gravy thickened with flour in the roasting pan and is shocked by their traditional roasts of meat, vulgarly extravagant to an Italian. He remarks that the English make good sweet pastry for pies, but his boiled suet pudding can hardly have transplanted well to an Italian climate.

For all his international airs, however, Leonardi is an Italian writing for Italians. With the benefit of fifty years' experience in and out of Italy, he freely adapts foreign recipes, using Italian ingredients like ricotta, and adding Parmesan cheese like a salt for seasoning. He emphasizes the excellence of Italian ingredients—the mussels from the Bay of Taranto, the beef of Tuscany, and the fresh fish which is available everywhere, so that cooks need never rely on salted fish, as in other countries. He uses copious quantities of the white truffles of Piedmont, he stuffs suckling pig with macaroni, and he shares the native partiality for little birds that was to shock English travelers. "They frequently eat kites, hawks, magpies, jackdaws, and other lesser birds," reports a contemporary guidebook. "Between Rome and Naples travellers are sometimes regaled with buffaloes and crows."

Leonardi's experience of Italian cooking was acquired in a princely household. In the early 1750s (after an apprenticeship in France with the epicurean Maréchal de Richelieu) he joined Michele Imperiali, Prince of Francavilla, the *cher amour* of Queen Amelia of Naples and a friend of Casanova. After enduring centuries of foreign domination, Naples, as capital of the newly independent Kingdom of the Two Sicilies, had become renowned for the virtuosity of its music and the gaiety of its masked balls. Where Versailles was wanton, Naples was openly licentious. "The dissipation of the Neapolitans is really disgusting," complained Lady Orford, Sir Horace Walpole's daughter-in-law. "All ranks seem to live only for tawdry show and idleness. Every day there are fireworks and music. . . ." John Moore, an English visitor who attended one of Prince Francavilla's parties, remarked on their luxury even on a fast day: "There were forty people . . . it was the most magnificent entertainment I ever saw, comprehending an infinite variety of dishes, a vast profusion of fruit, and the wines of every country." Leonardi, however, was apparently less impressed by his patron. He deplored the slovenly habit of serving made dishes, cold dishes, and roasts all at the same time; the practice is acceptable on a military cam-

paign, he says, but not when entertaining princes. Throughout his works, Leonardi upbraids Italians for their naiveté, and the best hope he holds out for them is that "in time" they may be capable of organizing a really grand dinner.

If Italian society was more "provincial" than French, it took correspondingly greater pride in regional cooking traditions. Like Martino and Scappi before him, Leonardi clearly had his own regional allegiances. He recommends zucchini *alla milanese* stuffed with breadcrumbs and béchamel, and a cassata *palermitana* made (as today) with ricotta. Naturally with his Neapolitan background Leonardi is keen on pasta, and he often bases his recipes on ready-made kinds, showing that the local pasta makers were already highly esteemed. But like any modern Italian cookbook, Leonardi also has a recipe

102

Leonardi has an agreeable style; his recipes are as much a pleasure to read as the results are to eat. If not exemplary about stating all quantities, he at least gives enough to indicate the broad outlines of a dish. His comment below on the Russian love of nettle soup is rare. Normally he says nothing about the countries he visits, keeping strictly to the cooking matter in hand; his book is the more professional, if less lively, because of it.

❖❖❖❖❖❖❖❖❖❖❖❖❖❖❖❖

# Zuppa russa di ortica

Leonardi likes to adapt foreign recipes, using Italian ingredients. Here he flavors the soup with Parmesan cheese, and even the eggs for the garnish are stuffed with an Italian cheese—ricotta.

*The Russians really love this soup and it is often served in noble households in St. Petersburg. To make it take the tips and tender leaves of nettles as fresh as possible, wash well and blanch for a moment in boiling water, then put under cold water, squeeze dry and chop coarsely. Heat a little chopped onion with a piece of butter, then add the nettles and cook a little, sprinkle with a good pinch of flour, pour over a good white stock made from a capon or good chicken cut in pieces. Cook gently and season with salt. Just before serving thicken the soup with eight egg yolks, stir in cream, pour into the terrine, add the pieces of capon or chicken and eight stuffed eggs fried in butter. It would be good to add a handful of grated Parmesan with the egg yolks and cream. If you want to add croutons of bread fried in butter to asparagus soup or this soup it will depend on the amount of vegetables used and on the soup. Note, however, that if you add bread you won't add either chicken or stuffed eggs.*

## Uove ripiene

*Cut the eggs in half, pound the yolks in a mortar, add a piece of butter, a little fresh ricotta or cold panada made very thick by beating three egg yolks, a handful of grated Parmesan, a little salt, ground pepper, nutmeg, powdered cinnamon, 4 raw egg yolks and one white. Mix well and stuff the eggs with this filling, pushing it well in. Roll in flour, dip in beaten egg, sprinkle with breadcrumbs and fry until a nice color.*

## RUSSIAN NETTLE SOUP

1 pound (500g) nettle leaves and tips
1 onion, chopped
2 tablespoons (30g) butter
2 tablespoons (20g) flour
1½ quarts (1½ L) chicken stock
salt and pepper

FOR LIAISON:

8 egg yolks
½ cup (1.25 dl) heavy cream
¼ cup (40g) grated Parmesan cheese (optional)

FOR GARNISH:

½ cup (100g) cooked chicken breast, diced
8 stuffed fried eggs (see next recipe)

OR

8 slices bread, crusts removed, diced
4-6 tablespoons oil and butter, mixed

In spring, young nettles make a delicious, tart soup. Sorrel or spinach are the nearest substitutes. This recipe serves 8.

If using nettles, wash them then blanch in boiling water for ½ minute and drain thoroughly. Spinach and sorrel need no blanching. Finely chop the leaves of them all.

In a kettle fry the onion in butter until soft, add the nettles, sorrel, or spinach, and cook gently until soft. Stir in the flour, then add the stock and bring to a boil, stirring. Season, cover, and simmer 15-20 minutes. The soup can be made up to 48 hours ahead and kept in the refrigerator, or it can be frozen.

TO FINISH: Prepare the garnish of chicken and eggs, or make the croûtons. Fry the diced bread in the oil and butter, stirring to brown evenly; drain the croûtons on paper towels and keep warm.

Reheat the soup. To add the liaison, mix the egg yolks and cream in a bowl. If using cheese, add it now, beating until smooth. Stir a little of the hot soup into the egg mixture, then stir this mixture back into the remaining soup in the pan. Heat gently until the soup thickens slightly. (Note: Do not boil or the soup will curdle.)

Taste for seasoning and pour into a hot soup tureen or individual bowls. Add the diced chicken and eggs, or croûtons, and serve at once.

STUFFED EGGS

8 hard-cooked eggs, shelled

FOR THE FILLING:

8 hard-cooked egg yolks
¼ cup (40g) grated Parmesan cheese
salt and pepper
grated nutmeg
cinnamon
3 raw egg yolks and 1 whole raw egg (all beaten to mix)

*(continued from previous page)*

OR

8  hard-cooked egg yolks
4  ounces (125g) fresh
   ricotta cheese

## FOR THE COATING:

½ cup (60g) flour seasoned
   with ½ teaspoon salt and
   pinch of pepper
2  eggs, beaten with 1 tablespoon oil and ½ teaspoon
   salt
¾-1 cup (100g) dry white
   breadcrumbs
deep fat (for frying)

These eggs make an excellent appetizer as well as a garnish for the soup. This recipe makes 8 stuffed eggs.

Halve the 8 hard-cooked eggs lengthwise, scoop out the yolks and sieve them.
If using the filling of Parmesan cheese, stir in the grated cheese with 3 of the sieved yolks, salt, pepper, nutmeg, and cinnamon to taste. Stir in the 3 raw egg yolks and 1 whole egg. Beat in the remaining sieved hard-cooked yolks. Fill egg halves and press them back together firmly.
If using the filling of ricotta cheese, season the cheese with salt and pepper and beat it until smooth. Beat in the 8 sieved, hard-cooked yolks. Fill egg halves as above.
Coat the filled eggs first in seasoned flour, then in the egg and oil mixture, then in the bread crumbs. Let the coated eggs dry 15 minutes. Or the eggs can be kept uncovered in the refrigerator for up to 8 hours.

TO FINISH: Heat the deep fat. Fry the eggs, a few at a time, in hot fat until golden brown. Drain finished eggs thoroughly on paper towels.

## *Pomidoro in chenef*

Leonardi identifies himself with Naples in this recipe—he was obviously proud of the local tomatoes and handles them with affectionate familiarity. Elsewhere he notes that a good *chenef* (for use in dumplings or stuffing) should be made of equal quantities of chicken, butter, and bread-crumbs, bound with egg yolks. Such simple recipes seem to come more easily to him than the exotica of France and Russia.

*Use small Sicilian tomatoes if available, or our own variety, but make sure they are the same size and plunge for a moment in boiling water to remove the skins; carefully hollow them out from the stalk end and stuff with a good cooked stuffing of chicken breast, not too full, and mix some grated Parmesan. Put slices of onion, carrot on the bottom of a casserole, then cover with bacon and ham, place the tomatoes on this with the hole facing downward, cover with more onion, carrot, bacon and ham. Season with salt and freshly ground pepper, moisten with very little good stock and cook with a quick heat on both sides, but remember they cook very quickly. Let them cool a little then remove without breaking, wipe with a cloth, put on a plate with the hole facing down and serve a little good sauce on top.*

## STUFFED TOMATOES

2  pounds (1kg) even-sized
   medium tomatoes, scalded
   and peeled
2  onions, sliced
2  carrots, sliced
2-3 slices bacon, diced
1  slice cooked ham, diced
salt and freshly ground
   pepper
¾-1 cup (2-2.5 dl) white stock

## FOR THE STUFFING:

6-8 slices (125g) bread, crusts
   discarded
1  cup (2.5 dl) water
1  cooked chicken breast (125g)
   ground
½ cup (125g) butter, softened
salt and freshly ground
   pepper
½ cup (75g) grated Parmesan
   cheese
3  egg yolks
Tomato sauce, for serving

The tomatoes may be served hot or cold; they are enough for 4–6 as an appetizer.

Cut the core from the tomatoes and scoop out the seeds with a teaspoon, leaving the hole as small as possible. Sprinkle the insides with seasoning. Set the oven at hot (400°F or 205°C).

FOR THE STUFFING: Soak the bread 5 minutes in water, squeeze it dry, then pull it into crumbs. Work the bread with the chicken in an electric food processor, or pound them in a mortar with a pestle until smooth. Beat in the butter and Parmesan with salt and pepper to taste, then stir in the egg yolks. Fill the tomatoes with the stuffing, taking care they do not split.
In a heavy-based casserole spread half the onion and carrot mixture and sprinkle with half the bacon and ham. Set the tomatoes on top, hole down, and sprinkle with the remaining vegetables, bacon, and ham. Sprinkle with salt and pepper and moisten with stock. Bake uncovered in the heated oven for 20–25 minutes or until just tender. (Note: The tomatoes overcook easily.)
Transfer the tomatoes to a platter, spoon the tomato sauce over them, and serve either hot or at room temperature.

for fresh pasta made with four or six eggs. His gnocchi and fettucine are layered with ham, Parmesan, and melted butter with a cream sauce on the side. Tagliolini are to be boiled for only six and a half minutes—an Italian habit that provoked a German traveling in Italy in 1804 to complain about rice and macaroni "too little boiled." Clearly he was not accustomed to *al dente* pasta.

Most significantly for Italian cooking, Leonardi is the first cook to record how the tomato was being used in southern Italy. He can lay claim to originating that classic Neapolitan combination, pasta and tomato; he cooks meatballs in tomato sauce, gives a recipe for chicken *alla siciliana* cooked with ham,

onions, herbs, and tomato sauce, and he stuffs tomatoes and explains how to dry them in the open air for a purée. His *sugo di pomodoro*, made with seeded tomatoes simmered slowly with onions, celery, garlic, basil, and parsley has not changed one iota today.

By the 1760s Leonardi had tired of Naples and spent the next decade or two on the move. Apart from a spell in Rome with the Cardinal de Bernis (who, as befitted a former French courtier, awarded a prize to the city's best cook, the *rosticciere* of Prince Borghese) Leonardi was abroad, first with Louis XV on his military campaigns and then with two Russian noblemen living in exile, Ivan Ivanovich Schuvalov

## Gatto di lasagne alla misgrasse

It has been claimed that this dish was invented in 1799 by a chef of Macerata in honor of the commander of the Austrian forces at Ancona, but the recipe must have a much older tradition as it is clearly familiar to Leonardi writing in 1790. It is a luxurious variation of the usual Bolognese lasagne layered with meat sauce and today is still regarded as a specialty of the region around Ancona.

*Entré. Make dough as for tagliolini [below] with the only difference that you add a nut of butter and do not roll out the dough so thinly. Cut out lasagne in 4 inch or 6 inch squares and cook in boiling salted water, dropping them one at a time at the point where the water is boiling hardest so they do not stick together. When they are cooked, drain, put in cold salted water then lay out on a clean cloth. Take a well-buttered casserole and sprinkle with breadcrumbs, then make a large star on the bottom with slices of ham, then spread the lasagne on the bottom and round the sides of the casserole so they come right up to the top and overlap the sides, alternating with layers of grated Parmesan, nuts of fresh butter, a little béchamel, a little sweetbread ragù and truffles cooked in very little liquid, powdered cinnamon, ground pepper and nutmeg. When the casserole is almost full, fold inside the lasagne that are hanging over the edge and cover with the same mixture, finishing with just butter and Parmesan; bake until a nice color in a fairly hot oven then turn out onto a plate and serve immediately.*

## Zuppa di tagliolini

*Make a dough with flour and 4 or 6 eggs and salt, depending on how much pasta you want to make, knead well until not too hard and not too soft; leave to rest a little then roll out paper thin either in one large sheet or in separate sheets. Leave to dry a little then roll up and cut into ribbons. Cook for 6½ minutes in boiling, salted water.*

## Ragù di animelle

Up to the tricks of his trade, Leonardi was aware that prunes make a handy, cheap substitute for the blackness of truffles. They also add a pleasant touch of sweetness to this dish.

*Blanch one or two calves' sweetbreads in boiling water and cut in large pieces, then put in a saucepan with some sliced truffles or prunes, according to the season, or both dried sweetbreads and prunes soaked in water to soften them, a piece of ham, a bit of butter, a bouquet of mixed herbs and cook; when it begins to dry out moisten with ½ glass champagne or other white wine and some couli and let it reduce by two-thirds, or sprinkle with a pinch of flour and moisten with the wine, and half couli and half white sauce; season with salt and ground pepper and boil gently. When everything is cooked add some blanched cooked chicken livers, some little stuffing balls or a few small cooked prawns; cook a little longer; remove the fat, and the ham and the bouquet of herbs and serve with lemon juice, either as a Terrine, or as an Entremet or to garnish an Entremet; but in this case use little sauce, no stuffing balls (chenef) and prawns, and cut the sweetbreads in large dice.*

## BAKED LASAGNE WITH SWEETBREADS AND TRUFFLES

pasta dough (see next recipe)

FOR THE FILLING:

2-3 tablespoons (30-45g) butter
½ cup (75g) browned breadcrumbs
2 slices cooked ham
sweetbread ragoût (see below)
béchamel sauce, made with 2 tablespoons (30g) butter, 2 tablespoons (20g) flour, 1¼ cups (3dl) milk, salt, pepper, and nutmeg
2-3 tablespoons (30-45g) butter
¾ cup (120g) grated Parmesan cheese
½ teaspoon ground cinnamon
¼ teaspoon grated nutmeg
salt and freshly ground pepper

Moule-à-manqué cake pan, baking dish, or shallow casserole (1quart or 1-liter capacity)

The lasagne serves 6 as a main dish.

Make the pasta dough and roll it out as thinly as possible. Cut it into 4-inch squares and leave to dry (on paper sprinkled with flour) for at least 2 hours. The dough can be made ahead, left to dry for 24 hours, then kept for up to a week in the refrigerator; it can also be frozen.

Thickly butter the cake pan or baking dish with 2–3 tablespoons (30–45 grams) butter and sprinkle with breadcrumbs. Cut large diamonds from the ham, discarding any fat, and arrange a star in the base of the mold. Make the sweetbread ragoût and the béchamel sauce for the filling.

TO COOK THE LASAGNE: Fill a roasting pan with salted water to a depth of 2–3 inches and bring to a boil. Drop in the lasagne and

poach just below boiling point, stirring occasionally so they do not stick, for about 6 minutes or until *al dente*. Transfer them to a bowl of cold water. (Note: To avoid sticking, do not cook too many lasagne at once.)

TO ASSEMBLE THE DISH: Drain some of the lasagne on paper towels and arrange them overlapping in a layer in the bottom of the mold. Line the sides of the mold also, letting strips of lasagne hang over the edge. Fill the mold with layers of sweetbread ragoût, béchamel sauce, sliced truffles, and drained lasagne, dotting the layers with butter and sprinkling with cheese, cinnamon, nutmeg, salt and pepper to taste. (Note: The cheese is already salty, so more salt may not be needed.) When the mold is full, fold in the strips of lasagne at the edge and cover with a final layer of lasagne. Dot the top with butter and sprinkle with the remaining cheese. The lasagne can be prepared up to 24 hours ahead and kept covered in the refrigerator, or it can be frozen.

TO FINISH: Bake the lasagne, uncovered, in a moderately hot oven (375°F or 190°C) for 30 minutes or until very hot and golden brown. Let cool slightly, then turn out onto a platter and serve at once.

## PASTA DOUGH

about 4 cups (500g) flour
1 teaspoon salt
4 eggs

Sift the flour onto a marble slab or board, make a well in the center, and add the eggs and salt. Work the eggs with the fingers of one hand, gradually drawing in the flour and adding more flour if necessary to make a smooth but slightly soft dough. Knead the dough thoroughly on a floured marble or board for 5 minutes or until it is very smooth and elastic. Cover it with an inverted bowl and let rest at least 1 hour. Roll it out according to individual recipe.

## SWEETBREAD RAGOÛT

1 pair (about 1 pound or 500g) calves' sweetbreads
small can truffles, with their liquor, or ¼ pound (125g) pitted prunes, cooked
1 tablespoon (15g) butter
1 slice (about 50g) uncooked ham or lean bacon
bouquet garni
½ cup (1.25dl) champagne or other dry white wine
about 1 cup (2.5dl) brown sauce, made with 1 cup real stock thickened with
1 teaspoon arrowroot or potato starch mixed with 1 tablespoon cold water
½ cup (125g) chicken livers, or chicken stuffing balls (see recipe for Stuffed Tomatoes, page 104), or a few shrimps
1 tablespoon (15g) butter
squeeze of lemon juice
salt and freshly ground pepper

The sweetbreads are delicious served as a main dish with rice or fresh noodles. This quantity would be enough for 2.

Soak the sweetbreads in cold water for 1–2 hours to whiten them. Put them in cold water, bring to a boil, and simmer for 5 minutes. Drain and clean them thoroughly, discarding all membrane and skin. Cut them into ½–1-inch pieces. Slice the truffles or prunes, reserving the truffle liquid. Butter the base of a heavy saucepan, set the ham or bacon in the bottom, then the sweetbreads and sliced prunes or truffles, with the liquid from the truffles. Add the bouquet garni, cover, and cook gently 10–15 minutes. Moisten with the champagne or white wine and brown sauce and simmer, uncovered, until reduced by two-thirds.

Meanwhile, if using chicken livers, blanch them by putting in cold water, bringing to a boil, and simmering 1 minute. Drain and sauté them in butter until brown but still pink in the center. Slice them. If using stuffing balls, cook them in a little stock, or fry them in butter until firm.

Discard the ham or bacon and the bouquet garni from the sweetbreads and season them to taste, adding a squeeze of lemon juice. Add the chicken livers, stuffing balls, or shrimps; continue cooking 1–2 minutes for the flavors to blend, then serve.

109

*Grigori Potemkin (right), a glutton who shared Catherine's taste for cabbage soup and rye bread, was the longest-lasting of her many lovers.*

and Grigori Orlov. Schuvalov (a notable Francophile) had been the lover of Empress Elisabeth of Russia, and Orlov the lover of Empress Catherine; they shared a passion for travel, and Leonardi toured with them, no doubt in the grand Russian style with the rest of their household in train. Schuvalov used to remark that the greatest privilege of a rich man was to eat well, and it was certainly through working for these two noblemen that Leonardi acquired his unique international experience. By 1783, when Orlov died, Leonardi was sufficiently distinguished to be called to Russia as steward to the Empress Catherine herself.

Catherine's court had the brilliance of Versailles and Naples but none of their blasé sophistication. The Russians reveled with childlike delight in their great palaces along the Neva, styled after French and Italian models but outdoing them all in splendor. Gold and jewels glittered everywhere; at a celebration for the birth of Catherine's grandchild, the British ambassador reported that "the dessert at supper was set out with jewels to the amount of upwards of two million sterling." This extravagance was sustained by an army of servants—many nobles kept 500 or more, and as steward of the imperial household Leonardi could have been responsible for double that number. However, far from being

# Rissole alla napolitana

The Arabs ruled Sicily until the end of the eleventh century and these turnovers, reminiscent of Greek *tiropetas* made with flaky phyllo dough, show the Arabic origin of many Italian pastries. Panzarotti filled with local cheese such as provatura (made with buffalo milk), marzolina (made with ewe's milk) and caciocavallo (made with cow's milk) are popular throughout southern Italy. They are always fried in lard, the common fat of the region, as it is cheaper than oil.

*Chop two fresh provatura cheeses, add a little Parmesan, some grated provatura, marzolina and caciocavallo, a slice of chopped ham sweated for a moment over the heat in a casserole, chopped parsley, no salt, ground pepper, nutmeg, two raw eggs and mix well. Roll out a sheet of pasta brisé made with butter or lard, either will do, about the thickness of a paolo [coin], put little heaps of the cheese mixture around the edge, brush with beaten egg, fold the pasta dough over, press down well and cut out little crescent-shaped ravioli with the pasta wheel. Before serving fry in very hot lard and serve golden brown at once. In Naples these rissoles are called panzarotti.*

## PANZAROTTI (FRIED CHEESE TURNOVERS)

FOR THE PASTRY DOUGH:

4 cups (500g) flour
1 teaspoon salt
½ cup (125g) butter or lard
⅓ cup (1dl) water

FOR THE FILLING:

1 fresh provatura cheese or ½ pound (250g) mozzarella, diced

¼ cup (30g) grated Parmesan cheese
½ cup (75g) grated provolone or Gruyère cheese
2 ounces (60g) prosciutto or cooked ham, chopped
1 tablespoon chopped parsley
pinch of ground nutmeg
freshly ground black pepper
2 eggs, beaten to mix
deep fat (for frying)

This makes 25–30 panzarotti.

FOR THE PASTRY DOUGH: Sift the flour onto a marble slab or board, make a well in the center, and add the butter or lard, salt, and 2–3 tablespoons water. Work the central ingredients with the fingertips until well mixed, then gradually draw in the flour using the whole hand. Add more water as necessary to make a dough that is soft but not sticky. Cover it and chill ½–1 hour.

FOR THE FILLING: Fry the ham over low heat, stirring, until the fat runs and it browns lightly. Let cool, then mix into the diced provatura, grated Parmesan, provolone, and parsley. Season to taste with nutmeg and pepper—salt is not needed as the ham and cheeses are already salty. Stir in the beaten eggs to bind the mixture.

On a floured board, roll out the dough to ⅛-inch thickness. About 1½ inches from the edge of the dough, place teaspoonsful of the filling at 2-inch intervals. Brush around the mounds of filling with water and fold over the edge of the dough to cover them. Press to seal and cut out the turnovers with a ravioli cutter. Repeat with more mounds of filling, gradually working toward the center of the dough. The turnovers can be kept covered in the refrigerator for up to 48 hours, or they can be frozen.

TO FINISH: Heat the deep fat to 360°F (180°C). Fry the turnovers, a few at a time, in hot fat until brown. Drain thoroughly on paper towels. Serve them as soon as possible.

# Manzo stufato

This famous dish is now known as *ragù napoletano* and a folklore has grown up around the ritual of preparing it for Sunday lunch: the long hours it must simmer until the gravy is rich and the meat tender. Leonardi recommends serving the meat and vegetables, with the sauce in a separate dish to accompany macaroni—a custom that is often followed today. Alternatively the meat may be chopped up small with the gravy to serve as a pasta sauce, showing the Italian preference for small pieces of meat that so distressed eighteenth-century English tourists.

*This is our version of stufato: it is a universal dish that is delicious when it is made well using good beef. For those who prefer fat meat use rib; those who like lean meat say that sirloin is better, so it is a matter of choice. This is how to make it: cut the meat in even pieces; take one ounce of fat bacon for every pound of beef and chop very finely, together with onion, scallion, parsley, two or three cloves of garlic depending on the amount of beef used, sweet marjoram and basil, all finely chopped. Put the chopped ingredients in a casserole, or as we say, in a stufarola with the beef, season with salt, pepper and fine spices. Cook over a low heat and when the juice in the pan has reduced add half a glass of boiling white wine. Let the liquid reduce again, add some stock and cook well covered in only a little liquid. When the meat is cooked remove the fat and season with salt to taste. Any vegetable goes well in this dish, such as celery, turnips, quince, pears, carrots, spring onions, truffles, tomatoes, mushrooms; it is particularly good with pears and tomato sauce. Boil the vegetables first and add to the meat when it is almost done so they finish cooking together. Pears and quinces should be cut in quarters and added uncooked to the meat. Fry turnips first in lard until golden brown. Tomato sauce is made*

*(continued from previous page)*

*in the following way, not just to use in a stufato but in other similar dishes, that is cut open whatever quantity of tomatoes you need, squeeze gently and put in a casserole with sprigs of parsley, basil, a few cloves of garlic, a little celery, sliced onion and a few scallions if you have them; put on the fire and boil gently for one hour, then rub through a sieve to obtain everything except the skins and the seeds and use this sauce as required.*

## STEWED BEEF

### FOR THE BRAISED BEEF:

4-pound (2kg) shell of beef,
   with some fat, cut in
   2-inch (5cm) pieces
¼-pound (125g) piece fat
   bacon, chopped
2 onions, finely chopped
2 scallions, finely chopped
2-3 cloves garlic, crushed
1 tablespoon chopped parsley
1 teaspoon chopped basil
1 teaspoon chopped marjoram
salt and freshly ground
   black pepper
1 teaspoon ground allspice
½ cup (1.25 dl) white wine
1-2 cups (2.5-5 dl) brown stock
2 pounds (1kg) macaroni,
   boiled (for serving)

### FOR THE GARNISH:

2 tablespoons (30g) lard or
   shortening
1 pound (500g) baby
   turnips trimmed
5-6 stalks celery, cut in
   2-inch (5cm) lengths
1 pound (500g) baby
   carrots, trimmed
8-10 scallions, cut in 2-inch
   (5cm) lengths
½ pound (250g) mushrooms,
   trimmed and quartered
1 pound (500g) firm pears
   peeled, quartered, and cored

### FOR THE TOMATO SAUCE (OPTIONAL):

2 pounds (1kg) ripe tomatoes,
   seeded and chopped
2 tablespoons (30g) lard or oil
1 onion, thinly sliced
1 scallion, chopped
1-2 cloves garlic, crushed
bouquet garni made of
   parsley sprigs, fresh basil
   leaves, and celery leaves

Given the quality of eighteenth-century beef, it is not surprising Leonardi uses the best cuts—sirloin or rib—but chuck or round can be substituted. Tomato sauce for serving is optional. The vegetables are not all needed in the garnish, but the wider the selection, the more attractive the dish. This recipe serves 8.

Set the oven at moderately low (325°F or 163°C). In a heavy-based casserole heat the bacon until the fat runs. Add the onions and scallions and cook gently until soft. Stir in the garlic, parsley, basil, and marjoram. Toss the meat in salt, pepper, and allspice until well coated, add to the pan, and cook briskly until the vegetables and meat just start to brown. Add the wine and boil until completely reduced. Add 1 cup (2.5 decilitres) of stock, cover tightly, and cook in the heated oven 3–3½ hours or until the meat is very tender. Add more stock during cooking if the mixture gets dry. At the end of cooking, the sauce should be thick and rich. Skim off any fat. The beef can be kept up to 3 days in the refrigerator, or it can be frozen. The vegetables are best added when the beef is reheated.

FOR THE GARNISH: Cook turnips in lard or shortening over brisk heat until brown but still firm (about 10 minutes). Blanch celery in boiling, salted water for 5 minutes and drain. Cook carrots in salted water 10–15 minutes until almost tender and drain. Blanch scallions in boiling, salted water for 2 minutes and drain.
Add turnips to the casserole 45 minutes before the end of cooking. Add pears and mushrooms 30 minutes before the end of cooking; celery, carrots, and scallions need 15–20 minutes' cooking with the meat. All the vegetables should be tender before serving. Taste the sauce for seasoning.

FOR THE TOMATO SAUCE: Fry the onion in the lard or oil until soft. Add the tomato, scallion, garlic, bouquet garni, salt, and pepper and simmer very gently, uncovered, for 15–20 minutes until the sauce is thick and pulpy. Strain and taste for seasoning.

TO SERVE: Pile the beef and vegetables on a platter and spoon the tomato sauce on top. Serve boiled macaroni separately.

## *Fegato di mongana alla veneziana*

This well-known dish is typical of good Italian cooking, where the flavors of simple ingredients are left to speak for themselves. Leonardi includes it as an "orduvre" but today it is served as a main course, with slices of toasted polenta (baked corn meal).

*Finely slice four or five onions and fry in a casserole with a nut of butter, a little oil, chopped scallions or spring onions, add the liver, salt, freshly ground pepper and chopped parsley and cook to perfection, making sure it is very juicy. Serve with its own gravy and plenty of lemon juice.*

*Polenta, made with yellow cornmeal, is the traditional accompaniment to calves' liver Venetian style. In the painting below, the dough is kneaded on a table-cloth to absorb excess moisture – still the best procedure.*

## CALVES' LIVER VENETIAN STYLE

2 pounds (1kg) calves' liver
2 tablespoons olive oil
4-5 (about 750g) onions, thinly sliced
3 tablespoons (45g) butter
salt and freshly ground pepper
1 tablespoon chopped parsley

For this recipe it is vital that the liver be sliced paper thin. Italians have been known to freeze the liver, then slice it with a mechanical bacon slicer, but the liver is hard to brown after freezing. The best implement is the old-fashioned, razor-sharp knife. This recipe serves 6.

Slice the liver as thinly as possible, discarding any skin and membrane. In a frying pan heat the oil and butter and fry the onions gently until soft but not brown. Add the liver, sprinkle with salt and pepper and cook, stirring occasionally until the liver and onions are brown. (Note: The speed of cooking is important. If cooked too slowly the liver will stew rather than browning. If cooked too fast it will be dry.)
Taste for seasoning, transfer to a platter, sprinkle with parsley, and serve at once.

## *Cassata palermitana*

Instead of being frosted with a glaze, today cassata Palermitana is often macerated in maraschino liqueur, but the ricotta filling flavored with indigenous Sicilian candied fruits and orange flower water is unchanged. Chopped chocolate is often added to the filling instead of being sprinkled on top.

*Take some good ricotta and mix with not too much white powdered sugar, a little cinnamon water and the same amount of orange flowers. Some people also mix in strips of candied lemon, orange flowers and chopped pistachio nuts; mix well. Line a casserole or a copper mold on the bottom or sides with sponge cake, put in the ricotta then cover with further slices of sponge cake. After half an hour turn onto a plate with a napkin on it; glaze with a light royal glaze; garnish the cassata with chocolate strands, pistachio nuts or other comfits in an attractive pattern, a few candied pears or other dried fruit; dry the glaze for a minute on the stove and serve cold.*

## CASSATA PALERMITANA

2 pounds (1kg) ricotta cheese
½ cup (100g) shelled pistachios
3 cups (360g) confectioners' sugar, sifted
2 teaspoons ground cinnamon
2 teaspoons orange flower water
1½ cups (300g) candied orange and lemon peel, finely chopped
9-inch (23cm) diameter sponge cake, weighing about 1 pound (500g)

FOR GARNISH:
glacé icing made with 2 cups (240g) confectioners' sugar
2-3 tablespoons water, and
1 teaspoon orange flower water
candied pears, apricots, cherries, grated chocolate, pistachios, for decoration

9-inch (23cm) springform pan

This recipe serves 10–12.

Split the sponge cake into three layers. Set one layer in the bottom of the pan, reserve another layer, and cut the third into strips to line the side of the mold.

FOR THE FILLING: If necessary blanch the pistachios for 1 minute in boiling water, drain, and skin them; coarsely chop them. Work the ricotta cheese through a sieve, then beat in the confectioners' sugar with the cinnamon and orange flower water. Stir in the candied peel and pistachios and spread the filling in the lined mold, pressing it down well. Set the reserved round of cake on top, cover with a pie pan base or flat plate and set a 1-pound (500-gram) weight on top. Chill overnight.

TO FINISH: Remove the plate from the cassata, set it on a rack and remove the springform pan sides. For the icing, sift the confectioners' sugar into a bowl and beat in enough water with the orange flower water to make a stiff paste. Set the bowl in a pan of hot water and stir until the icing is tepid; it should just coat the back of a spoon. If not, add more sifted confectioners' sugar or water until it is the right consistency. Pour the icing over the cake and spread with a metal spatula so the sides of the cake are coated. (Note: Work quickly as the icing sets fast.)
Decorate the top of the cake with grated chocolate, pistachios, and candied fruits, transfer to a platter with a napkin or paper doily, and serve.

trained, most of these "servants" were serfs whose status is conveyed by a stark advertisement from a St. Petersburg journal of the time: "To be sold: a girl of 16 of good behavior, and a second-hand, slightly used carriage."

During Leonardi's time at court the lead was taken by Prince Grigori Potemkin, Orlov's successor to Catherine's favors. He thought nothing of spending 20,000 roubles (then about £60,000 sterling) on a dinner followed by artistic entertainment. At one party the whole of St. Petersburg talked about a soup of sterlet (a type of sturgeon) which cost 3,000 roubles and was served in a bathtub of massive silver. A grand dinner would begin with oysters specially imported from Denmark, and in summer Russia's own rivers yielded a superb harvest of fish. In winter, before Christmas, the frozen Neva was the setting for a mile-long market where large quantities of frozen meat were sold. "It would be difficult for even a nice epicure to perceive the difference," remarked an English commentator in 1804, in what must be the first endorsement of frozen foods.

Fresh or frozen, many of the grander ingredients came from afar. "I have frequently seen at the same time sterlet from the Volga, veal from Archangel, mutton from Astrachan, beef from the Ukraine, and pheasants from Hungary and Bohemia," reported William Coxe during a trip through Russia in 1778. Out of season, the cost of a melon in a Moscow market could rise fortyfold, having been sent by land carriage from the Caspian, a thousand miles away. The Empress Catherine grew fruits and vegetables in her own hothouses, which must have been extravagant to heat during the long Russian winter. One March dinner in St. Petersburg was graced by a real cherry tree laden with fruit—"But flavor is lacking from the prodigals of the greenhouse," the great French chef Carême was later to remark of his spell at the Russian court. Catherine herself is said to have had simple tastes, reserving a grand display for formal occasions. In private she kept to cabbage (a taste she shared with Potemkin), rye bread, rusks, and plenty of strong coffee.

Leonardi stayed only a few years in Russia, complaining that he could not stand the climate, then returned to the welcoming sun of Italy, probably reaching Rome in 1787. After the publication of *L'Apicio* in 1790, he spent a few years with the Duke of Gravina in Naples, but he had chosen the wrong moment to abandon the opulence of Russia. When Napoleon's armies invaded Italy, the duke scuttled hastily back to his native Sicily and Leonardi was left to fend for himself. Possibly he may have kept a taverna; certainly it was a bad time for anyone whose livelihood depended on the patronage of the rich.

The latter days of Leonardi's career are obscure. He may have had some of the adventures he describes in the preface to *Giannina ossia la cuciniera della alpi* (Giannina or the Alpine Cook). Giannina was an innkeeper at Mont Cenis who had married a French cook and traveled with him in Russia, central Europe, and on the high seas, working for the East India Company. More likely Leonardi stayed in Italy, perhaps cannibalizing *L'Apicio moderno*, for the recipes in *Giannina* and in two or three other works which bear his name proved to be no more than adaptations of *L'Apicio*. In deference to the vogue for chinoiserie, one of these books was called *Tonkin*, but disappointingly it treats not of Chinese cooking but of the sweet liqueurs and candied fruits then in fashion on the credenza (the ornamental side table dating from the Renaissance).

*L'Apicio moderno* remains his master work, and a master work it certainly is. However, its ultimate importance for Italian cooking lies not in its French recipes and techniques, much as they added depth and breadth to native traditions, but in its elaboration of cooking as a discipline demanding skill and dedication. Italians had not seen a cookbook of such ambition since the time of Scappi, and in those 250 years the indigenous tradition of cooking owed its survival to its deep roots in Italian homes rather than to the inspiration of cookbooks. As Leonardi himself wrote, "Pride has been a reason why Italian cooking has deteriorated in the last two centuries; cooks are afraid people would think them ignorant if they were caught consulting a cookbook." Leonardi restored leadership to his "boundless profession" (as he called it), building on the same modest repertoire of meat, pasta, vegetables, and desserts as had featured in Martino and Scappi. The fact that Italian cooking has come so far from there, finding its major expression in 1880 with the classic *La Scienza in cucina* by Pellegrino Artusi, owes much to the initiative of Francesco Leonardi.

*Poor fishermen consume a hasty meal of pasta in this 1801 view of the Bay of Naples, the city where Leonardi began and ended his career.*

# Amelia Simmons

flourished 1796

The first cookbook written by an American for Americans appeared in Hartford, Connecticut, in 1796 and was entitled quite simply *American Cookery.* It was a modest little volume of some 130 recipes, making none of the extravagant claims to erudition that were customary in Europe, but seeking rather "the improvement of the rising generation of females in America." The book reads like a personal collection of time-honoured recipes which, after passing from hand to hand for several decades, had finally made its way into print. More an aide-memoire for an experienced cook than a manual of instruction for the novice, it skates over everyday techniques to concentrate instead on party dishes like turtle or calf's head, rich cream desserts, and huge fruit cakes. About the author nothing is known except her name, Amelia Simmons, and her statement that she is an orphan.

All the cookbooks then available in America had originated in England and none had the American recipes offered by Amelia Simmons. She uses corncobs to smoke bacon and suggests cranberry sauce as an accompaniment to turkey. She gives the first recipes for Indian slapjacks, "johny" or hoe cake, and three versions of Indian pudding, all using cornmeal, an American staple the English regarded with disdain. Benjamin Franklin, writing in the *London Gazetteer* in 1766, felt compelled to protest:

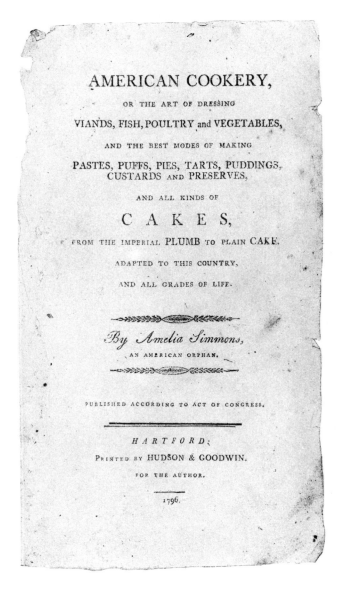

AMERICAN COOKERY,

OR THE ART OF DRESSING

VIANDS, FISH, POULTRY and VEGETABLES,

AND THE BEST MODES OF MAKING

PASTES, PUFFS, PIES, TARTS, PUDDINGS, CUSTARDS AND PRESERVES,

AND ALL KINDS OF

CAKES,

FROM THE IMPERIAL PLUMB TO PLAIN CAKE.

ADAPTED TO THIS COUNTRY,

AND ALL GRADES OF LIFE.

*By Amelia Simmons,*

AN AMERICAN ORPHAN.

PUBLISHED ACCORDING TO ACT OF CONGRESS.

HARTFORD:

PRINTED BY HUDSON & GOODWIN.

FOR THE AUTHOR.

1796.

*Benjamin Franklin, Amelia Simmons's contemporary and enthusiastic advocate of things American.*

"Pray, let me, an American, inform the gentleman, who seems ignorant of the matter, that Indian corn, take it for all in all, is one of the most agreeable and wholesome grains in the world and that johny cake or hoe cake, hot from the fire is better than a Yorkshire muffin." The contemporary English cook would have found some of Amelia's vocabulary equally odd; fat for making pastry is "shortening," biscuits have become "cookies" (from the Dutch *koekje*), and scones are called "biscuits." Her cook-

Opposite:
*Detail of "The Residence of David Twining" (1787). The artist, David Hicks, was born in 1780 and in this painting, done from memory in the 1840s, he stands as a child looking at the Bible beside his foster parents, the Twinings. The farm was in Pennsylvania, but the same essentials of prosperity—the stock animals, the poultry, the work horses and horses for riding, the barns, the well, and the cider press — would have been familiar to Amelia Simmons in New England.*

117

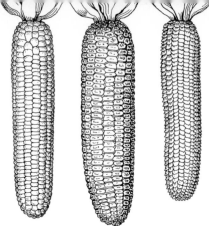

for bass, shad, codfish, blackfish, and salmon. The greatest innovation is in her cakes. To tea cakes, wiggs (buns flavored with caraway) and gingerbread, which are all of obvious English origin, she adds federal pan cake, buckwheat cakes (to be found on many a colonist's breakfast table), and election cake, with its vote-winning flavorings of wine and brandy, known to the future president John Adams as early as 1756. The other uniquely American cake found in Amelia's book is Independence cake, a fruitcake raised with yeast and grandly decorated with gold leaf. From the recipe's enormous yield (it starts with twenty pounds of flour), it would seem that this cake was made only once a year to crown a town's festivities on "the Glorious Fourth" of July.

At the time Amelia wrote her book, several leaders of the infant Republic—Franklin, Adams, and Jefferson for example—had been introduced through their diplomatic missions to a more cosmopolitan diet. Franklin and Jefferson continued to flirt with French cooking but in the year of *American Cookery*'s publication, Adams dined with a Massachusetts friend and declared that his "salted Beef and shell beans with a Whortleberry Pudden and Cyder was a Luxurious Treat." The ultimate accolade bestowed on New England cooking came from the French gastronome Brillat-Savarin (exiled from his country by the revolution) who in 1794 was lavishly entertained near Hartford, Connecticut. A farmer and his four daughters prepared for him "a superb piece of corned beef, a stewed goose, a magnificent leg of mutton, a vast selection of vegetables, and at either end of the table two huge jugs of cider."

This was just the food familiar to Amelia Simmons, for her book was published in Hartford. As a child, she probably boarded with a respectable family, since in her preface she says that "the orphan, tho' left to the care of virtuous guardians, will find it essentially necessary to have an opinion and a determination of her own." Her determination to produce a cookbook is all the more admirable in view of her probable position as domestic and cook and her semi-literate state—she explains that she lacked "an education sufficient to prepare the work for the press." Her practical education was another matter;

book is also the first in the world to use a chemical raising agent called pearl ash—a substance akin to baking soda and derived from potash.

*American Cookery* was such a success that a second edition appeared in the same year. In it Amelia Simmons is at pains to explain that she has had trouble with her publisher—she hopes that "this second edition will appear, in a great measure, free from those egregious blunders, and inaccuracies . . . which were occasioned either by the ignorance, or evil intention of the transcriber for the press." The second edition is indeed very different from the first. Three of the six beef recipes are for steak—a first hint of what was to become an American addiction—and Amelia repairs the almost total omission of fish from the first edition with recipes

*A Hare or Rabbit trussed for Roasting*

*A Hare or Rabbit for Roasting or Boiling*

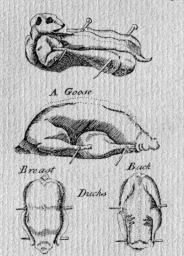

*A Goose*

*Breast*      *Back*

*Duchs*

Reflecting her heritage, Amelia Simmons's recipes hark back to an earlier age. Like the first European cooks she tends to write in note form, and the interpretation of some of her recipes is a matter of guesswork; those given here are among the most explicit.

## Chouder

Amelia Simmons's chowder is not the soup we know, but a stew of fish and crackers fried in salt pork with scarcely a trace of liquid—large quantities of water or milk were not added until considerably later. The name almost certainly comes from the Breton expression *faire chaudière*, meaning to make a fish stew in a caldron. Such a stew was taken by Breton fishermen to Nova Scotia and eventually traveled down the coast to New England. By the mid-eighteenth century it had found its way back to England as "chouder." One version similar to this recipe of Amelia Simmons's, but baked like a pie with a top crust, appears in the 1770 edition of Hannah Glasse's *Art of Cookery*. The mangoes mentioned here as accompaniment were presumably pickled or in a chutney; perhaps Amelia was thinking of her own optimistic recipe for making so-called mangoes out of green melons.

*Take a bass weighing four pounds, boil half an hour; take six slices raw salt pork, fry them till the lard is nearly extracted, one dozen crackers soaked in cold water five minutes; put the bass into the lard, also the pieces of pork and crackers, cover close, and fry for 20 minutes; serve with potatoes, pickles, apple-sauce or mangoes; garnish with green parsley.*

## FISH CHOWDER

4-pound (2-kg) whole sea bass, rockfish, bluefish, haddock, or any other white fish
water
1 teaspoon salt
12 (about 60g) unsalted crackers
6 slices (about 250g) salt pork
2 tablespoons chopped parsley (for sprinkling)
boiled potatoes, pickles, applesauce, or mango chutney (for serving)

This recipe serves 6.

Set the oven at moderate (350°F or 177°C). Wash the fish, put it in a baking dish, and add enough cold water to half cover, with the salt. Cover with buttered paper and bake in the heated oven for 50–60 minutes or until the fish flakes easily; let it cool. Take the fish from the bones, discarding the skin, and divide it into fairly large pieces.
Pour about 1 cup (2.5 deciliters) cold water over the crackers, leave 5 minutes to soak and drain off the excess.
In a large skillet fry the salt pork until lightly browned and all the fat has been extracted. Add the fish and soaked crackers, stir carefully, and cover tightly. Cook over moderate heat for 10–12 minutes, stirring occasionally, until the fish and crackers are lightly browned and all the fat has been absorbed. Taste for seasoning, sprinkle with chopped parsley, and serve with boiled potatoes and pickles, applesauce, or mango chutney.

## To alamode a round

By the end of the eighteenth century the original meaning of *à la mode* (fashionable) had become irrevocably associated in cooking with a large cut of beef braised with wine and bones to make a rich gravy. In a primitive kitchen even this basic dish was not easy, hence Amelia Simmons's warning to place the meat on top of the bones to avoid scorching on the bottom of the pan. She seals the pot with dough to prevent steam from escaping during cooking, then leaves the meat to marinate overnight in the wine before setting the pot to "hang on" the fireplace crane in the morning. The breadcrumbs added at the end would probably have been browned by holding a shiny tin sheet to reflect the heat of the fire onto the meat.

*Take fat pork cut in slices or mince, season it with pepper, salt, sweet marjoram and thyme, cloves, mace and nutmeg, make holes in the beef and stuff it the night before cooked; put some bones across the bottom of the pot to keep from burning, put in one quart Claret wine, one quart water and one onion; lay the round on the bones, cover close and stop it round the top with dough; hang on in the morning and stew gently two hours; turn it, and stop tight and stew two hours more; when done tender, grate a crust of bread on the top and brown it before the fire; scum the gravy and serve in a butter boat, serve it with the residue of the gravy in the dish.*

(continued from previous page)

## BRAISED BEEF

⅓ pound (160g) pork fat, ground or finely chopped
1 teaspoon freshly ground black pepper
2 teaspoons salt
1 teaspoon marjoram
1 teaspoon thyme
½ teaspoon ground cloves
½ teaspoon ground nutmeg
½ teaspoon ground mace
5-6-pound (2½-3-kg) boned round or rump of beef, rolled
1½-2 pounds (750g-1kg) beef bones, split
3 cups (7.5 dl) red Bordeaux wine
2 cups (5 dl) water
1 onion, quartered
½ cup (60g) dry white breadcrumbs (to finish)

### FOR THE SEALING DOUGH:

6-7 tablespoons (about 1 dl) water
1 cup (125g) flour

This recipe serves 8–10.

Mix the pork fat with the pepper, salt, marjoram, thyme, and spices. With a pointed knife cut deep incisions in the beef and stuff them with the fat mixture. Put the bones in the bottom of a Dutch oven or heavy casserole, set the beef on top, add the wine, water, and onion and cover. Stir enough water (about 3 tablespoons) into half the flour to make a soft paste—do not beat or the paste will become elastic. Seal the gap between casserole and lid with the paste and leave in the refrigerator overnight.

The next day set the oven at moderately low (325°F or 163°C). Cook the meat 2 hours, remove the lid, and turn the beef. Make more paste with the remaining flour and water, reseal the lid and continue cooking the meat 1–2 hours longer—a long thin cut will take less time than a thick squat one. Transfer the beef to a heatproof platter or a roasting pan, sprinkle with the breadcrumbs, and baste with a little cooking liquid; broil until browned, then keep hot. Strain the cooking liquid into a saucepan, skim off the fat, and bring it to a boil. Taste it for seasoning and serve separately as gravy with the meat.

## Pumpkin

This recipe, labeled simply pumpkin, is in fact a pie, though Amelia Simmons includes it in her section on puddings. Her first version, containing large amounts of cream, must have been for parties and the second, made with milk and molasses, for everyday. Despite its bitterness, blackstrap molasses was often used for sweetening, since outside areas where sugar and maple syrup were produced, it was far cheaper. Molasses (known to the English as treacle) and rum were one of the main bones of contention during the War of Independence, for the British insisted on placing a high import duty on the raw product. As John Adams said: "I know not why we should blush to confess that molasses is an essential ingredient in American independence."

*No. 1. One quart [pumpkin] stewed and strained, 3 pints cream, 9 beaten eggs, sugar, mace, nutmeg and ginger, laid into paste No. 7 or 3, and with a dough spur, cross and chequer it, and baked in dishes three quarters of an hour.*
*No. 2. One quart of milk, 1 pint pumpkin, 4 eggs, molasses, allspice and ginger in a crust, bake 1 hour.*

## PUMPKIN PIE

### FOR THE PASTRY:

3 cups (375g) flour
½ teaspoon salt
½ cup (125g) butter
⅓ cup (80g) shortening or lard
6-7 tablespoons (about 1 dl) water

### FOR THE FILLING:

3 cups (7.5 dl) heavy cream
4 eggs, beaten to mix
3 cups (7.5 dl) cooked, strained pumpkin
1¼ cups (300g) sugar
1 teaspoon ground nutmeg
1 teaspoon ground mace
2 teaspoons ground ginger

Two 9-inch (22-cm) pie pans

This is the first, and richer, of the fillings; it and the pastry are enough for two 9-inch pies.

TO MAKE THE PASTRY: Sift the flour into a bowl with the salt, add the butter and shortening or lard, and cut the fat into small pieces with a pastry cutter or two knives. Rub in with the fingertips until the mixture forms crumbs. Add 6 tablespoons cold water, stir, then press the mixture together, adding more water if necessary to make a dough that is soft but not sticky. Chill 30 minutes.

FOR THE FILLING: Beat the cream with the eggs into the cooked pumpkin and stir in the sugar with the nutmeg, mace, and ginger. Set the oven at moderate (350°F or 177°C).

Roll out two-thirds of the pastry, line the pie pans, and fill with the pumpkin mixture. Roll out the remaining pastry and cut two ¾-inch bands; reserve them. Cut the remaining pastry into narrow strips and decorate the tops of the pies with a lattice. Lay the reserved pastry bands around the edges of the lattice. Bake the pies in the heated oven for 1 hour or until the filling is firm.

PHILLIS' AMBROSIA.

ARKWRIGHT JONNY CAKE MEAL.
GROUND BY GRANITE STONES.

Overleaf:
*"The Fourth of July Picnic at Weymouth Landing,"* painted by Susan Merrett, shows the kind of communal gathering where Amelia Simmons's vast Independence Day cake made with twenty pounds of flour would have been appreciated.

The remoteness of the southern housewife from the actual business of cooking was reflected in the position of the kitchen, which was often built apart from the main house so that the fire would not add to the oppressive summer heat. In New England, however, the kitchen invariably formed part of the main house. In old farmhouses, it was the principal living room, where all could benefit from the warmth of the great central fireplace whose flues also heated upper and adjacent rooms. All cooking was done around this kitchen fireplace. A central fire was usually kept going constantly, and during the day one or two smaller fires would be kindled on each side to boil a kettle of water for washing and cleaning. Controlling the heat was tricky and cooks learned early which logs had a fierce heat that died quickly and which were steady-burning. All but the most primitive kitchens were equipped with a crane, hinged to swing outward, from which pots and kettles could be suspended at variable heights

at that time in the United States, year-round supplies of household goods were not assured and a knowledge of such basic skills as sewing, brewing, candle-dipping, and soap-making were important. Since the cold northern climate severely limited the growing season, the life of the family also depended on stores laid down for the winter. Yankee cooks were fiercely proud of their skill with pickles and preserves, a necessity raised to an art and *American Cookery* makes much use of preserved ingredients such as salt pork, dried apples, raisins, and cornmeal. It also includes an attractive selection of fruit jams and jellies as well as the ubiquitous pickled cucumbers.

Further south, on the plantations of Virginia and the Carolinas, the situation was very different. Slave labor meant that cooking could be done on a considerably larger scale, making possible the southern tradition of hospitality. Thomas Jefferson remarked that not once had he been forced to dine alone with his family at Monticello—visitors doubtless craved his ice creams as much as his conversation—and George Washington complained that Mount Vernon was "little better than a well-resorted inn." The families who could afford to entertain on such a scale were few, but even modest households generally kept a slave or two who could prepare time-consuming southern specialities like beaten biscuits. For Amelia Simmons, quickly-made dishes like pancakes, or the "alamode" beef that looked after itself for hours over a low fire, were more practical. When Adams succeeded Washington as president in 1797, the difference in the scale of official entertainment was observed at once.

*A woodcut of an orchard and a cider press. In the early days cider was the universal drink in New England, and no farm was without its cider apple trees and press.*

over the fire. For roasting, meat and fowl were skewered on a spit. Turning the meat was a hot and dull job, assigned to the smaller children and eventually taken over by some crude mechanism such as a string that wound back on itself, or a weighted pulley.

121

For frying Amelia would have used skillets, called spiders, with three feet to hold them firm in the ashes. For browning the tops of puddings there were flat iron salamanders to be heated red-hot. Baking could be done by simply burying a covered pot in hot ashes and this was the original function of the Dutch oven; the base and lid were thoroughly heated before the fire, then the pie, bread, or cake was put inside and the oven surrounded by glowing embers. Amelia Simmons's recipes assume the use of an oven and most kitchens boasted at least a reflecting oven—a shiny tin box open on the fireside to focus the heat. The best ovens were made of brick, preheated with logs whose ashes were raked out before cooking began. Some brick ovens were constructed at the side of the fire with a door in the fireplace so the wood-smoke went up the chimney; others were built separately, outside the house.

Most housewives baked their own bread but Frances Trollope, writing in *Domestic Manners of the Americans* in 1832, remarks that despite its excellence, it is not eaten in great quantities; instead, Americans "insist upon eating horrible half-baked hot rolls both morning and evening." Amelia Simmons does not elaborate upon the art; she probably regarded the kneading and baking of bread as a basic technique which children learned at their mother's knees. Where knowledge was required was in choosing ingredients. Grain was often poorly harvested or badly kept—Amelia's one bread recipe is

devoted to the somewhat dubious task of making "good bread with grown flour" (i.e., from sprouted wheat). In extreme cases rye could develop the ergot fungus containing LSD, thought to be the cause of several early epidemics of hysterical visions known as St. Anthony's Fire.

Only in towns could the yeast for bread and coffee-cakes be bought at the baker's and even then its strength and freshness varied. Experienced cooks like Amelia made their own at home from "emptins" (another term unknown in England), a type of yeast made from the lees or emptyings of wine or beer. Later, in the West, pioneers relied on sourdough starter, made from mashed potatoes left to ferment, then "fed" from time to time with flour and water. Good starter was believed to improve with age and a pot of vintage starter was a treasured present to brides. So precious was this means of making bread that the gold rush miners earned the name "sourdoughs" from their habit of taking the pots to bed to prevent the yeast from dying in the icy air.

It is extraordinary to think that when *American Cookery* was printed in 1796, the complex French cuisine described first by La Varenne and then by Menon had been flourishing for 150 years. Recipes for gooseberry tart and bread pudding seem centuries as well as oceans apart from such fancies as Menon's *paupiettes de boeuf à l'estouffade aux capucines confites* (stuffed beef rolls braised and garnished with pickled nasturtium seeds). The contrast with England, however, was not so sharp; familiar "ham and beef-steaks appear morning, noon and night," reported Mrs. Trollope, though she found the combinations of dishes very strange. "I have seen eggs and oysters eaten together; the sempiternal ham with apple-sauce; beef-steak with stewed peaches; and salt fish with onions." The English preoccupation with cake-baking, preserving, and cooking codfish—all in an economical fashion—was generally shared by American cooks, as shown by the continuing success in America of established English works like Hannah Glasse's *The Art of Cookery* and Susannah Carter's *The Frugal Housewife*, which were useful even though they called for some ingredients unavailable in the New World and ignored others that were common.

However, the demand for a genuinely American cookbook is shown by the flood of imitations that followed Amelia's pioneer effort. The first was a special American edition of *The Frugal Housewife* in 1803, in which the publisher changed the original

124

## A Nice Indian Pudding

Indian pudding now means a spiced cornmeal pudding sweetened with molasses, but in the early days it referred to any pudding made with Indian meal (i.e., cornmeal). Amelia Simmons gives three versions, the first sweetened with sugar and raisins, the second similar to the modern one, and the third a mixture of milk and meal that was probably only lightly sweetened and intended to be served with meat.

*No. 1. 3 pints scalded milk, 7 spoons fine Indian meal, stir well together while hot, let stand till cooled; add 7 eggs, half pound raisins, 4 ounces butter, spice and sugar, bake one and half hour.*

*No. 2. 3 pints scalded milk to one pint meal salted; cool, add 2 eggs, 4 ounces butter, sugar or molasses and spice q.s.* [quantum sufficit; i.e., to taste] *it will require two and half hours baking.*

*No. 3. Salt a pint meal, wet with one quart milk, sweeten and put into a strong cloth, brass or bell metal vessel, stone or earthern pot, secure from wet and boil 12 hours.*

## INDIAN PUDDING

3 cups (75 dl) milk
½ teaspoon salt
¼ cup (50g) yellow cornmeal
2 tablespoons (30g) butter
1 egg, beaten to mix
¼ cup (60g) sugar or ¼ cup (7 cl) dark molasses
½ teaspoon ground cinnamon
½ teaspoon ground ginger

shallow baking dish
(1-quart or 1-liter capacity)

This is the second, classic version of Indian pudding given in

*American Cookery.* Today New Englanders would add ¼ cup (7 centiliters) more molasses and would serve it with whipped cream or vanilla ice cream; it serves 6.

Set the oven at moderate (350°F or 177°C). Scald the milk with the salt. Stir in the cornmeal gradually, and cook over low heat for 5 minutes, stirring constantly, until it thickens like cooked cereal. Let cool to tepid, stir in the butter until melted, followed by the egg, sugar or molasses, and spices.

Pour into a buttered shallow baking dish and bake in the heated oven for 1¼–1½ hours or until the pudding is set. Serve warm.

## Independence Cake

The cryptic instructions for this are typical of many of Amelia Simmons's recipes. She gives only some general comments on cake-making, such as "in all cakes where spices are named it is supposed that they be pounded fine and sifted; sugar must be dried and rolled fine; flour, dried in an oven; eggs well beat or whipped into a raging foam"—surely an exhausting business. The common raising agent was yeast, giving a texture closer to a coffeecake than a modern fruitcake, and the huge quantity of mixture in this recipe must have been baked in several pans. The mention of gold leaf for decorations shows that the cake

was intended for a very special occasion; box probably refers to the leaves of the shrub used in hedges. The frosting is taken from another of Amelia Simmons's cake recipes.

*Twenty pound flour, 15 pound sugar, 10 pound butter, 4 dozen eggs, one quart wine, 1 quart brandy, 1 ounce nutmeg, cinnamon, cloves, mace, of each three ounces, two pound citron, currants and raisins 5 pound each, 1 quart yeast; when baked, frost with loaf sugar; dress with box and gold leaf.*

*To frost* [the cake]. *Whip 6* [egg] *whites, during the baking, add 3 pound of sifted loaf-sugar and put on thick, as it comes hot from the oven. Some return the frosted loaf into the oven, it injures and yellows it, if the frosting be put on immediately it does best without being returned into the oven.*

## INDEPENDENCE CAKE

2 packages dry or 2 cakes (30g) compressed yeast
¾ cup (2 dl) lukewarm milk
4 cups (500g) flour
1 cup (250g) butter
1½ cups (350g) sugar
2 eggs, beaten to mix
½ teaspoon ground nutmeg
1 teaspoon ground cinnamon
½ teaspoon ground cloves
1 teaspoon ground mace
⅓ cup (75g) chopped candied citron peel
¾ cup (150g) currants
¾ cup (150g) raisins
¼ cup (7 cl) sweet white wine
¼ cup (7 cl) brandy

FOR THE FROSTING:

1 egg white
1 cup (120g) confectioners' sugar

8-inch (20-cm) springform pan

## THE FRUGAL HOUSEWIFE, OR Complete Woman Cook.

WHEREIN

The Art of Dreſſing all Sorts of Viands,
with Cleanlineſs, Decency, and Elegance,

Is explained in

Five Hundred approved RECEIPTS, in

| Roaſting, | Paſties, |
| Boiling, | Pies, |
| Frying, | Tarts, |
| Broiling, | Cakes, |
| Gravies, | Puddings, |
| Sauces, | Syllabubs, |
| Stews, | Creams, |
| Haſhes, | Flummery, |
| Soups, | Jellies, |
| Fricaſſees, | Giams, and |
| Ragoos, | Cuſtards. |

Together with the BEST METHODS of

| Potting, | Drying, |
| Collaring, | Candying, |
| Preſerving, | Pickling, |

And making of ENGLISH WINES.

To which are prefixed,

Various BILLS OF FARE,

For DINNERS and SUPPERS in every Month of the Year;
and a copious INDEX to the whole.

By SUSANNAH CARTER,
Of CLERKENWELL.

LONDON.

Printed for F. NEWBERY, at the Corner of St. Paul's Church-Yard.

BOSTON:
Re-Printed and Sold by EDES and GILL, in Queenſtreet.

---

*(continued from previous page)*

This is an unusual method of mixing a yeast dough, based on Amelia Simmons's recipe for loaf cakes; the finished cake is moist and close textured. Amelia Simmons must have served it at once because the frosting discolors after a day or two; however the flavor of the cake (without frosting) mellows if it is kept in an airtight container for a month or more. The quantities here produce a cake for 12–14; Amelia's original would serve about twenty times that number.

Sprinkle the yeast over the lukewarm milk and let stand 5 minutes or until dissolved. Sift 1 cup (125 grams) of the flour into a bowl, make a well in the center, and add the yeast mixture. Stir, gradually drawing in the flour to make a smooth batter. Cover and leave this sponge in a warm place for 40 minutes or until bubbles dot the surface.

Cream the butter, beat in the sugar, and continue beating until the mixture is light and soft. Beat in the eggs, one at a time. Sift the remaining flour with the nutmeg, cinnamon, cloves, and mace. Toss the candied peel, currants, and raisins with a little of this flour so they are thoroughly coated. Set the oven at moderately hot (375°F or 190°C) and grease the cake pan.

Stir the flour into the butter mixture in three batches, alternately with the wine and brandy, adding the candied and dried fruits with the last addition of flour. Stir in the yeast sponge. Pour the mixture into the prepared cake pan.

Bake in the heated oven for ¾ hour, lower the heat to 325°F (163°C) and continue cooking 1¼–1½ hours or until a skewer inserted in the center comes out clean. If the cake begins to brown too much during cooking, cover the top with foil.

While the cake is cooking make the frosting; stiffly beat the egg white and beat in the sifted confection-ers' sugar, a tablespoon at a time. When the cake is cooked, turn it out at once on a wire rack and cover with frosting, letting it drip down the sides; the heat of the cake will cook the frosting slightly and set it. If the cake is to be kept more than a day, it should be frosted with a regular boiled frosting just before serving.

## Gingerbread Cake

Amelia Simmons seems to have been fond of gingerbread as she gives more recipes for it than any other contemporary cookbook. This particular gingerbread is raised with pearl ash (a potash that was the forerunner of baking soda). Potash could be made cheaply from the vast American forests and by the end of the eighteenth century it had become a substantial export, used in the manufacture of soap, cloth, and glass.

*Three pounds of flour, a grated nutmeg, two ounces ginger, one pound sugar, three small spoons pearl ash dissolved in cream, one pound butter, four eggs, knead it stiff, shape it to your fancy, bake 15 minutes.*

## GINGERBREAD COOKIES

10 tablespoons (150g) butter
about ¾ cup (2 dl) light cream
1 egg, beaten to mix
1 teaspoon baking soda
4-4½ cups (500-550g) flour
1 teaspoon ground nutmeg
1 tablespoon ground ginger
⅔ cup (160g) sugar

Cutters for cookies or gingerbread men

This recipe makes a firm cookie-type dough that is rolled and cut out into shapes. It makes about thirty 3-inch cookies, which tend to be hard and dry, like Creole "planche" cookies.

Heat the butter with the cream until melted and let cool to tepid. Stir in the egg with the baking soda. Sift the flour with the nutmeg and ginger into a bowl, stir in the sugar, and make a well in the center. Pour the liquid ingredients into the well in the flour; gradually work in the flour to make a firm dough, adding a few drops of cream if necessary. Turn out the dough on a floured board or marble slab and knead until it is smooth and peels easily from the board. Chill for 20 minutes.

Set the oven at moderately hot (375°F or 190°C) and grease a baking sheet. Roll out the dough to ⅜ inch thickness and stamp out cookies, gingerbread men, or other shapes. Set on the prepared baking sheet and bake in the heated oven for 20 minutes or until lightly browned around the edges. Transfer to a rack to cool. Store in an air-tight container.

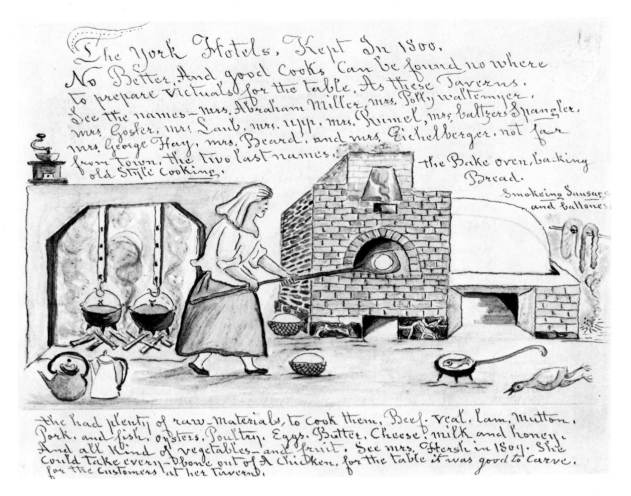

The York Hotels, Kept In 1800.
No Better, And good Cooks Can be found no where
to prepare victuals for the table, As these Taverns,
See the names — Mrs. Abraham Miller, Mrs. Polly waltemyer,
Mrs. Gosler, Mrs. Laub, Mrs. Upp, Mrs. Rumel, Mrs. baltzers Spangler,
Mrs. George Hay, Mrs. Beard, and Mrs. Eichelberger, not far
from town, the two last names!    old style Cooking.

the Bake oven, baking
Bread.
Smokeing Sausage
and Gallones.

the had plenty of raw Materials, to Cook them, Beef, veal, lam, mutton,
Pork, and fish, oysters, Poultry, Eggs, Butter, Cheese, milk and honey,
And all kind of vegetables — and fruit. See mrs. Hersh in 1809. She
Could take every bone out of A Chicken, for the table it was good to Carve,
for the customers at her Tavern.

This primitive rendering by Lewis Miller, a carpenter, shows some of the cooking techniques used in a Pennsylvania hotel around 1800. The open brick oven was used for baking bread. At the far right a smaller fire slowly smokes the sausages hanging above it.

version not a whit but simply tacked on an appendix of thirty recipes. Although some overlapped with those in *American Cookery*, others had not appeared in print before; *The Frugal Housewife* makes the first mention of crullers, "whaffles," cornmeal mush, cranberry tarts, doughnuts, and maple syrup. The American publisher of Hannah Glasse's *The Art of Cookery* was not to be outdone; two years later he too brought out an American edition with a special chapter of recipes copied unabashedly, word for word, from the appendix to *The Frugal Housewife*. Even more blatantly, the whole of *American Cookery* was reproduced in 1805 under the title *New American Cookery*, purportedly "by a Lady" and with not a word of acknowledgment to Amelia Simmons. For the next twenty years, American cookbooks were explicit or furtive adaptations of English classics or of *American Cookery* and its imitator, *The Frugal Housewife*. Indeed, Amelia Simmons herself was not entirely innocent of plagiarism, as she had picked up several of her more English recipes (like the

syllabub in which the cow is milked directly into the dessert to froth it) from Susannah Carter.

The popularity of the first American cookbooks (Amelia's recipes continued in print until 1831) shows that a native style of cooking was practiced with enthusiasm and pride. Certainly, in the nearly 200 years between the landing of the Mayflower and the appearance of *American Cookery*, cooking had come far from its European origins. Most traditional American dishes, such as hoe cakes, succotash, and chowder had already become established; pies were such a passion that the flat wooden boards used as plates in the early days had a "pie side" for dessert. When at last recipes for these favorites appeared in print, Amelia Simmons described only a very small part of the new cooking. Nonetheless, in her modest way she was the first person to give American cooking its own identity. The stilted charm of her book is far more evocative of early American life (often but one step removed from pioneer existence) than many a more professional production.

# Antonin Carême

1783–1833

Antonin Carême is probably the greatest cook of all time. Born in 1783, just before the French Revolution consigned the static elegance of the Versailles court to oblivion, his work reflects the freedom of thought and action that flooded France during the years that followed. He had the intellectual ability to analyze cooking old and new, to simplify methods and menus, and to define every aspect of the art that today is known as *haute cuisine.* He also had a practical brilliance which led him to become the most sought-after chef of his generation, with an international career in the capitals of Europe. Like Napoleon he combined, on his own level, a classic sense of order with romantic ambitions and a flair for self-dramatization.

*The ornamental hâtelets or skewers of Carême's time are still echoed in the frilled toothpicks topping hamburgers and club sandwiches.*

Carême's achievement is all the more amazing considering that he was totally self-educated, born in the gutter as the child of a hard-drinking laborer. At the age of ten, Marie-Antoine (or Antonin as he called himself) was turned out onto the harsh streets of Paris with the words: "Go, my child, and fare well in the world. Leave us to languish; poverty and misery are our lot and we will die as we have lived. But for those like you, with quick wits, there are great fortunes to be made." This paternal confidence was not misplaced; with a touch of the astuteness which was to mark his career, Carême knocked on the door of a modest cookshop where he was taken in, fed, and engaged to serve a six-year apprenticeship. His ability must have shown early for in 1800, at the age of seventeen, he went to work

Opposite:
*The spacious kitchens of the Brighton Pavilion, built for the Prince Regent at the beginning of the nineteenth century, followed the oriental theme of the rest of the buildings. Note the splendid array of copper pans (which can still be seen), and the metal covers on the central table for keeping food hot during its long journey to the dining room. Carême cooked here for a couple of years; but his flamboyant French style was cramped by conservative British tastes, and he became homesick.*

LE CUISINIER.

for Bailly, one of the most famous *pâtissiers* of the day. Carême has nothing but praise for Bailly, a generous man who allowed him to study in the *Cabinet des Gravures*, where he taught himself both to read and to draw.

At the time, the profession of *pâtissier* was at least as prestigious as that of *cuisinier*. Pastrycooks were responsible for *pièces montées*, the great decorative centerpieces that were the crowning glory of grand dinners. Carême excelled at these flights of fancy; in his first two books, *Le Pâtissier royal* and *Le Pâtissier pittoresque*, both published in 1815, he produces hundreds of designs for rustic pavilions, ruins, cascades, temples, forts, windmills, and other ornate creations. He insisted that "the fine arts are five in number—painting, sculpture, poetry, music, architecture—whose main branch is confectionery." Such miniature fantasies, their components surrealistically colored and shaped to look anything but themselves, make a mockery of nature, but they certainly appealed to Carême's patrons.

*The Prince de Talleyrand was a statesman, gourmet, and Carême's employer for many years.*

His two-year training with Bailly completed, Carême rapidly attracted the attention of the most famous statesman of the time, the Prince de Talleyrand. Talleyrand was a man of many parts; wit and bon viveur, he achieved the unusual distinction of acting as foreign minister both to Napoleon and to the restored monarch, Louis XVIII. He kept one of the best tables in Paris; for an hour each morning he conferred on the menu of the day with Carême, who reported that "M. de Talleyrand understands the genius of a cook; he respects it, he is the best judge of subtle improvements, and his expenditure

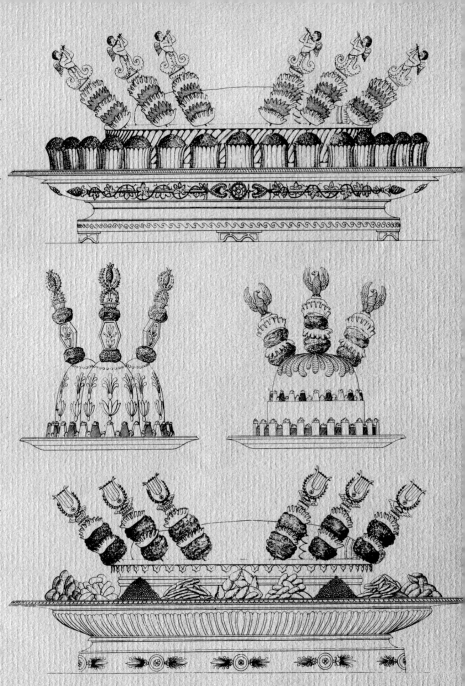

Overleaf:
*This design for a towering, seven-tiered buffet table appears in Carême's* Le Maître d'hôtel français, *but even he seems to have quailed at the thought of carrying it out as it was never made. The dishes shown include soups, fish, roasts, cold meats, jellies, and blanc-manges, as well as some of Carême's favorite* pièces montées *(center, right, and left). They were usually made of almond paste colored in violet, green, orange, yellow, and brick-red, the details picked out in chocolate. The effect must have been stunning indeed, though today such contrived designs in food have little appeal.*

*The presentation of food was one of Carême's greatest enthusiasms. He reduced the motley garnishes that had survived from the Renaissance, topping his dishes with ornamental* hâtelets *threaded with colorful ingredients like truffles, cockscombs, and crayfish, then mounted his creations on* socles *or bases (usually inedible), both shown clearly here.*

combines wisdom with generosity." Carême had been engaged as *pâtissier*, but he was determined to learn from Boucher, Talleyrand's chef, the art of the *cuisinier*. After twelve years beside Boucher, the pupil had outclassed his master, partly by working in the shadow of all the top chefs of the day as one of the *extras* called in to help on special occasions.

The early 1800s, when France was gripped in the desperate struggle for control of Europe, were hardly the most propitious for the arts of good living. The great days of the noble households were over, and the deliberately restrained tone of Empire fashions and furniture was carried into the kitchen where provisions and the staff to cook them were greatly reduced. But necessity is the mother of invention; forced to economize, cooks made better use of their time and of the ingredients available; the extravagant old cullis was abandoned in favor of an espagnole sauce (resembling the one used today) and the huge main dishes of the *ancien régime* were forgotten. Undaunted by this relative austerity, gourmets formed dinner clubs and a new breed of writer appeared—the gastronomic critic. Grimod de la Reynière, for example, wrote the *Almanach des gourmands* (an annual miscellany of food history and gossip) and the most famous gastronome of all, Anthelme de Brillat-Savarin, regularly visited Talleyrand's table, where he was apparently so preoccupied by the food that he rarely uttered a word.

By the end of the Napoleonic wars in 1815 both *haute* and *bourgeoise cuisine* would have been recognizable to a modern cook, thanks largely to the influence of Carême and his great rival, Beauvilliers. In contrast to Carême, who was the last of the great chefs in private service, Beauvilliers made his name as a restaurateur, being the first to "combine an elegant dining-room, smart waiters, and a choice cellar with superior cooking"—all at the cost, Brillat-Savarin reports, of an "inflated bill." Beauvilliers died in 1820, before competition between the two cooks could become bitter—in his last years he

"The Reckoning": then, as now, good eating was expensive.

Many of Carême's recipes are of inordinate length, not because they are complicated, but because he describes each step in the minutest detail. With the notable exception of the recipes in *Le Pastissier françois* written in 1653, these are the first old recipes that a novice can follow with ease.

✦✦✦✦✦✦✦✦✦✦✦✦✦✦✦✦

## Potage d'automne

Almost all Carême's soups are based on well-flavoured consommé, which he makes with chicken or beef, veal, and vegetables. For traveling, Carême recommends boiling the consommé until reduced to a thick, sticky juice (meat glaze) then leaving it to set. When cut in cubes it could be diluted with water for use—primitive bouillon cubes.

100. Caisse à bain-marie.

*Cut as for julienne the white of four leeks, the yellow leaves of two bunches of celery and those of a thinly sliced lettuce; after washing them well, toss them into the boiling consommé; add half a liter of baby peas, a pinch each of sugar and crushed pepper, two large soup spoons of flour, mixed to a soft smooth paste with cold stock; stir the soup with a large spoon, so the consommé thickens smoothly; after an hour and a half of simmering, pour the soup into a tureen containing little croutons, made according to the rule.*

## AUTUMN SOUP

white part of 3 medium leeks cut in julienne strips
leaves of 2 celery hearts, cut in julienne strips
½ head romaine lettuce, cut in julienne strips
2 quarts (2 L) well-flavored consommé
1 cup (150g) uncooked green peas
pinch of sugar
pinch of white pepper
salt (optional)

FOR LIAISON:

⅓ cup (40g) flour
¾ cup (2dl) cold consommé

FOR CROUTONS:

6 slices bread (crusts discarded), diced
½ cup (120g) butter

If this soup is made even in part with homemade consommé or stock, the flavor will be greatly improved. Frozen peas can be substituted for fresh ones. This recipe serves 8.

Wash and drain the leek, celery, and lettuce strips. Bring the consommé to a boil. Mix the flour with the ¾ cup (2 deciliters) consommé for the liaison and blend until smooth. Add to the boiling consommé, stirring constantly, and simmer 2–3 minutes or until consommé is thickened and smooth. Add the leek, celery, and lettuce strips with the peas, sugar, and pepper and simmer, uncovered, for 15–20 minutes or until the vegetables are tender. Taste the

soup for seasoning, adding salt and more pepper if necessary.
Meanwhile heat the butter and fry the croûtons, stirring, until browned on all sides. Drain them thoroughly on paper towels and keep warm. If serving in a tureen, put in the croûtons and pour over the soup; if serving in bowls, spoon the soup into the bowls and serve the croûtons separately.

## Sauce au beurre à l'italienne

Most of Carême's sauces take at least twelve hours because they are made step-by-step from basic sauces that are simmered slowly to concentrate their flavor. *Sauce italienne*, based on the comparatively quick *sauce au beurre* which follows, is one of the simplest. Carême recommends serving it with broiled or poached fish. The olive oil from Aix-en-Provence and the butter from Isigny in Normandy called for here are still reputed to be the best.

*After having chopped a little parsley, several mushrooms, a truffle, a touch of garlic, take a fragment of bay leaf and thyme, a whole clove, a little coarsely ground pepper, some grated nutmeg and some salt; after sautéing this seasoning with a little sweet butter over a moderate heat, you add a glass of champagne, then strain out the fragments of herbs and the clove; transfer your mixture into a pan in a water bath containing a large spoonful of butter sauce prepared in the usual way, two spoonfuls of good oil from Aix, some Isigny butter, the juice of a lemon, and serve. The sauce should be highly flavored.*

135

(continued from previous page)

## Sauce au beurre

In one of the many pertinent remarks scattered throughout his recipes, Carême comments that butter sauces must be seasoned with discernment as their ingredients are so delicate.

*In a saucepan put a small soup spoon of flour and a little Isigny butter. After mixing in the flour with a wooden spoon, you add half a glass of water or consommé, a little salt and grated nutmeg, and the juice of half a lemon; stir the seasoning over a high heat and, as soon as it boils, take the sauce from the heat and mix in a good nut of Isigny butter; the sauce should then be velvety, very smooth and of a good flavor. A little good regular vinegar can be substituted for the lemon juice.*

## BUTTER SAUCE À L'ITALIENNE

½ bay leaf
sprig of thyme or ½ teaspoon dried thyme
1 whole clove
2½ tablespoons (40g) butter
2 tablespoons chopped parsley
3 mushrooms, finely chopped
1 truffle, finely chopped (optional)
½ clove garlic, crushed
pinch of grated nutmeg
salt and pepper
½ cup (1.25 dl) champagne butter sauce (see below)
2 tablespoons olive oil
juice of ½-1 lemon

The amount of lemon juice needed for this sauce depends on the size of the lemon and its acidity. Serve the sauce with broiled or poached fish for 4.

Tie the bay leaf, thyme, and clove with thread or wrap them in a piece of cheesecloth. In a heavy-based pan melt 1 tablespoon of the butter and add the parsley, mushrooms, truffle (if using), garlic, tied herbs, nutmeg, and a little salt and pepper. Sauté over medium heat 1–2 minutes until the mushrooms are soft. Add the champagne, simmer 5 minutes, and discard the bay leaf, thyme, and clove.
Put the butter sauce (see below) in the top of a double boiler or in a saucepan placed in a roasting pan of hot water. Stir in the champagne and flavorings, then gradually stir in the oil. When the sauce is smooth, add the remaining butter in small pieces and stir until incorporated. Add lemon juice to taste with more salt and pepper if needed. (Note: This sauce separates easily and should be made over hot, not boiling water, so the pan is never more than hand hot.) The sauce is served tepid.

## BUTTER SAUCE

2 tablespoons (20g) flour
½ cup (120g) butter
¾ cup (2 dl) water or consommé
pinch of salt
pinch of grated nutmeg
juice of ½ lemon or 2 tablespoons wine vinegar

This sauce can be served in place of hollandaise; it will not have quite the same butter flavor and texture as good hollandaise, but it is less likely to curdle. Without adding the *italienne* flavoring, it serves 3.

In a heavy-based pan put the flour with 2 tablespoons of the butter and stir over low heat until the butter is melted. Add the water or consommé, blend well, then add salt, nutmeg, and lemon juice or vinegar and bring to a boil, stirring. As soon as the mixture thickens, take it from the heat and beat in the remaining butter, in small pieces. It may be necessary to warm the pan slightly to incorporate all the butter, but do not heat it too much or the sauce will curdle. Taste it for seasoning. Reheat the sauce or keep it warm in the top of a double boiler and never allow it to boil; it should be served tepid.

was more famous than Carême, having scored a triumph in 1814 with his *L'Art du cuisinier*, regarded as the first worthy successor in seventy years to Menon's *La Cuisinière bourgeoise*. Carême was still known as a *pâtissier* rather than a *cuisinier*, but behind the scenes in the great houses he had already developed the *haute cuisine* so elegantly described in his later books.

The better to establish himself, Carême left Talleyrand's household in 1815 and crossed the Channel to work for the Prince Regent, the eccentric arbiter of England's taste. The prince gave Carême every consideration, remarking graciously on one occasion that the "dinner last night was superb, but you will make me die of indigestion," to which Carême rejoined: "Prince, my duty is to tempt your appetite, not to control it." However, the Prince was not tempted for long; Carême was depressed by the climate and the attitude of his fellow cooks, who resented the attention paid to this foreign interloper. Above all, he found the English generally ignorant of the finer points of good cooking (though the leftovers of Carême's pâtés, offered illicitly after a banquet, commanded a high price). In Carême's opinion the recent influx of French chefs into England had had little effect. "The essentials of English cooking," he wrote, "are the roasts of beef, mutton, and lamb; the various meats cooked in salt water, in the manner of fish and vegetables . . . fruit preserves, puddings of all kinds, chicken and turkey with cauliflower, salt beef, country ham, and several similar ragouts—that is the sum of English cook-

## Poulets sautés à la castillane

Sautés were invented at the beginning of the nineteenth century, possibly by Carême himself. They involve cooking meat or poultry, either partly or completely, before adding a little liquid, so that a concentrated sauce is obtained without any lengthy reduction at the end of cooking. The heat must be carefully controlled if the meat is to sauté without burning, and this had not been possible before the invention of stoves with flat, evenly-heated tops and the development of a special sauté pan with a heavy base and straight sides, still a standard part of French kitchen equipment. In using tomatoes in this recipe, Carême was ahead of his time as they were not popular in cooking until mid-century.

*Take a pound of Bayonne ham or, better still, ham from Malaga, cut in small dice; sauté it in butter so it browns lightly; add to it two chickens, cut in pieces, and cook so that they stiffen without coloring; add four onions, cut in rounds, two boxes of mushrooms, fluted, several stems of parsley, a clove of garlic, and a bouquet garni; let the chickens cook briskly without catching on the bottom of the pan; ten minutes before serving, throw in six tomatoes, cut in two and the seeds discarded; just before serving, deglaze the pan and serve with the garnish and the concentrated cooking liquid from the chickens.*

47. Plat à sauter (v. p. 42).

## SAUTÉ OF CHICKEN À LA CASTILLANE

1½ tablespoons (25g) butter
½ pound (250g) raw, lightly smoked ham, diced small
1 frying chicken (about 3 pounds or 1½ kg), cut in pieces
2 onions, cut in rounds
½ pound (250g) mushrooms, stems trimmed level with caps
2 stems parsley
½ clove garlic, crushed
bouquet garni
salt and pepper
3 medium (250g) tomatoes, peeled, quartered, and seeded
½ cup (1.25 dl) chicken stock

This recipe is deceptively simple, as a great deal depends on careful cooking of the chicken so that it cooks fairly fast without browning. Canadian bacon is the best substitute for mildly smoked raw ham; Virginia ham is too salty. This recipe serves 4.

In a sauté pan or large skillet, melt the butter and sauté the ham over medium heat until lightly browned. Put the pieces of chicken, skin side down, on the ham and sauté for 5 minutes or until the flesh is firm and white, but not brown. Add the onions, mushrooms, parsley, garlic, and bouquet garni and sprinkle with salt and pepper. Continue cooking over medium heat, stirring occasionally and turning the chicken pieces, for 20 minutes or until the onions are soft and the chicken pieces are tender. Add the tomatoes, lifting the chicken pieces on top of them, and continue cooking 10 minutes. Transfer the chicken to a platter and keep warm. Add the stock to the pan and bring to a boil, stirring to dissolve the pan juices. Taste for seasoning, spoon the sauce and garnish over the chicken, and serve.

## Jambon braisé et glacé à la piémontaise

This braised ham is typical of the splendid *grosses pièces* that formed the centerpieces of grand dinners. A *mirepoix* is a mixture of diced vegetables, used to give flavor to a braise.

*Take a good Bayonne or Westphalia ham—it must be lightly cured and of the best quality; trim off some of the fat and put the ham to soak in plenty of water. For a ham of less than a year old, 24 hours is sufficient; then wash it, drain and wrap it in a napkin that you tie tightly. Put it in a large* braisière *[heavy casserole], fill it with water and add four carrots, as many onions, two bouquets garnis of bay leaf, thyme, basil, a whole clove and a little mace. Then start boiling over a very hot stove; skim off a light foam; cover the* braisière *and place it so that the ham just simmers steadily for three hours. Then drain it, peel off the skin and place it on the bottom of a large oval pan in which you simmer it an hour in a* mirepoix *moistened with a large spoonful of consommé, half a bottle of good Chablis and half a glass of old cognac, all worked through a sieve. It is essential to taste the ham before the cooking in this* mirepoix *is finished, because if the flesh is slightly salty, it is better to let it cook completely in the first cooking, because the* mirepoix *will firm the flesh, giving it more flavor, but also concentrate the salt it contains. Experience must guide the practitioner in his work: theory can illuminate, but that is all; practice is the heart of the matter. Then glaze the ham in the oven in the heavy oval pan. Set the ham on a platter on a bed of rice* à la piémontaise, *made with 1½ pounds of rice. Decorate the shank of the ham with a frill and serve with it an espagnole sauce, mixed with the* mirepoix *from which all the fat has been skimmed. Serve grated Parmesan cheese separately.*

## BRAISED HAM À LA PIÉMONTAISE

a whole uncooked country
   ham (12-16 pounds or 5-7 kg)
rice à la piémontaise
   (see next recipe)
1½ cups (250g) grated
   Parmesan cheese (for
   serving)

FOR SIMMERING:

4 carrots, quartered
4 onions, quartered
large bouquet garni
2 teaspoons basil
2 whole cloves
2 blades mace

FOR BRAISING:

3 tablespoons (45g) butter
3 carrots, diced
3 onions, diced
3 stalks celery, diced
2 cups (5 dl) consommé
2 cups (5 dl) Chablis or
   other dry white wine
½ cup (1.25 dl) cognac

FOR BROWN SAUCE:

3 tablespoons oil
2 carrots, diced
2 onions, diced
3 tablespoons (30g) flour
3½ cups (8.5 dl) beef stock
salt and pepper (optional)

Paper frill (for decoration)

It is essential to use a mildly cured ham for this recipe—Virginia and other salty hams are not suitable. Carême's espagnole sauce takes nearly a day to make, so a quick brown sauce is suggested as a substitute; a modern espagnole sauce, taking 2–3 hours, is given in Escoffier's recipe for *tournedos chasseur*. Depending on the size of the ham, this recipe serves 12–16.

Scrub the ham, trim off some of the fat, and soak it for 24 hours in cold water. Drain, wrap it tightly in cheesecloth, put it in a large pot with the quartered carrots and onions, bouquet garni, basil, cloves, and mace. Add water to cover, bring quickly to a boil, skim, add the lid, and simmer constantly, allowing 15 minutes per pound and 15 minutes more. Let it cool slightly.

Meanwhile, in a heavy-based pan melt the butter for braising and gently cook the diced carrots, onions, and celery for 5–7 minutes until soft but not brown. Add the consommé, Chablis, and cognac; cover and simmer 30 minutes. Purée the mixture in a blender or work it through a sieve and pour it into a large oval casserole. Peel the skin from the ham and discard. Put the ham in the casserole on top of the purée, bring to a boil, cover, and braise in a moderate oven (350°F or 177°C) for 1 hour.

FOR THE BROWN SAUCE: In a heavy-based pan heat the oil and sauté the carrots and onions until soft but not brown. Add the flour and cook over high heat, stirring constantly, until the flour is well browned; do not allow it to burn. At once add 3 cups (7.5 deciliters) of the stock and bring to a boil, stirring. Skim the sauce and leave it to simmer ½ hour. Add ½ cup (1.5 deciliters) more stock, skim again, and continue simmering 15–20 minutes or until the sauce is glossy and the consistency of thin cream; strain it and taste for seasoning. When the ham is cooked, transfer it to a roasting pan and spoon over enough brown sauce to baste the ham. Roast it in a very hot oven (425°F or 218°C) for about 20 minutes or until browned, basting again halfway through cooking. Skim all fat from the cooking liquid and add it to the brown sauce. Bring it to a boil and taste for seasoning. Spread the *rice à la piémontaise* in a large platter and set the ham on top. Decorate the

shank of the ham with a paper frill. Serve the sauce and a bowl of grated Parmesan cheese separately.

## *Riz à la piémontaise*

The rice of Carolina had already made its mark by Carême's time, but the blanching and washing needed show that its quality was very different from today.

*Wash in warm water a pound and a half of Carolina rice several times; after blanching it a few seconds, drain it and simmer three-quarters of an hour in a pan, mixing it with twelve ounces of butter, three large spoonsful of good consommé, a little coarsely ground pepper and two soup spoons of grated Parmesan; when turning it out on the platter, sprinkle it lightly with the same cheese.*

## RICE À LA PIÉMONTAISE

3½ cups (1½ pounds or 750g)
   long-grain rice
1½ cups (375g) butter
3½ cups (8.5 dl) consommé
3 cups (7.5 dl) water
salt and freshly ground
   black pepper
1 cup (125g) grated Parmesan
   cheese

This recipe serves 12–16.

In a very large heavy-based pan melt the butter, add the rice, consommé, water, and a little salt and pepper and sprinkle with 3–4 tablespoons grated cheese. Cover and simmer 20–25 minutes until all the liquid is absorbed. Let stand, covered, for 10 minutes, then stir lightly to fluff up the grains and taste for seasoning. Spread the rice in a large hot platter and sprinkle with the remaining cheese before placing the ham on top.

*Les audiences d'un Gourmand.*

Talleyrand, he was a veteran of the celebrity-studded international gatherings that determined the fate of Europe after the Napoleonic Wars.
Returning to Paris in 1823, Carême entered upon the last and most important phase of his life, when through his cookbooks he established himself as the doyen of his profession. The first of these books, *Le Maître d'hôtel français*, had appeared in the previous year; in it Carême describes the hundreds of menus which he personally had created and cooked in the capitals of Europe—eloquent testimony to his boast that he could work faster and more efficiently than anyone else.
Modesty was never Carême's greatest virtue; he once denounced his colleagues for their "miserable works which degrade our national cooking. Why are you so small in talent and so mean in invention?" The ideal cook, he explains, should have "a discerning and sensitive palate, perfect and exquisite taste, a strong and industrious character; he should be skillful and hardworking and unite delicacy, order, and economy." His strictures would be merely bombastic were it not for the ruthless singleness of mind with which he put them into practice. Carême himself ate little and touched no alcohol. He seems to have had no time for his family, for he makes but one isolated reference to a daughter and does not so much as mention a wife.
In the years that followed the publication of *Le Maître d'hôtel français*, Carême enjoyed an Olympian fame. His dinners were an occasion to remember. One of them, cooked in the summer of 1828, has been recaptured by Lady Morgan (a peripatetic Irish novelist) who reported that Carême was working for a Rothschild "at a salary beyond what any sovereign in Europe might be able to pay, even though assisted by Monsieur Rothschild, without whose aid so many sovereigns would scarcely be able to keep cooks at all." As for the meal: "To do justice to the science and research of a dinner so served would require a knowledge of the art equal to that which produced it . . . every meat presented in its natural aroma; every vegetable in its own shade of verdure." The climax of the meal was a *plombière* "with the hue and odour of fresh gathered nectarines [which] satisfied every sense and dissipated every coarser flavour." Iced bombes such as a *plombière* (based on almond milk and whipped cream, topped with fresh fruit purée) were favorites of Carême's. They offered great scope for his decorative talents and his recipes can hardly be bettered today.

ing." A more accurate description of old-fashioned English fare could hardly be penned today.
Two years of England were enough for Carême and in 1818 he returned to Paris where further tempting offers awaited him. He joined the staff of Czar Alexander but, predictably, Russia proved no more to Carême's taste than England. Like Leonardi before him Carême found the climate trying. Fresh produce was available for only four months of the year—an insupportable restriction for one of Carême's talents. So he returned to France and in 1820 went to Vienna to work for the British ambassador. Here Carême was much more at home. He noted with satisfaction that the ingredients and general standard of cooking were second only to Paris. Vienna had been the scene of earlier triumphs when Carême had cooked at the congress of 1815—like

## Garnitures de petites carottes à la flamande

Carême was famous for his simple ways with vegetables. He insisted that they should never be over-cooked and went so far as to cut root vegetables in cylinders so that they cooked evenly.

*Cut a bunch of new carrots in little cylinders with a vegetable cutter, then blanch and refresh them and cook them with consommé, a little butter and some sugar. When reduced to a glaze, just before serving add a pinch of chopped, blanched parsley, and serve them mixed together.*

### BABY CARROTS À LA FLAMANDE

1 pound (500g) baby carrots
1½ cups (3.75 dl) consommé
1 tablespoon (15g) butter
2 teaspoons sugar
1 tablespoon chopped parsley

Carême shapes and cooks parsnips, turnips, and cucumbers in the same way as carrots, and as an attractive garnish he suggests mixing them all together with a little béchamel sauce. This recipe will serve 4.

With a large apple corer, cut the carrots into cylinders, trimming the tops and roots. Put the carrots in a pan of cold water, bring to a boil, and cook for 2 minutes. Drain and refresh under cold water. In a pan add the carrots to the consommé, butter, and sugar and simmer until the carrots are almost tender. Cook over high heat until the liquid is reduced to about 1 tablespoon and makes a shiny glaze. Meanwhile twist the parsley in the corner of a piece of cheesecloth, pour boiling water over it, and squeeze it dry; the parsley will be bright green. Add it to the carrots, toss to mix, and serve.

## Soufflé parisien aux fraises

Classic soufflés were Carême's invention, though puddings made fluffy with meringue had been known for many years. It was thanks to new ovens heated by air draft instead of the old method of filling with hot coals that the constant heat needed for a true soufflé could be maintained. The *croustade* or pastry case was not eaten; it was made with the same straight sides as our soufflé dishes, and in fact inspired them.

*After hulling a large basket of good strawberries, crush them. Work them through a fine sieve to obtain a purée; mix a pound and a half of powdered sugar with eighteen stiffly whipped egg whites. When all is well blended, stir in the strawberry purée until thoroughly mixed. Pour the mixture into a croustade of eleven inches diameter and three and a half inches in height; surround it with three buttered sheets of paper. This croustade is cooked in advance, as for a croustade of hot pâté à la financière, but it should be rolled very thin. It can also be cooked at the same time as the soufflé and works just as well but the soufflé must be cooked a little longer. I prefer the croustade to be cooked in advance. Put the soufflé in a moderate oven and give it a good hour's cooking. When it is ready to serve, put red-hot cinders on a large baking sheet. Take the soufflé from the oven and place it on the hot cinders so it stays puffed. Meanwhile, cover it with powdered sugar and glaze it with a red-hot iron; then carry it very quickly to the dining room. Lift it with the help of a pan lid, and set it on a platter, which should be covered with a fine damask napkin. Take off the paper holding up the soufflé and serve it at once. Soufflés of raspberries, gooseberries, and mirabelle or greengage plums are made in the same way.*

## STRAWBERRY SOUFFLÉ

1 pint (250g) strawberries, hulled
½–¾ cup (125–175g) sugar
5 egg whites
confectioners sugar (for sprinkling)

Soufflé dish (1½-quart or 1½-liter capacity)

Without a special salamander or very hot broiler, it is impossible to glaze a soufflé, so sprinkle it instead with confectioners' sugar before serving. The mixture is so simple that the flavor of the soufflé depends enormously on the quality of the strawberries, which should be highly perfumed. If not, add a little kirsch or lemon juice to the purée. This quantity serves 4. A sauce of fresh strawberry purée is an excellent accompaniment.

Purée the strawberries in a blender or work them through a sieve. Add ¼–½ cup (60–120 grams) sugar, depending on their sweetness. Butter the inside of the soufflé dish and sprinkle it with granulated sugar, discarding the excess. Set the oven at moderate (350°F or 177°C).

Up to an hour before serving, stiffly whip the egg whites. Add the remaining ¼ cup (60 grams) sugar and continue beating until this meringue mixture is glossy and holds a tall peak. Stir a little meringue into the strawberry purée, mixing it well, then add the purée to the remaining meringue; fold them together as lightly as possible. Spoon the soufflé mixture into the prepared mold—it should reach the top of the mold—and bake it in the heated oven for 25–30 minutes or until puffed and brown. The center should still be slightly concave. Sprinkle the top with confectioners' sugar, and serve it at once.

141

# Gâteau pithiviers

The origins of puff pastry are obscure; it is thought to have come from Italy or Spain where it may have been inspired by the Arab skill with sweet pastries (their wafer-thin pastry is made quite differently, however). Puff pastry was familiar to La Varenne, who made it more or less by the classic method, and Carême was a master at it, famous for his lightness of hand. He lists a dozen variations of the puff pastry *gâteau pithiviers*, which is still made today. "Turns" refers to the rolling and folding process by which the pastry is made and a litron is an old 12-ounce measure. The white glaze referred to at the end of the recipe was probably a sugar coating. The aveline almonds called for in the filling are regular or sweet almonds, different from the bitter almonds occasionally called for in small quantities to add piquancy (as in the macaroons mentioned in this recipe).

*Make half a litron of puff pastry dough. When it has had eight turns, divide it in two, giving two-thirds of the volume to one piece, then roll this out large enough to cut a round nine inches in diameter. Pile the trimmings from this round on the remaining pastry, and make with it another round of seven inches diameter; place it on a baking sheet. Then lightly moisten the edges of the round and spoon the filling on top. Spread it evenly to within an inch of the border of the pastry, then carefully cover the filling with the other pastry round, pressing it on the base in order to stick the edges together and prevent the filling from escaping during cooking. Flute the edge of the gâteau, marking the pastry with the point of a knife at half an inch from the filling. Lightly gild the top, then mark a palm leaf, or a rose, or simply some even stripes. Put it in a hot oven. When it is browned, move it nearer*

*the mouth of the oven so that the pastry can dry without browning. After three-quarters of an hour of cooking (the base of the pastry should be very crisp, otherwise this type of gâteau is not good to eat) cover it evenly with sugar so it can be glazed by making a little hot flame at the mouth of the oven; or give it a white glaze. After pounding eight ounces of aveline almonds (blanched), add six ounces of fine sugar, four of Isigny butter, two of bitter macaroons, four egg yolks, and a tiny pinch of salt. When all is well beaten, add four spoonsful of whipped cream.*

## GÂTEAU PITHIVIERS

puff pastry made with 1½ cups (200g) flour, ¾ cup (180g) butter, pinch of salt, ½ teaspoon lemon juice, and ⅓-½ cup (1-1.25 dl) ice water

1 egg, beaten to mix with ½ teaspoon salt (for glaze)

granulated sugar (for sprinkling)

### FOR FILLING:

¾ cup (125g) whole blanched almonds, ground

⅓ cup (80g) sugar

¼ cup (60g) unsalted butter, softened

1 macaroon, crushed

2 egg yolks

tiny pinch of salt

¼ cup (7cl) heavy cream, whipped until it holds a soft peak

Bitter almond macaroons (as called for by Carême) are not available so if the filling seems tasteless, add a few drops of almond extract. Any classic French cookbook will give the method for making puff pastry. The gâteau serves 6.

FOR THE FILLING: Pound the ground almonds in a mortar with a pestle or in a bowl with the end of a rolling pin until the oil is released, making them slightly sticky. Stir in the sugar, add the butter, and pound until very smooth and pastelike. Add the crushed macaroon, egg yolks, and salt and continue pounding until the mixture is very smooth and holds together. Gently stir in the whipped cream.

Set the oven at hot (400°F or 205°C). Cut off two-thirds of the dough. Roll out the large piece ¼ inch thick into a 10-inch round. With a sharp knife cut it out to a 9-inch round and reserve. Pile the trimmings one on top of another and add to the remaining one-third of dough. Roll out the remaining dough ¼ inch thick into an 8-inch round and cut a 7-inch round from it, discarding the trimmings.

Set the 7-inch round on a baking sheet and brush a 1-inch strip around the edge of the round with egg glaze, without allowing it to drip down the sides. Pile the filling in the center and spread it to within an inch of the edge of the dough. Set the 9-inch round on top and press the edges firmly together to seal both rounds so the filling cannot escape. Holding the back of a knife parallel to the board, score the edges of the pastry with horizontal cuts to encourage it to rise and with the knife held vertically pull in the edges at regular intervals to form scallops. Mark the top of the gâteau with curved lines radiating from the center like a flower, and make a hole in the center for steam to escape. Brush the top lightly with glaze.

Set the gâteau in the top of the heated oven and bake it for 20 minutes or until the pastry is puffed and browned. Turn down the heat to moderate (350°F or 177°C), set the gâteau in the bottom of the oven, and continue baking 30 minutes or until the gâteau is very crisp. Transfer it to a wire rack to cool and serve warm or cold.

*Carême had cooked as an* extra *in most of the great kitchens of Paris and must have been familiar with those of the Tuileries palace shown here, probably little altered by the time this picture was* *made a few decades later. Roasts turn before a huge fire, while in the cool* garde manger *(right), cooks build up the gelatin or sugar-based* pièces montées *that were Carême's pride.*

However, it was aspics, with their elaborate molds and garnishes, that gave full rein to his pastrycook's passion for display. The cold buffet, though dating back to the *credenza* of Renaissance Italy, did not really catch on in France until after the revolution. Carême was its most brilliant exponent. In *Le Cuisinier parisien*, published in 1828, he lays down the principles for making classic *chaudfroids* and aspic dishes, an art which has not significantly developed since then. But even the great can make mistakes and it was with aspic that Carême once had a major disaster. The isinglass (a type of gelatin) failed to arrive and, foolishly, Carême tried to mold his charlottes without it; to his chagrin they wobbled so dangerously when turned out that they were unusable. He never forgot the disgrace nor allowed it to happen again.

His last book was *L'Art de la cuisine française au* *dix-neuvième siècle*, an exhaustive survey of classic French cooking as perfected by Carême himself and followed with little change until the end of the century. In this book he develops several hundred versions of today's *potages* and institutes the custom of garnishing meat with meat and fish with fish, dispensing with the sweetbreads and cockscombs which had survived from the fifteenth century. The basic sauces—espagnole, béchamel, and velouté— would be familiar to today's chefs, as would Carême's 100 and more variations. Carême has been criticized for extravagance, but in fact it was he who simplified menus; he once described his ideal meal as beginning with vegetable soup, followed by roast or braised fillet of beef served with glazed vegetables or rice and a simple *jus* as gravy. Then would come poached or gratinéed fish, or a fish stew, a roasted fowl with vegetables, pastries,

LAU BIEN VENUE

L'ARRIVÉE.

*Un Anglais attaqué du Spleen, vient se faire traiter en France.*

LE DÉPART.

*...du spleen par la Cuisine Française, l'Anglais retourne à Londres...*

*The English suspicion of French cooking was mutual. In this French cartoon an emaciated Englishman, racked with indigestion, goes to take a cure in France (left) and returns (right) reeking of garlic, his enormous paunch supported on a wheelbarrow.*

salad, and a dessert. Not until the end of the century did such an admirably classic menu become the rule set by another outstanding chef, Escoffier.

Carême was in poor health while he was writing *L'Art de la cuisine*—the first three volumes appeared in 1833, the year of his death, and two volumes were added later by his friend and colleague Plumérey. Carême had exhausted himself in his dedication to cooking. Rising before dawn to choose the freshest vegetables and fruits from the market, he was on constant duty until ten or eleven at night, and before retiring, no matter how late the hour, he jotted down his progress during the day—notes that doubtless formed the basis of his books. Sometimes he would sleep hardly at all, as the sauces for an important dinner were started at 3 a.m. Added to this, conditions of work were exhausting. "Imagine yourself in a large kitchen at the moment of a great dinner," he relates. "See twenty chefs coming, going, moving with speed in this caldron of heat,

look at the great mass of charcoal, a cubic meter for the cooking of entrées, and another mass on the ovens for the cooking of soups, sauces, ragouts, for frying and the water baths. Add to that a heap of burning wood in front of which four spits are turning, one of which bears a sirloin weighing forty-five to fifty pounds, the other fowl or game. In this furnace everyone moves with speed; not a sound is heard, only the chef has a right to speak and at the sound of his voice, everyone obeys. Finally the last straw: for about half an hour, all windows are closed so that the air does not cool the dishes as they are being served, and in this way we spend the best years of our lives. We must obey even when physical strength fails, but it is the burning charcoal that kills us."

But not for one moment did Carême regret it. "Charcoal kills us, but what does it matter? The shorter the life, the greater the glory," he declared. A man apart, sensitive, egotistical, his personality comes across with a burning intensity that defies criticism. His practical experience was unrivaled; soups, sauces, aspics, pastries, and ices—he was a specialist in them all. Carême's writing covers *haute cuisine* in its entirety—he was interested in anything and everything to do with food. But his observations (unlike those of so many inquisitive minds) never lack force; no matter what the subject, Carême has that uncanny knack of reaching the heart of the matter that is the mark of genius.

144

............et je prétends, dans ma reconnoissance,
Dérobant les Lauriers d'un Jambon de Mayence,
D'une couronne un jour décorer ton bonnet.

Monsieur delincavit.                    Bovinet Sculpsit.

# Isabella Beeton

1836–1865

The most successful European cookbook ever published is *Household Management* by Isabella Beeton. Always referred to simply as "Mrs. Beeton," the book has been repeatedly updated in successive editions and is still in print today, more than 100 years after the original was written. Even more astonishingly, though the book packed over 1,500 recipes into an exhaustive survey of every imaginable household art from selecting servants to table setting, Mrs. Beeton was only twenty-four when she produced it.

Into that twenty-four years she had crammed more practical experience than most women have in a lifetime. Isabella Mary Mayson was born in London in 1836, the eldest of what was to become a family of twenty-one children. When she was five her father died and her mother, left with four small girls, soon remarried. Bella's stepfather was Henry Dorling, clerk of the racecourse at Epsom and a widower who also had four children. As the family expanded, they overflowed into what must be one of the most unconventional dwellings on record—the racecourse grandstand. In other respects, however, their upbringing was typical of the Victorian middle class: Bella was coached by excellent masters (an education that was to stand her in good stead) and as she grew older she must have been entrusted with much of the housekeeping. In one of her letters she complains that no sooner had one small brother or sister been nursed back to health, than it was the turn of another to fall sick.

By the time she met Samuel Beeton at age nineteen, Bella was a self-confident, handsome young woman with blue eyes, whose humor failed to conceal the strength of her nose and chin. Sam was Bella's perfect complement: brilliant, mercurial, and a trifle neurotic, but with a rising reputation as a young publisher; without the other, neither would have achieved the success they did. Determined to be a model wife, Bella set herself to learning the theory

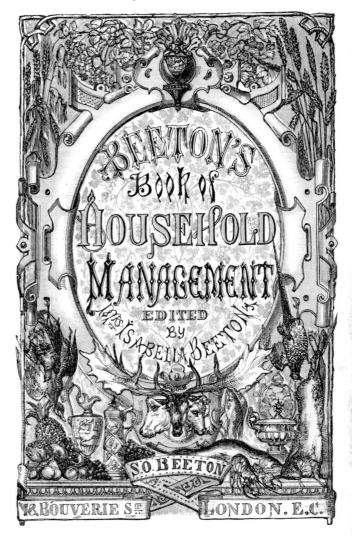

Opposite:
*Isabella Mayson, who as Mrs. Beeton became a byword for Victorian respectability, was brought up in one of the most unconventional homes on record—the grandstand of Epsom racecourse. Only on a few days a year, however, was it as crowded as in this famous picture by W. P. Firth of Derby Day.*

The cruet set (right) includes a bottle of
Worcestershire sauce, typical of the
convenience foods recommended by Mrs.
Beeton.

Even by the florid standards of the day,
this massive silver soup tureen (below)
must have bordered on the vulgar.

of cooking and housewifery, and scarcely was she
married in 1856 than Sam set her to work on *The
Englishwoman's Domestic Magazine.*

This publication was one of several that appealed to
the new middle class of the industrial age. Thrift and
respectability ruled their lives, so the magazine
debated such questions as "Can we live on £300 a
year?" and tirelessly instructed ladies in dressmak-
ing, bead-work, and the improvement of their
minds. On this subject Mrs. Beeton has surprisingly
liberated views, extolling America, where women
can become "preachers, public speakers, lecturers

and medical practitioners." One of the most successful features of *The Domestic Magazine* was a
correspondence column of readers' letters and
recipes—there was even a "soup *à la cantatrice*,"
dubbed "good for the voice," contributed by the
singer Jenny Lind. Borrowing ideas from other
authors such as the respected Eliza Acton, Mrs.
Beeton was able to embark on her master work. She
claimed to have tried all the recipes in *Household
Management,* though it is hard to believe that in the
midst of constant writing, trips abroad with her
husband, and the birth of two children (both of
whom died in infancy), she could also have found
time to test an average of fifteen recipes a week for

two years. The work was overwhelming and Mrs.
Beeton was the first to admit it. "I must frankly
own," she declares in her preface to *Household
Management*, "that if I had known beforehand that
this book would have cost me the labour it has, I
should never have been courageous enough to
commence it."

*Household Management* appeared in installments in
1859 and as a book in 1860. It is a pleasure to read.
In contrast to the flowery phrases that were then the
fashion, Mrs. Beeton writes succinctly and with an
enviable fluency. She strikes just the right note of
reassuring authority and she has a sense of order
which places her far ahead of her competitors. She is
the first to list the quantities of ingredients, cooking
time, and servings with every recipe. Much of the
generation to whom *Household Management* was
addressed had been born and bred in towns, so Mrs.
Beeton carefully states the approximate season for
each recipe (something that any country woman
would have known from childhood) and directs her
readers how to do their marketing. Naturally she
devotes little space to preserving, the pride of the
country housewife, as it presupposes a well-stocked
kitchen garden. Convenience foods like mushroom
ketchup are given Mrs. Beeton's blessing, as is baking powder, which had been commercially available
since about 1850. Before then cooks used an unreliable mixture of baking soda and an acid ingredient
like buttermilk or molasses.

Mrs. Beeton does her best to anticipate every even-
tuality, and many a modern hostess would agree
with her that "The half-hour before dinner has
always been considered as the great ordeal through
which the mistress, in giving a dinner-party, will
either pass with flying colours, or, lose many of her
laurels." She is at her best on picnics, a recreation

Mrs. Beeton's recipes, with their carefully listed ingredients, cooking time, servings, and approximate cost, have served as models for many years. She subordinates a very Victorian weakness for italics to the need for clarity—unlike the Queen herself, who peppered her writing with triple underlinings and exclamation marks. Several of her cooking methods may appear unorthodox, but they work perfectly in practice.

## Ox-tail Soup

All traditional English cookbooks have two recipes for oxtail soup, one thick and the other clarified with egg white to make a consommé for special occasions. This is the thick, everyday version which is almost a meal in itself.

*INGREDIENTS.—2 ox-tails, 2 slices of ham, 1 oz. of butter, 2 carrots, 2 turnips, 3 onions, 1 leek, 1 head of celery, 1 bunch of savoury herbs, 1 bay-leaf, 12 whole peppercorns, 4 cloves, a tablespoonful of salt, 2 tablespoonfuls of ketchup, ½ glass of port wine, 3 quarts of water.*

*Mode.—Cut up the tails, separating them at the joints; wash them, and put them in a stewpan, with the butter. Cut the vegetables in slices, and add them, with the peppercorns and herbs. Put in ½ pint of water, and stir it over a sharp fire till the juices are drawn. Fill up the stewpan with the water, and, when boiling, add the salt. Skim well, and simmer very gently for 4 hours, or until the tails are tender. Take them out, skim and strain the soup, thicken with flour, and flavour with the ketchup and port wine. Put back the tails, simmer for 5 minutes, and serve.*

*Time.—4½ hours.*
*Average cost, 1s. 3d. per quart.*
*Seasonable in winter.*
*Sufficient for 10 persons.*

## OXTAIL SOUP

2 tablespoons (30g) butter
2 oxtails (about 2 pounds or 1kg each), cut in joints
½ pound (250g) uncooked lean ham or Canadian bacon, diced
2 carrots, sliced
2 medium white turnips, sliced
3 onions, sliced
1 large leek, sliced
small bunch of celery, sliced
2-3 sprigs parsley
1 teaspoon thyme
1 bay leaf
12 peppercorns
4 whole cloves
3½ quarts (3½ l) water
1 tablespoon salt
¼ cup (7cl) port wine
2 tablespoons tomato ketchup

### FOR THICKENING:

⅓ cup (80g) butter
⅓ cup (40g) flour

This recipe can easily be converted into a stew by adding only half the quantity of water. It serves 10.

In a large kettle melt the butter and add the oxtails, ham or bacon, carrots, turnips, onions, leek, celery, parsley, thyme, bay leaf, peppercorns, cloves, and 1½ cups (3.75 deciliters) of the water. Cook over high heat, stirring, until the juices are drawn from the meat and have evaporated to form a thick brown liquid in the bottom of the pan. Add the remaining water, cover, and bring slowly to a boil. Skim well, add the salt, and simmer, covered, for 4-5 hours until the meat is very tender and falling off the bones. Skim the soup and stir it from time to time.
Take out the tails and reserve them. Strain the liquid and if possible chill it overnight so the fat solidifies on top; skim it. It should measure about 2½ quarts (2½ liters) but if it has evaporated too much add more water.
To thicken the soup, melt the butter in a saucepan and stir in the flour. Cook until well browned and stir in the liquid. Bring to a boil, stirring, and replace the oxtails. Stir in the port wine. Mix a little of the hot liquid with the ketchup and stir into the soup. Taste for seasoning, simmer 5 minutes, and serve.

## Moulded Pears

This is one of the first mentions of commercial gelatin; before Mrs. Beeton's time, cooks had to rely on the natural gelatin they could boil from bones, or on isinglass (prepared from fish)—a substance similar to gelatin but less easy to use.

*INGREDIENTS.—4 large pears or 6 small ones, 8 cloves, sugar to taste, water, a small piece of cinnamon, ¼ pint of raisin wine, a strip of lemon-peel, the juice of ½ lemon, ½ oz. of gelatine.*

*Mode.—Peel and cut the pears into quarters; put them into a jar with ¾ pint of water, cloves, cinnamon, and sufficient sugar to sweeten the whole nicely; cover down the top of the jar, and bake the pears in a gentle oven until perfectly tender, but do not allow them to break. When done, lay the pears in a plain mould, which should be well wetted, and boil ½ pint of the liquor the pears were baked in with the wine, lemon-peel, strained juice, and gelatine. Let these ingredients boil quickly for 5 minutes, then strain the liquid warm over the pears; put the mould in a cool place, and when the jelly is firm turn it out on a glass dish.*

*Time.—2 hours to bake the pears in a cool oven.*
*Average cost, 1s. 3d.*
*Sufficient for a quart mould.*
*Seasonable from August to February.*

(continued from previous page)

## PEAR MOLD

4 large or 6 small (800-900g) firm pears, peeled, cored, and quartered
2 cups (5 dl) water
½ cup (120g) sugar, or to taste
8 cloves
2-inch (5-cm) piece cinnamon stick
1 envelope (7g) gelatin
strip of lemon peel
juice of ½ lemon
¾ cup (2 dl) port wine

Plain mold or deep dish (6-cup or 1½-liter capacity)

For this dish it is important to choose pears that are firm and full of flavor when cooked. The raisin wine mentioned by Mrs. Beeton was very sweet and usually brewed at home; port is the nearest equivalent and has the advantage of coloring the mold deep pink. This recipe serves 6.

Set the oven at low (300°F or 150°C). Put the pears with the water, sugar (the amount needed depends on the sweetness of the pears), cloves, and cinnamon into a casserole or heatproof pot and cover tightly. Bake in the heated oven for 1–1½ hours or until the pears are very tender (cooking time depends very much on their ripeness). Let them cool slightly. Reserve the juice. Wet the mold and arrange the quarters of pears, rounded side down, in the bottom. Chill ½ cup (1.25 deciliters) of pear juice in a bowl, sprinkle over the gelatin, and let stand 5 minutes until spongy.
Put remaining juice in a pan with the lemon peel, lemon juice, and port wine and simmer 5 minutes. Pour the hot liquid into the gelatin and stir until dissolved. Let cool to tepid, and strain some of the mixture over the pears to form a layer that just covers them. Chill until

Opposite:
*In this early-Victorian photograph a middle-class group gathers for tea in poses held rigid for the camera. At the time, tea was taken after a six or seven o'clock dinner (hence the lamp on the table).*

set, strain in the remaining liquid, and chill until firmly set. A short time before serving, pull the mixture gently away from the sides of the mold with the fingers to break the air lock, set a platter upside down on top, and unmold onto the platter.

# Rhubarb and Orange Jam (to resemble Scotch Marmalade)

Adding inexpensive rhubarb to stretch oranges is an economical ruse typical of Mrs. Beeton, and so is the optimistic designation "to resemble Scotch marmalade," considered by many to be the best kind—perhaps because marmalade originated in Dundee. As it turns out, the unorthodox combination is at least as good as any citrus marmalade.

*INGREDIENTS.—1 quart of finely-cut rhubarb, 6 oranges, 1½ lb. of loaf sugar.*

*Mode.—Peel the oranges; remove as much of the white pith as possible, divide them, and take out the pips; slice the pulp into a preserving-pan, add the rind of half the oranges cut into thin strips, and the loaf sugar, which should be broken small. Peel the rhubarb, cut it into thin pieces,*

Overleaf:
*The royal family led the fashion for picnics for which Mrs. Beeton caters with such gusto. Her picnic for forty included a dozen different meats and no fewer than ten dozen bottles of liquid refreshments.*

*put it to the oranges and stir altogether over a gentle fire until the jam is done. Remove all the scum as it rises, put the preserve into pots, and, when cold, cover down. Should the rhubarb be very old, stew it alone for ¼ hour before the other ingredients are added.*

**Time.—**¾ to 1 hour.
**Average cost,** *from 6d. to 8d. per lb. pot.*
**Seasonable** *from February to April.*

## RHUBARB AND ORANGE JAM

6 navel oranges
2 pounds (1kg) rhubarb thinly sliced
3 cups (660g) sugar

Heatproof glasses or jars, and paraffin wax

This recipe makes about two 1-pint (5-deciliter) jars of jam.

Using a vegetable peeler, remove the rind from 3 of the oranges and reserve. Remove the pith with a serrated-edge knife, cutting with a sawing motion. Using the same knife, remove both rind and pith from remaining 3 oranges and discard.
Cut reserved rind into thin slices. Slice all the oranges; put them in a heavy-based pan (not aluminum) with the rhubarb and sliced orange peel and heat gently, stirring, until the juice runs from the rhubarb. Warm the sugar in a low oven (250°F or 122°C) for 5–10 minutes. Add the sugar to the orange and rhubarb mixture and heat gently, stirring until the sugar has dissolved. Bring to a boil and boil rapidly without stirring, skimming occasionally, until the jam gives a jell test. Take from the heat, pour into hot sterilized jars, and let cool. When cold, seal with paraffin wax, cover with paper, and store in a cool, dry place.

RHUBARB.

the Victorians pursued with unflagging energy despite the inclement English weather. Mrs. Beeton's "bill of fare for a picnic of 40 persons" includes six roasts of lamb and beef, a ham, various roast birds, several assorted pies and salads, and a collared calf's head, not to mention more than seventeen dozen puddings, cakes, and breads, plus half a pound of tea. That indispensable English accompaniment to lamb, "a bottle of mint sauce, well corked," is not forgotten, nor is a mysterious stick of horseradish—surely not to be grated on the spot. The staggering beverage allowance of ten dozen bottles, both alcoholic and non-alcoholic, certainly necessitated her laconic instruction to "take three corkscrews."

The fact that forty should be considered a normal number for a picnic reflects the size of the average Victorian family; Mrs. Beeton's flock of twenty

brothers and sisters was unusual even for those days, but several offspring, plus the odd maiden aunt or two, made ten at table a normal occurrence in most families. Mrs. Beeton casts a fascinating light on the life of such households. A family whose income is £1,000 a year, she says, might expect to employ a cook, an upper housemaid, nursemaid, under housemaid and a manservant at a total cost of between £60 and £65 a year. "It is desirable," she cautions, "unless an experienced and confidential housekeeper be kept, that the mistress should herself purchase all provisions and stores for the house." Youngsters ate in the nursery and Mrs. Beeton recommends her simplest cakes as "suitable

for children" and even gives them their own Christmas pudding. The French chef Ude, who worked in England earlier in the century, was convinced that this habit of limiting children to plain food "so they are not introduced to their parents' table till their palates have been completely benumbed by the strict diet observed in the Nursery and Boarding-Schools," was responsible for the generally abysmal standard of English cooking.

Ude belonged to a different world from Mrs. Beeton. He was one of several French chefs working for the fast-living aristocracy, who maintained retinues of foreign servants and as many as four chefs, including a Frenchman for sauces and an Englishman for roasts. The most famous of these chefs was Alexis Soyer, who set the tone at the fashionable Reform Club during the 1840s with his lamb cutlets Reform—chops coated in breadcrumbs

## Beef-Steaks and Oyster-Sauce

Oysters have long been used to enrich meat and poultry and they have only recently become expensive. As late as the 1830s, Sam Weller remarked in *Pickwick Papers*: "The poorer a place is, the greater call there seems to be for oysters. . . . Blessed if I don't think that ven a man's wery poor, he rushes out of his lodgings, and eats oysters in reg'lar desperation."

*INGREDIENTS.—3 dozen oysters, ingredients for oyster sauce, 2 lbs. of rump-steak, seasoning to taste of pepper and salt.*

*Mode.—Make the oyster sauce, and when that is ready, put it by the side of the fire, but do not let it keep boiling. Have the steaks cut of an equal thickness, broil them over a very clear fire, turning them often, that the gravy may not escape. In about 8 minutes they will be done, when put them on a very hot dish; smother with the oyster sauce, and the remainder send to table in a tureen. Serve quickly.*

*Time.—About 8 to 10 minutes, according to the thickness of the steak.*
*Average cost, 1s. per lb.*
*Sufficient for 4 persons.*
*Seasonable from September to April.*

## Oyster Sauce

It is amusing to find Mrs. Beeton subscribing to the ancient fallacy that beating mixtures in one direction makes them lighter.

*INGREDIENTS.—3 dozen oysters, ½ pint of melted butter, made with 1 teaspoonful of flour, 2 oz. butter, ⅓ pint of milk, a few grains of salt.*

*Mode.—Open the oysters carefully, and save their liquor; strain it into a clean saucepan (a lined one is best), put in the oysters, and let them just come to the boiling-point, when they should look plump. Take them off the fire immediately, and put the whole into a basin. Strain the liquor from them, mix with it sufficient milk to make ½ pint altogether, and make the sauce. Mix the butter and flour smoothly together on a plate, put it into a lined saucepan, and pour in the milk. Keep stirring it one way over a sharp fire, let it boil quickly for a minute or two. Put in the oysters, which should be previously bearded, if you wish the sauce to be really nice. Set it by the side of the fire to get thoroughly hot, but do not allow it to boil, or the oysters will immediately harden. Using cream instead of milk makes this sauce extremely delicious. When liked add a seasoning of cayenne, or anchovy sauce; but, as we have before stated, a plain sauce should be plain, and not be overpowered by highly-flavoured essences; therefore we recommend that the above directions be implicitly followed, and no seasoning added.*

*Average cost for this quantity, 2s.*
*Sufficient for 6 persons. Never allow fewer than 6 oysters to 1 person, unless the party is very large.*
*Seasonable from September to April.*

## STEAK WITH OYSTER SAUCE

2 pounds (1kg) sirloin or porterhouse, cut in steaks 1 inch (2.5cm) thick
salt and pepper
oyster sauce (see below)

The steak is less likely to dry out during cooking if it is brushed with oil or melted butter; this amount serves 3.

Make the sauce and keep it hot over very low heat or in the top of a double boiler; do not overcook it or the oysters will harden. Broil the steaks 4–5 inches from the heat, allowing 3–4 minutes on each side for rare steak; turn the steaks three or four times during cooking and sprinkle each side after broiling with salt and pepper. Transfer the steaks to a hot platter, coat them with a little of the sauce, and serve the rest separately.

## OYSTER SAUCE

¾ pint (about 18) standard oysters, with their liquor
½ cup (1.25 dl) milk
2 teaspoons flour
2 tablespoons (30g) butter
a little salt

Mrs. Beeton's urging to add no seasoning but salt to this sauce is very English in its simplicity; the ingredients stand by themselves and must be the finest quality. If you prefer, the sauce can be spiced with cayenne or nutmeg. This quantity makes 1½ cups (3.75 deciliters) sauce.

Put the oysters in a saucepan, bring them just to a boil—they should look plump—and let cool slightly. Strain the liquor and add enough milk to it to make ¾ cup (2 deciliters). Discard the beards from the oysters (American oysters may not have to be bearded). Work the flour and butter on a plate with a fork or the end of a metal spatula until smooth. Put in a heavy-based pan with the milk and bring to a boil, stirring constantly. Simmer 2 minutes, take from the heat, and add the oysters and a little salt to taste.

## Scotch Shortbread

Good shortbread, with its high proportion of butter, should have a crumbly, almost granular texture.

INGREDIENTS.—*2 lbs. of flour, 1 lb. of butter, ¼ lb. of pounded loaf sugar, ½ oz. of caraway seeds, 1 oz. of sweet almonds, a few strips of candied orange-peel.*

Mode.—*Beat the butter to a cream, gradually dredge in the flour, and add the sugar, caraway seeds, and sweet almonds, which should be blanched and cut into small pieces. Work the paste until it is quite smooth, and divide it into six pieces. Put each cake on a separate piece of paper, roll the paste out square to the thickness of about an inch, and pinch it upon all sides. Prick it well, and ornament with one or two strips of candied orange-peel. Put the cakes into a good oven, and bake them from 25 to 30 minutes.*

Time.—*25 to 30 minutes.*
Average cost, *for this quantity, 2s.*
Sufficient *to make 6 cakes.*
Seasonable *at any time.*
Note.—*Where the flavour of caraway seeds is disliked, omit them, and add rather a larger proportion of candied peel.*

## SCOTCH SHORTBREAD

1 cup (250g) butter
3 cups (375g) flour
¼ cup (60g) sugar
1½ teaspoons caraway seeds, or
   2 tablespoons (30g) sliced
   or chopped candied
   orange peel
2 tablespoons (30g) slivered
   almonds, finely chopped
1 tablespoon sliced or
   chopped candied orange
   peel (for topping)

For a sweeter cookie add ¼ cup more sugar. The recipe makes two 6-inch squares of shortbread.

Set the oven at moderate (350°F or 177°C). Cream the butter, stir in the flour, sugar, caraway seeds if using, and chopped almonds, and work the mixture with the hand to form a ball. Turn it out on a floured marble slab or board and knead it with the heel of the hand until very smooth and it peels in one piece from the board. Divide the mixture in two, set each piece on the baking sheet, and pat or roll it to a 6-inch square. Pinch the edges to flute them and mark each square into bars. Press the candied peel lightly into the top. If omitting caraway seeds, add extra portion of candied peel.
Bake the squares in the heated oven for 30 minutes or until very lightly browned. Let cool slightly on the baking sheets, and cut along the lines to form bars. Then transfer to a rack to cool completely. Store in an airtight container.

## To Make Good Plain Buns

This is one of the many recipes in *Household Management* that uses baking powder, invented only a few years before the book was published. Mrs. Beeton was quick to realize that standardized baking powder was more predictable than baking soda and worked at once, unlike yeast which could take hours to raise dough.

INGREDIENTS.—*1 lb. of flour, 6 oz. of good butter, ¼ lb. of sugar, 1 egg, nearly ¼ pint of milk, 2 small teaspoonfuls of baking-powder, a few drops of essence of lemon.*

Mode.—*Warm the butter, without oiling it; beat it with a wooden spoon; stir the flour in gradually with the sugar, and mix these ingredients well together. Make the milk lukewarm, beat up with it the yolk of the egg and the essence of lemon, and stir these to the flour, &c. Add the baking-powder, beat the dough well for about 10 minutes, divide it into 24 pieces, put them into buttered tins or cups, and bake in a brisk oven from 20–30 minutes.*

Time.—*20–30 minutes.*
Average cost, *1s.*
Sufficient *to make 12 buns.*
Seasonable *at any time.*

## PLAIN MUFFINS

¾ cup (180g) butter
2 cups (250g) flour
½ cup (120g) sugar
½ cup (1.25 dl) milk
2 egg yolks
few drops lemon extract
1½ tablespoons baking powder

12 muffin tins

These plain muffins are made differently from the usual method. Flavorings such as raisins, fresh blueberries, grated orange peel, and nuts can easily be added. This recipe makes 12 muffins.

Grease the muffin tins and set the oven at moderately hot (375°F or 190°C). Cut the butter in pieces, put it in a bowl over a pan of hot water, and stir until melted but not oily. Take the bowl from the heat and gradually stir in the flour and sugar. Heat the milk to tepid and stir it into the egg yolks and lemon extract. Stir the milk mixture into the flour mixture, add the baking powder, and beat 10 minutes by hand or 5 minutes in an electric mixer with a dough hook. Divide the mixture into 12 pieces, then put them into the prepared tins. Bake in the heated oven for 30–35 minutes or until the muffins are firm to the touch and browned. Let cool slightly in the pans. They are best eaten with butter while still warm.

This mid-nineteenth-century kitchen shows some effects of the industrial revolution; it is lighted by gas jets (center and left), metal items like the coalscuttle and molds abound, and gadgets like the grinder (beside the door) are just coming into use. The fire is enclosed behind bars, anticipating the closed range, but cooking pots still hang from the traditional crane and the roast spins steadily before the fire on a string weighted to keep it turning, as in Renaissance Italy.

and diced ham, sautéed, and served with a brown sauce flavored with pickles and red currant jelly. Like other French chefs in England, Soyer had had to adapt his style to the tastes of his masters, who preferred square meals with plenty of meat and game, culminating in that quintessentially English dish, the savory.

Soyer created innumerable kitchen gadgets and bottled sauces and wrote several cookbooks. What distinguished him from other chefs, however, was his concern for the lower end of the social scale. *A Shilling Cookery* aimed "to bring every wholesome kind of cheap food to the notice of the poor, so that, with a little exertion, they may live, and live well, with the few pence they earn, instead of living badly at times and most extravagantly at others." Beside him Mrs. Beeton, cocooned in the bourgeois world of the Victorian family, shows a disturbing complacency. Like her spiritual grandmother, Mrs. Glasse, nothing can shake her conviction that "British is Best."

This chauvinism was encouraged by the queen, to judge from the books written by her cook, Charles Francatelli, who favored dishes *à l'anglaise* (plainly boiled). Francatelli's forte was desserts and in *The Royal Confectioner*, published in 1856, he advocates the curious custom (also described by Mrs. Beeton) of setting out dessert before a dinner begins. "Fashion, upheld by good sense, in placing the dessert permanently on the table before the company are seated, has introduced a beneficial as well as a charming innovation." Francatelli's cakes, creams, and compotes are by no means as elaborate as Carême's, but one still wonders how they held up in the heat and jostle of a grand dinner which could last for three or four hours.

Grand as these French cooks were, Mrs. Beeton far outdid them in scope and to this day none has bettered her thorough grasp of the subject. *Household*

THE BRITISH DOMESTIC.
PHASE SECOND.—HER COOKERY.

"Don't want no cookery books. I don't. I could tell yer all wot's in 'em on my 'ead."

*In the days of copper boilers, it was not unknown for outsize puddings to be cooked in the same receptacle as the laundry.*

# Christmas Plum-Pudding (Very Good)

Christmas puddings should be made several weeks ahead and traditionally every member of the household stirs the mixture. Charms are added—a bachelor's button, spinster's thimble, rich man's sovereign, lucky horseshoe, etc.—indicating the fortune of the finder when the pudding is served. Mrs. Beeton's note about preparing several puddings at once is typical of her practical approach to entertaining. To stone means to pit.

INGREDIENTS.— 1½ lb. of raisins, ½ lb. of currants, ½ lb. of mixed peel, ¾ lb. of bread crumbs, ¾ lb. of suet, 8 eggs, 1 wineglassful of brandy.

Mode.—*Stone and cut the raisins in halves, but do not chop them; wash, pick, and dry the currants, and mince the suet finely; cut the candied peel into thin slices, and grate down the bread into fine crumbs. When all these dry ingredients are prepared, mix them well together; then moisten the mixture with the eggs, which should be well beaten, and the brandy; stir well, that everything may be very thoroughly blended, and press the pudding into a buttered mould; tie it down tightly with a floured cloth, and boil for 5 or 6 hours. It may be boiled in a cloth without a mould, and will require the same time allowed for cooking. As Christmas puddings are usually made a few days before they are required for table, when the pudding is taken out of the pot, hang it up immediately, and put a plate or saucer underneath to catch the water, that may drain from it. The day it is to be eaten, plunge it into boiling water, and keep it boiling for at least 2 hours; then turn it out of the mould, and serve with brandy-sauce. On Christmas-day a sprig of holly is usually placed in the middle of the pudding, and about a wineglassful of brandy poured round it, which, at the moment of serving, is lighted, and the pudding thus brought to table encircled in flame.*

Time.—*5 or 6 hours the first time of boiling; 2 hours the day it is to be served.*
Average cost, 4s.
Sufficient *for a quart mould for 7 or 8 persons.*
Seasonable *on the 25th December, and on various festive occasions till March.*
Note.—*Five or six of these puddings should be made at one time, as they will keep good for many weeks, and in cases where unexpected guests arrive, will be found an acceptable, and, as it only requires warming through, a quickly-prepared dish.*

## CHRISTMAS PUDDING

½ loaf (½ pound or 250 g) white bread
4 cups (750 g) raisins
1⅓ cups (250 g) currants
1 cup (250 g) mixed chopped candied peel
¾ pound (375 g) beef suet, ground
8 eggs, beaten to mix
½ cup (1.25 dl) brandy

FOR SERVING:

⅓–½ cup (1–1.25 dl) brandy
sprig of holly

Heatproof mold or bowl (not aluminium), 2-quart (2-liter) capacity

The "few days" suggested by Mrs. Beeton is the minimum time the pudding should be made ahead; like fruit cakes, the flavor of plum pudding matures if kept for several months. Most modern recipes add ½ cup (125 grams) sugar and spice to taste. This recipe serves 10.

Butter the mold or bowl. Discard the crusts from the bread and work it to crumbs a little at a time in a blender, or rub it through a wire sieve. In a large bowl put the raisins, currants, candied peel, breadcrumbs, and suet and stir until thoroughly mixed. Add the eggs and the ½ cup (1.25 deciliters) brandy and continue stirring until well mixed. Spoon the mixture into the prepared mold, pressing each spoonful down well with the back of the spoon.

Cut a round of brown paper and one of foil 4 inches larger than the rim of the bowl. Butter the brown paper and put both rounds together, foil up. Make a 1-inch pleat across the center (this allows for expansion) and lay over the mold, buttered side down. Tie securely with string, leaving a loop for easy removal when cooked.

Place the mold in a deep saucepan, add boiling water to cover, and add the lid. Boil steadily for 5–6 hours, adding more boiling water when necessary so the pudding is always covered. It is important that it boil constantly.

Lift out the pudding and let it cool. Discard the foil and brown paper, replace with freshly buttered brown paper and foil, and store in a dry place.

TO SERVE: Cook the pudding in boiling water to cover or in the top of a steamer for 2 hours longer.

Turn it out on a hot platter. Heat the brandy, pour it over the pudding, and flame. Add a sprig of holly on the top of the pudding and serve at once with brandy sauce.

## Plum-Pudding Sauce

As Mrs. Beeton says, this is a very rich and excellent sauce, a highly alcoholic version of the usual hard sauce.

*INGREDIENTS.—1 wineglassful of brandy, 2 oz. of very fresh butter, 1 glass of Madeira, pounded sugar to taste.*

*Mode.—Put the pounded sugar in a basin, with part of the brandy and the butter; let it stand by the side of the fire until it is warm and the sugar and butter are dissolved; then add the rest of the brandy, with the Madeira. Either pour it over the pudding, or serve in a tureen. This is a very rich and excellent sauce.*

*Average cost, 1s. 3d. for this quantity.*
*Sufficient for a pudding made for 6 persons.*

## BRANDY SAUCE

¼ cup (7 cl) brandy
⅓ cup (80 g) butter
about ⅓ cup (80 g) sugar
¼ cup (7 cl) Madeira

Makes about 1 cup (250 grams) sauce, enough for 6.

Put the butter and sugar in a saucepan with half the brandy and heat gently, stirring constantly, until the sugar has melted and the mixture is liquid. Do not let it become too hot or the butter will be oily. Take it from the heat and stir in the remaining brandy and Madeira. Pour the sauce over the pudding or serve it in a separate sauceboat.

*Management* immediately proved the type of best seller for which all publishers yearn. From the first it needed no advertising; sales picked up steadily by word of mouth, then continued year after bumper year. Sam lost no time in making the most of such a hot property. Isabella had a third child, to their joy a healthy son. She revised *Household Management* yet again to appear as a dictionary, completing the work in January 1865. Two weeks later she died of puerperal fever after giving birth to their fourth child. Samuel Beeton was overwhelmed; his financial affairs went from bad to worse and without his wife's steadying hand he was unable to cope. In 1886 he went bankrupt and was forced to sell his copyrights to the publishers Ward, Lock and Tyler. It was they who made *Household Management* the continuing success it has been, revising it constantly to suit changing tastes. At the turn of the century, for example, Herman Senn, a professional chef, dropped many of Mrs. Beeton's more basic dishes, substituting delicate little Edwardian molds and garnishes. His example has been followed so relentlessly that in the latest edition, published in 1960 (and reprinted a dozen times since then), virtually the only trace remaining in *Household Management* of the original author is her name. Happily the virtues and virtuosity of the real Mrs. Beeton can still be appreciated in the facsimile edition brought out in 1968 by Jonathan Cape.

Written when the "dear Queen" was the proud symbol of British supremacy, *Household Management* reflects both the best and the worst of the Victorian age. Mrs. Beeton can sound insufferably priggish when she lets her desire to instruct run away with her, and any housewife who could live up to her standards would be a paragon indeed. But it is impossible not to be interested by her recipes, amused by her anecdotes and happy turns of phrase, and amazed by the sheer overwhelming detail of the book. Nothing is forgotten, nothing left to chance, not even the temperature of the dining room, which (says Mrs. Beeton) should be "about 68 degrees"— a directive which most English homes have studiously ignored.

# Fannie Farmer

1857–1915

"Cookery," wrote Fannie Merritt Farmer, "is the art of preparing food for the nourishment of the body." To that forthright if somewhat forbidding statement she added: "Progress in civilization has been accompanied by progress in cookery." The year was 1896, the place Boston—a city believed by many of its citizens to be "the hub of the universe"—and the writer a thirty-nine-year-old semi-invalid who had already earned a considerable reputation as the dynamic principal of the Boston Cooking School. But no one imagined that through *The Boston Cooking-School Cook Book*, Fannie Farmer's name would become a household word.

Her rise to fame can be traced to a chance question about the "heaping" spoons and cups by which cooks had always measured ingredients. "Couldn't they be level?" asked one of her students. The alert Fannie, ever trying to take the guesswork out of cooking, was quick to realize the implications. She also outlawed such traditional measures as butter "the size of an egg" and "wineglasses" of liquid. By vigorous promotion through her school, books, newspaper columns, and lectures, she swept aside the remnants of the cumbersome European system of measuring ingredients by weight and set Americans firmly on the course of level measurement by volume.

Fannie Farmer was born in Boston in 1857, the eldest of the four daughters of John Franklin Farmer, "a stately man of great charm but little practical ability," according to his great-niece, Wilma Lord Perkins. The Farmers were of "untainted New England stock, Unitarian and bookish" and the family was warm and close-knit. When she was thirteen, Fannie suffered a paralytic stroke that put an end to all hopes of a college education. For a time she was a paid mother's helper but everyone could see that her ability and determination destined her for a more challenging career. Fannie's married sister discovered a teacher-training school which did not require a high school diploma of its students, and in 1887, at the age of thirty, Fannie enrolled in the Boston Cooking School for a two-year course. After graduation she stayed on as assistant to the principal, who died a year later. The trustees then elected Fannie to replace her.

Despite Fannie's physical handicap—she was permanently lame—she proved an energetic and capable director. She encouraged her students to experiment with new dishes, she was constantly testing new products, and hardly surprising, she was

## THE ORIGINAL
# Fannie Farmer
## COOK BOOK
### 1896

A facsimile of the first edition of
THE BOSTON COOKING-SCHOOL COOK BOOK
by Fannie Merritt Farmer

Hugh Lauter Levin Associates, New York

*distributed by*
CROWN PUBLISHERS, INC.
419 Park Avenue South, New York, N.Y. 10016

Opposite:
*A teacher training class at the Boston Cooking School lines up for the graduation photo, displaying the tools of their profession. Note the ingenious tabletop, which can be raised from a comfortable level for dining to worktop height.*

passionately concerned with invalid cookery. "As a teacher," said Mrs. Perkins, "Fannie was incomparable, if at times something of a trial to her devoted students. They used to sigh that she would almost always ask, after a recipe had been tested and retested, 'Could it be better?'"

Obsessed with accuracy, Fannie Farmer soon found inadequate the school textbook written by a predecessor, Mrs. Lincoln. Not only were the recipes too few to make it a comprehensive work of reference, but by Fannie's standards the instructions were scanty. She worked hard on a replacement, and her nephew Dexter Perkins, then a boy of six, remembers his aunt limping up and down the room as she dictated the manuscript to his mother. Family tradition has it that the day she delivered the manuscript to her chosen Boston publishing house (Little, Brown), Fannie dressed with care for once, even to white gloves. Initially aloof, Little, Brown finally agreed to act as her agent; Fannie was to pay all the costs of producing the book, they were to supervise its production and distribution. According to Mrs. Perkins, the book "remained in Fannie Farmer's possession and was never on a royalty basis." Some three million copies, in eleven editions, have been published since the first print order of 3,000 copies in 1896. Little, Brown paid dearly for its doubts; when Fannie died in 1915, over half her $161,000 estate was in copyrights.

The reasons for the success of *The Boston Cooking-School Cook Book* are plain. Fannie's instructions are simple enough for any novice to follow, and needless to say, the measurements are precision itself. The recipes range from general favorites like doughnuts to such New England specialities as baked beans and chowder, with a heavy emphasis on cakes and desserts. Fannie is firm on how to make good bread (a subject "of no small importance"), her instructions on broiling, boiling, and the like are exhaustive, and she is deeply interested in nutrition and the scientific principles lying behind cooking techniques. To some modern minds, however, Fannie may seem a bit of a kill-joy; the nearest she gets to admitting that eating can be a pleasure as well as a necessity is to suggest adding flowers to an invalid's tray.

For seventy years a theme of sobriety and thrift had dominated American household works, ever since Lydia Child had written *The American Frugal Housewife* in 1829 and dedicated it to "those who are not ashamed of economy." Mrs. Child's contemporary and equal in influence, Eliza Leslie, was more easy-going, but her half-dozen works are also pervaded by a similar emphasis on respectability and virtue. Both ladies well knew how the vicissitudes of the American economy—banks that went under, crops that failed—could fell the middle class. To these sermons on self-help, Catharine Beecher, whose sister wrote *Uncle Tom's Cabin*, added a tone of militancy. The two sisters founded several schools for girls, and in 1845 Catharine published *A Treatise on Domestic Economy for Use in the Home*, a pioneer work in home economics. "Let the young women of this nation find that domestic economy is placed in schools on equal or superior grounds to

Fannie Farmer's recipes follow the style we use today. Her instructions are terse and to the point and need little or no adaptation for the modern kitchen. Curiously, for someone so precise about measurements, she seldom says how many servings a recipe yields. Her vagueness about oven heat and baking times may be attributed to the idiosyncracies of the wood or coal burning ranges which required as much care and feeding as a household pet. However, later editions of her books did take into account the advances made in standardizing kitchen appliances, and readers knew if "Fannie" said a cake took thirty minutes to bake at 350°F in Boston, it probably took the same time in Boise, Idaho.

## Devilled Scallops

The American love of do-it-yourself cooking showed early and Fannie Farmer's *Chafing Dish Possibilities*, published in 1898, had a ready sale. This recipe exemplifies her sparing use of seasonings; seldom in her book does she call for more than salt and pepper, mustard, onions, shallots, and a few herbs such as parsley, thyme, and bay leaf.

*Clean one pint scallops, heat to boiling point, drain, and reserve liquor. Melt three tablespoons butter, add two tablespoons flour, mixed with one-half teaspoon salt, one-fourth teaspoon mustard, and a few grains cayenne. Pour on gradually the reserved liquor. When sauce begins to thicken, add the scallops. Serve with brown bread sandwiches.*

## DEVILLED SCALLOPS

1 cup (½ pound or 250g) bay or sea scallops with their liquor
3 tablespoons (45g) butter
2 tablespoons (20g) flour
½ teaspoon salt
¼ teaspoon dry mustard
pinch of cayenne
8 thin slices buttered whole wheat bread (for serving)

This recipe serves 2.

Add enough water to scallop liquor to make ⅔ cup (2 deciliters). Put the scallops with the liquid in a chafing dish or saucepan, heat until almost boiling, and drain, reserving the liquid. Melt the butter in the pan, stir in the flour, salt, mustard, and cayenne, and cook until foaming. Add the liquid, blend well, and heat, stirring, until the sauce thickens. Add the scallops, turning them so they are well coated with sauce, and heat gently until very hot. Serve at once with thinly sliced bread and butter as accompaniment.

## Glazed Sweetbreads Lucullus

Foreign cooking was not Fannie's forte—she cooks pasta to a mush and refers to French-style tournedos steaks as "tornadoes." However, Americans of her day did consume parts of the animal which are ignored today—sweetbreads, tripe, and brains—and in this respect, at least, the diet was closer to the European than it is now. In the following recipe, Fannie takes several shortcuts that would make a French chef shudder, like using canned artichokes, but the results amply justify her methods.

*Trim sweetbread and parboil in Sherry wine until plump, the time required being about one-half hour. Keep covered during the cooking, turning twice. Cool and cut in pieces. Put one and one-half tablespoons butter in frying pan, and when melted add one-half teaspoon beef extract. Cook sweetbread in mixture until glazed, turning frequently. Drain canned artichoke bottoms and reheat; then arrange on circular pieces of sautéed bread. Place pieces of sweetbread on each and pour around Lucullus Sauce made by adding one cup chopped sautéed mushrooms to one cup tomato sauce.*

## GLAZED SWEETBREADS LUCULLUS

1½ pounds (750g) or 1½-2 pairs sweetbreads
¾ cup (2dl) sherry
2½ tablespoons (40g) butter
½ teaspoon meat glaze, or ½ cup (1.25 dl) brown stock boiled until reduced to ½ teaspoon
4 canned or frozen artichoke bottoms, cooked

FOR CROÛTES:

4 slices bread
2 tablespoons oil
2 tablespoons (30g) butter

FOR LUCULLUS SAUCE:

½ pound (250g) mushrooms, chopped
1 tablespoon butter
1 cup (2.5 dl) tomato sauce
salt and pepper

Fannie Farmer does not specify what to do with the sherry after cooking the sweetbreads, but it is excellent added to the sauce. The tomato sauce she used was probably canned. This recipe serves 4.

THE WATKINS NO. 21A

*"A place for everything and everything in its place," was the theory behind this built-in kitchen cabinet of 1912. Flour was stored in the glass container (upper left) and flowed into the sifter. The* *pull-out shelf at center was for kneading and shaping dough, and the finished product was kept in the bread safe (lower right). Cleaning the contraption must have been a nightmare.*

# Boston Baked Beans

This dish has survived from colonial days, when beans, pork, and molasses were among the most abundant staples in the kitchen. In Puritan households, the beans were baked all day Saturday to serve fresh in the evening; they were warmed over for Sunday breakfast and served cold for the midday meal, thus enabling the cook to observe the ban against working on the Sabbath.

*Pick over one quart pea beans, cover with cold water, and soak over night. In morning, drain, cover with fresh water, heat slowly (keeping water below boiling point), and cook until skins will burst—which is best determined by taking a few beans on the tip of a spoon and blowing on them, when skins will burst if sufficiently cooked. Beans thus tested must, of course, be thrown away. Drain beans, throwing bean-water out of doors, not in sink. Scald rind of one-half pound fat salt pork, scrape, remove one-fourth inch slice and put in bottom of bean-pot. Cut through rind of remaining pork every one-half inch, making cuts one inch deep. Put beans in pot and bury pork in beans, leaving rind exposed. Mix one tablespoon salt, one tablespoon molasses, and three tablespoons sugar; add one cup boiling water, and pour over beans; then add enough more boiling water to cover beans. Cover bean-pot, put in oven, and bake slowly six or eight hours, uncovering the last hour of cooking, that rind may become brown and crisp. Add water as needed. Many feel sure that by adding with seasonings one-half tablespoon mustard, the beans are more easily digested. If pork mixed with lean is preferred, use less salt.*
*The fine reputation which Boston Baked Beans have gained, has been attributed to the earthen bean-pot with small top and bulging sides in* *which they are supposed to be cooked. Equally good beans have often been eaten where a five-pound lard pail was substituted for the broken bean-pot.*
*Yellow-eyed beans are very good when baked.*

## BOSTON BAKED BEANS

2 pounds (1kg) dried pea beans
½ pound (250g) fat salt pork
1 tablespoon salt
1 tablespoon molasses
3 tablespoons sugar
1½ teaspoons dry mustard (optional)

5-quart (5-liter) bean pot or deep casserole

As an accompaniment, this recipe makes 10–12 servings.

Pick over the beans, cover with cold water, and leave to soak overnight. Drain them, put in a pan with water to cover, add the lid, and bring slowly to a boil. Cook, keeping just below boiling point, for 2½ hours, or until the beans burst when a few are lifted on a spoon and you blow on them. Add more water during cooking if the beans get dry.
Set the oven at low (250°F or 122°C). Blanch the salt pork by bringing it to a boil in cold water. Drain it, score the rind deeply at half-inch intervals, and cut a thin slice from the bottom. Drain the beans, discarding the cooking liquid. Put the slice of pork in the bottom of the bean pot or casserole, add the beans, and bury the piece of pork in them, leaving the rind exposed—the pot should be almost filled. Mix the salt, molasses, sugar, and mustard, if used, with a cup of boiling water and pour it over the beans. Add more boiling water to cover, add the lid, and bake the beans in the heated oven for 6–8 hours, uncovering them during the last two hours so the pork rind becomes crisp.

*(continued from previous page)*

Soak the sweetbreads for 2–3 hours in cold water; drain and rinse them. Blanch them by putting in cold water, bringing to a boil, and simmering 2 minutes. Drain them, rinse, and remove any ducts and skin. Put them in a small pan with the sherry, cover, and simmer 25–35 minutes or until very tender. Drain them, reserving the sherry if you like. Press between two plates and let cool. Cut the sweetbreads in thick slices.

FOR THE CROÛTES: Cut large rounds from the slices of bread, fry them in the oil and butter until brown on both sides, drain on paper towels and keep warm.

FOR THE SAUCE: Sauté the chopped mushrooms in the butter over low heat until all the moisture has evaporated; add the tomato sauce and sherry if you like. Bring to a boil and add salt and pepper to taste.

To heat the artichoke bottoms, melt 1 tablespoon of the butter in a pan and heat the artichokes gently without browning. In a frying pan melt the remaining 1½ tablespoons butter, and add the meat glaze. Put in the sliced sweetbreads and sauté over medium heat, turning often, until glazed and golden brown. Set an artichoke bottom on each croûte, top with the sliced sweetbreads, and arrange on a deep platter. Spoon around the sauce and serve.

164

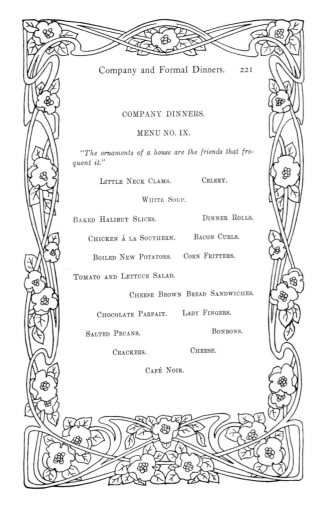

*Cooking always came first with Fannie Farmer. In this excerpt (below) from a letter of 19 November 1912, to a former student, she talks of little else.*

*This dinner is one of the fifty-one menus for different occasions that appeared in Fannie Farmers' A Book of Good Dinners, published in 1905. In typical period fashion, each is preceded by a quaint aphorism.*

chemistry, philosophy, and mathematics, and they will blush to be found ignorant of its first principles," she proclaims.

These proselytizing ladies were active at a time of drastic change in the status of American women. Now that the land was tamed, a wife was no longer caught up with her husband in the adventures of settling America. The family, from being a self-contained unit that could, if need be, produce its own food, weave its own cloth, and make its own soap and candles, was in most areas becoming part of a more urban community. Now more intellectual skills were demanded of the housewife, plus the ability to adapt to the exigencies and allurements of town life. Lydia Child and Eliza Leslie deplored idle, spendthrift women, and their tactic was to elevate them to the status of "homemaker" and so

Company and Formal Dinners. 221

COMPANY DINNERS.

MENU NO. IX.

*"The ornaments of a house are the friends that frequent it."*

LITTLE NECK CLAMS. CELERY.

WHITE SOUP.

BAKED HALIBUT SLICES. DINNER ROLLS.

CHICKEN À LA SOUTHERN. BACON CURLS.

BOILED NEW POTATOES. CORN FRITTERS.

TOMATO AND LETTUCE SALAD.

CHEESE BROWN BREAD SANDWICHES.

CHOCOLATE PARFAIT. LADY FINGERS.

SALTED PECANS. BONBONS.

CRACKERS. CHEESE.

CAFÉ NOIR.

emphasize the dignity and importance of their duties. Catharine Beecher was to improve upon this title by labeling the housewife a "domestic scientist." The conviction that household management was a serious subject to be learned in school rather than picked up at home is quite apparent from *The Boston Cooking-School Cook Book*, which is clearly intended to be studied as a text as well as used in the kitchen.

After eleven years of running the Boston Cooking School, the restrictions of training teachers became irksome and Fannie opened her own "Miss Farmer's School of Cookery." She was a striking figure—blue eyes, pince-nez, red hair greying handsomely at the temples, "slender and firmly corseted," a student of 1912 has recalled. Fannie's reputation was by now considerable, and the demonstration lectures she gave twice weekly attracted 200 people. Toward the end, when her illness recurred, she spoke from a wheelchair, her knees sticking straight out and covered with a lap robe. Even in her younger days, an assistant did most of the cooking, partly to save Fannie's limited strength and partly, said Mrs. Perkins, because "she was too impatient to cook a whole meal." She must often have been too busy; in a letter of 1912, she notes that "Miss Allen has two waitress's classes on Monday. One in the

A.M. and one in the P.M. Next week we shall be running sixteen hospital classes, sixteen private-classes and we start our third marketing class. With the special lessons we are more than busy." Fannie herself wrote regularly for *Woman's Home Companion*, and one year she lectured in over thirty cities, as far as the Pacific Coast.

Amid all these activities, which would have over-taxed many a healthier person, Fannie also found time to write half a dozen other cookbooks includ-ing her own favorite, *Food and Cookery for the Sick and Convalescent* ( the subject of lectures she gave at the Harvard Medical School), and *A New Book of Cookery*, published in 1912. The latter book shows a different, more sophisticated side to her cooking—

flourishing of Fannie Farmer's local readers put away a lot of food. Her typical family dinner menu called for soup, roast, an "entrée" or composed dish, vegetables, a salad, and dessert. Such abundant fare was typical of middle-class America, although the choice of dishes varied enormously, depending on

*True to form, Fannie holds up a stan-dard cup containing sugar, carefully measured and leveled in the prescribed manner. At right a nervous young student tries out an orange gelatin dessert.*

perhaps the result of the many visits she made with her family to New York restaurants, when each would order a different dish and taste carefully to guess the recipe. Dishes like jellied poached eggs, sweetbreads Lucullus, and coupe Caruso belong clearly to the French tradition that flourished at Delmonico's, the Astor, the Knickerbocker, and the Waldorf, whose dining room was then ruled by the legendary Oscar.

Turn-of-the-century America was a place of con-spicuous consumption, not limited to the appetite of the preposterous Diamond Jim Brady, whose stomach was discovered to be six times the standard size. However superciliously Bostonians might regard New Yorkers and French taste, the more

Martha Hayes Luddey

## Celery and Cabbage Salad

By the end of the nineteenth century, urban Americans took almost for granted the constant supply of fresh vegetables from the South and California, made possible by the railroads. "Salads . . . constitute a course in almost every dinner," remarks Fannie, and they were—and still are—more popular than in Europe.

*Remove outside leaves from a small solid white cabbage and cut off stalk close to leaves. Cut out centre and with a sharp knife shred finely. Let stand one hour in cold or ice water. Drain, wring in double cheese cloth, to make as dry as possible. Mix with equal parts celery cut in small pieces. Moisten with Cream Dressing and refill cabbage. Arrange on a folded napkin and garnish with celery tips and parsley between folds of napkin and around top of cabbage.*

## Cream Dressing

*½ tablespoon salt.*
*½ tablespoon mustard.*
*1¼ tablespoons sugar.*
*1 egg slightly beaten.*
*2½ tablespoons melted butter.*
*¾ cup cream.*
*¼ cup vinegar.*

*Mix ingredients in order given, adding vinegar very slowly. Cook over boiling water, stirring constantly until mixture thickens, strain and cool.*

## CELERY AND CABBAGE SALAD

1 small solid green cabbage
5-6 stalks celery
several sprigs parsley
boiled dressing (see below)

A little cabbage goes a long way and these quantities are enough to serve 12–14.

Remove the outside leaves of the cabbage and trim the stem so the cabbage sits firmly. With a sharp knife, hollow out the center from the top, leaving a thin shell. Finely shred the leaves and soak in ice water for an hour. Thinly slice the celery stalks, reserving the tops. Drain the cabbage, put it in a cloth or double cheesecloth, and wring it dry. Add the celery and mix with boiled dressing. Pile enough mixture into the cabbage shell to fill it and decorate the top with parsley sprigs. Set the cabbage on a folded napkin on a platter and decorate the folds of the napkin with the celery tops and more parsley.

### BOILED DRESSING

½ tablespoon salt
1½ teaspoons mustard
4 teaspoons sugar
1 egg, beaten to mix
2½ tablespoons (40g) melted butter
¾ cup (2dl) heavy cream
¼ cup (7cl) vinegar

This recipe makes about 1¼ cups (3 deciliters) dressing.

In the top of a double boiler put the salt, mustard, and sugar and with a wooden spoon stir in the egg, melted butter, and cream. Gradually stir in the vinegar. Put the pan over boiling water and cook, stirring constantly, until the dressing thickens enough to coat the back of a spoon. Take from the heat, strain, and let cool, stirring occasionally.

## Entire Wheat Bread

Entire wheat flour, the equivalent of today's stone-ground whole wheat flour, was milled from the "entire" grain and so contained the protein-rich germ removed from all-purpose flour. As an invalid she had been more than casually interested in nutrition, and as a teacher she stressed the importance of protein "in the dietary," though she never mentioned vitamins, which were not discovered until the twentieth century. Gem pans are miniature loaf pans.

*2 cups scalded milk.*
*¼ cup sugar or ⅓ cup molasses.*
*1 teaspoon salt.*
*¼ yeast cake dissolved in*
*¼ cup lukewarm water.*
*4⅓ cups entire wheat flour.*

*Add sweetening and salt to milk, cool, and when lukewarm add dissolved yeast cake and flour; beat well, cover, and let rise to double its bulk. Again beat, and turn into greased bread pans, having pans one-half full; let rise, and bake. Entire Wheat Bread should not quite double its bulk during last rising. This mixture may be baked in gem pans.*

## WHOLE WHEAT BREAD

1 cake (15g) compressed yeast or 1 package dry yeast
¼ cup (7cl) lukewarm water
2 cups (5dl) milk
¼ cup (60g) sugar or ⅓ cup (9cl) molasses
2 teaspoons salt
6-6½ cups (600-650g) stone ground whole wheat flour
1 egg beaten with ½ teaspoon salt (for glaze)-optional

9x5x4 inch (22x12x10cm) loaf pan
or 8 individual loaf pans

This recipe makes 1 large loaf or 8 individual ones.

## (continued from previous page)

Sprinkle or crumble the yeast over the warm water and let stand 5 minutes or until dissolved. Scald the milk, let cool to lukewarm, and stir in the sugar or molasses with the salt. Put 4½ cups (450 grams) of the flour into a bowl, make a well in the center, and add the yeast and milk mixtures. Stir with the hand and gradually draw in all the flour. Sprinkle the remaining flour on a board. Turn the dough out onto the board and knead it, working in the flour, for 5 minutes or until smooth and elastic, adding a little more flour as necessary. Place the dough in a greased bowl, turn it so the top is greased also, and cover with a damp cloth. Put the dough to rise in a warm place for 1–1½ hours or until doubled in bulk.

Grease the loaf pans and set the oven at hot (400°F or 205°C) for small loaves or moderately hot (375°F or 190°C) for a large one. Knead the dough lightly to knock out the air, shape it into 1 large or 8 small loaves, and set in the pans—they should be filled half full. Cover and leave the dough to rise again for 25–35 minutes or until risen almost to the top of the pans. Brush the loaves with egg glaze. Bake in the heated oven, allowing 30–35 minutes for small loaves or 55–60 minutes for the large one. When done, the bread sounds hollow when tapped on the bottom. Cool the loaves on a wire rack.

## Cream Pie

Cream pie is not a pie at all, but a cake baked in layer pans. Originally, it was probably baked in a pie pan. This recipe is typical of Fannie Farmer's many cake recipes; accurate though she was about spoon and cup measurements, it was not until later editions that she added details on the size of cake pans or baking temperatures.

⅓ cup butter.
1 cup sugar.
2 eggs.
½ cup milk.
1 ¾ cups flour.
2 ½ teaspoons baking powder.

*Cream the butter, add sugar gradually, and eggs well beaten. Mix and sift flour and baking powder, add alternately with milk to first mixture. Bake in round layer cake pans. Put Cream Filling between layers and sprinkle top with powdered sugar.*

## French Cream Filling

Fannie was not above endorsing selected products or equipment. The Dover egg beater mentioned in this recipe was one favored utensil.

¾ cup thick cream.
¼ cup milk.
¼ cup powdered sugar.
White one egg.
½ teaspoon vanilla.

*Dilute cream with milk and beat until stiff, using Dover egg-beater. Add sugar, white of egg beaten until stiff, and vanilla.*

## BOSTON CREAM PIE

⅓ cup (80g) butter
1 cup (220g) sugar
2 eggs, beaten to mix
1¾ cups (220g) flour
2½ teaspoons baking powder
½ cup (1.25 dl) milk
French cream filling (see below)
confectioners' sugar

Three 9-inch (22-cm) cake pans

This recipe makes one 9-inch cake.

Set the oven at moderate (350°F or 177°C) and grease and flour the cake pans. Cream the butter, gradually beat in the sugar, and continue beating until the mixture is blended thoroughly. Gradually beat in the eggs, a little at a time, and beat until the mixture is smooth and light. Sift the flour with the baking powder. Stir the flour into the egg mixture in three batches, alternately with the milk. Divide the mixture among the three prepared pans and spread evenly over the bottom. Bake in the heated oven for 25–30 minutes or until the mixture springs back when lightly pressed with a finger-tip and draws away from the sides of the pan. Turn the cakes out onto a rack to cool. A short time before serving, sandwich them with the French cream filling, sprinkle the top generously with confectioners' sugar, and set the cake on a platter.

## FRENCH CREAM FILLING

1 cup (2.5 dl) heavy cream
¼ cup (30g) confectioners' sugar
½ teaspoon vanilla
1 egg white

This recipe makes about 2 cups (5 deciliters) filling.

Beat the cream until it holds a soft peak, add the sugar and vanilla, and continue beating until stiff. Stiffly beat the egg white and fold into the cream.

## Fudge

*Melt one tablespoon butter, add one-half cup milk and one and one-half cups sugar; stir until sugar is dissolved, then add five tablespoons prepared cocoa, or two squares unsweetened chocolate. Stir constantly until chocolate is melted. Heat to boiling point and boil twelve minutes, stirring occasionally to prevent burning. Extinguish flame, add one teaspoon vanilla, and beat until the mixture is creamy. Pour into a buttered pan, cool, and mark in squares.*

## FUDGE

4 tablespoons (60g) butter
1 cup (2.5dl) milk
3 cups (660g) sugar
10 tablespoons (75g) cocoa powder or 4 squares (4 ounces or 125g) unsweetened chocolate, chopped
2 teaspoons vanilla

8-inch (20-cm) square cake pan

This recipe makes 1½ pounds (750 grams) fudge.

Butter the pan. Melt the butter in a large saucepan and add the milk and sugar. Cook over gentle heat, stirring, until the sugar dissolves. Add the cocoa powder or the chopped chocolate and continue stirring over low heat until the cocoa dissolves or the chocolate melts. Bring to a boil and boil steadily for 12 minutes, stirring occasionally to prevent scorching, or until the mixture reaches the soft ball stage (240°F or 115°C on a sugar thermometer).
Take from the heat and add the vanilla. Beat the fudge for 1–2 minutes or until the mixture loses its shine and stiffens slightly. Do not overbeat or the fudge will harden. Pour at once into the prepared pan and leave to cool slightly. Mark into squares with a knife.

*On the back of a recipe for "Butterfly Teas," part of the course menu for 13 November 1912, Fannie sketched this outline for decorating the little cakes.*

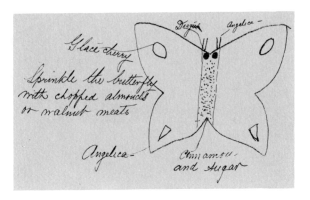

local tradition and ethnic tastes. No country has had such a long and rich harvest of regional cookbooks as the United States—a heritage which dates back to 1824 (when Mrs. Randolph wrote her classic *The Virginia Housewife*) and which still prospers today in the books and locally printed paperbacks of clubs and church groups. Even Fannie's *Boston Cooking-School Cook Book*, which from its first appearance in 1896 had a general appeal, still belonged unmistakably to New England, no less than Amelia Simmons's *American Cookery* written exactly a century earlier.
During that hundred years the average American kitchen had been transformed. The great open fireplace that was so wasteful of wood had vanished, and in its place stood a castiron range with an oven and space on top for heating pots. In the first edition of *The Boston Cooking-School Cook Book*, Fannie mentions only coal or wood as fuel for these stoves, but the Boston Gas Company had already opened a showroom in 1875. In those days before thermostats, the standard way to test the heat of an oven was with the hand. A student relates how, gold watch at the ready, Miss Farmer would time the moment when the heat forced her hand out of the oven: 20–30 seconds was the allowance for a "quick" oven and 45–60 seconds for a slow one. Into the oven, year round, went chickens raised in incubators and meat from cattle fattened by new feeding methods. Fruit and vegetables, now reaching the great American cities by train, were more likely to come fresh from the grocers than from the housekeeper's "put-up" winter stock of preserves. Ships no longer called at Boston to take ice from Wenham Lake to all corners of the earth; the technique of icemaking had been mastered and the domestic refrigerator was soon to arrive. The great food-processing and canning industries were developing, along with

169

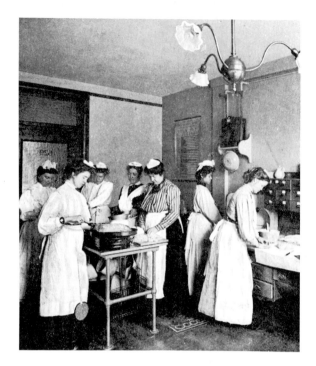

brand names like Knox's gelatin, Quaker rolled oats, and Baker's chocolate.

In England thirty years earlier, Mrs. Beeton had been preoccupied with much the same revolution in household management, and there are many parallels between her book and Fannie Farmer's. Both women were writing for a family market where good living had to be combined with economy. Both were concerned with teaching the basics of cooking to a wide audience. But where Mrs. Beeton is chatty and digresses into the past, Miss Farmer sticks firmly to the task immediately before her. In a world of increasing mechanization and uniformity, cooking was becoming an intellectual discipline which it was the duty of a conscientious housewife

to assimilate, be she rich or poor. "It is my wish," Fannie wrote in her introduction to *The Boston Cooking-School Cook Book*, "that this book may not only be looked upon as a compilation of tried and tested recipes, but that it may awaken an interest through its condensed scientific knowledge which will lead to deeper thought and broader study of what to eat." Carême would have applauded the sentiment, but he would have been astonished at the direction in which it led Fannie Farmer. The American insistence on accuracy in cooking is the antithesis of the free-wheeling French spirit in which chefs rarely measure ingredients but rely on experience and flair in putting them together. This contrast is still apparent today; while most Americans clamor for cookbooks with step-by-step

instructions, the French housewife seems content with a few cursory remarks.

Despite the passage of almost eighty years, "Fannie Farmer" still commands an enormous following. First revised by Fannie herself (to include the use of gas and electricity) her book has been repeatedly updated. Recent editions take account of freezers, meat thermometers, and blenders and although the original size has been doubled to 3,000 recipes, the book has been treated with much more sympathy than Mrs. Beeton's, doubtless because the editing has remained within the family. Fannie Farmer may have had her limitations as a practical cook—ironically, the family considered her cooking talents inferior to those of her sister May or of the family housekeeper—but her gift for organization and for communicating ideas to others was outstanding, as was her intellectual grasp of cooking as a science. Her standards of precision have had an incalculable effect on modern American cooking, earning for Fannie Farmer the nickname "mother of level measurement," and a permanent place in the history of cooking.

Around 1910 a Frenchman visited Fannie Farmer's school in Boston. He reported:

"The second school that I saw is a cooking school. A woman rented a few rooms in some house or other, had a luxurious brochure printed on Holland-type paper – and *voilà* a new school. The director – Miss Farmer – is a lady in her forties, very lively, fair, with gold-framed glasses gleaming on her nose, a pretty little lace cap on her head, a bodice of white piqué and a white apron. She explains her system, which is very simple.

"Irish girls arrive from their homeland, knowing nothing and seeking a situation. For the sum of three or four dollars, Miss Farmer has them into the kitchen for two weeks, and they come out cooks. That's not all: she also teaches them to wait at table, instructs them in clean teeth, neat nails, tidy hair, and tells them how to pick up table crumbs, etc.

"But the school has been founded for another purpose: to teach middle and upper class girls how to do their own cooking, and how to run a house. They enrol in groups of eight, which makes a class. They pay a dollar or a $1.50 a lesson. There are six courses, consisting of ten lessons each.

"I saw these girls putting on their cap and apron as they arrived. The seemed to be having great fun playing housekeeper. 'They come here the moment they're engaged,' Miss Farmer tells me. 'And you see they do the work themselves, prepare their lunch, take turns serving it, and eat it. There's no better way of teaching.'

"I ask Miss Farmer if her students follow the 60 lessons right to the end. 'Most of them do,' she says. 'There's a great deal to be learnt! In the first course, we show them how to lay a fire, how to use a gas stove, how to cook potatoes and eggs and bake bread and apples, how to filter coffee, and how to make bread dough, simple soups and a few puddings. The second and third course is a more advanced cooking. The fourth is on pastries, salads and desserts. In the fifth course students learn how to serve, as before giving orders to others one must know how to carry them out oneself. So my students learn how to clean tables, polish floors, sweep up and dust, make butter balls, stack dishes, cups and glasses in cupboards, clean silver, arrange table decorations for all kinds of occasions, make Russian tea, English tea, iced tea, serve guests, make sandwiches, choose different wines and liqueurs – in a word, they learn French-style service. The sixth course is cooking for nurses. I go with students into a hospital and do a demonstration in the public ward. Then I train them to do shopping, and to buy supplies. So they learn about prices. From time to time, French chefs come and help – those from the best hotels in Boston, and sometimes from a transatlantic liner. The chef from the *Touraine*, for instance, has come several times from New York between crossings, and gives lessons to my girls.'"

*L'Amérique moderne*, by Jules Huret, Paris 1911.

# Auguste Escoffier

1846–1935

More than seventy years after its publication, Escoffier's Le Guide culinaire remains a standard work of reference in French professional kitchens. The photograph (left) catches Escoffier in one of his rare off-duty moments.

Escoffier has been hailed as the king of chefs and the chef of kings. He was the undisputed culinary leader in the thirty years before World War I, when crowned heads, led by the Prince of Wales (later Edward VII) toured the fashionable resorts of Europe accompanied by the beauties of the day, and when the *Wagons-Lits* company ran a regular service from St. Petersburg to Cannes. Escoffier was also the chef of chefs, defining for his profession the art of modern French cooking, reducing to essentials the elaborate structure of *haute cuisine* inherited from Carême.

London, Paris, Cannes, Monte Carlo, Nice, Lucerne —at one time or another between 1880 and the war, Escoffier headed the finest kitchens in them all. The situation was very different from the days of Carême; restaurants, from being a generally inferior alternative to dining at home, had taken the lead. No longer did the great chefs work in private houses

*The great hotelier César Ritz was the perfect partner for Escoffier. Their association lasted almost forty years and extended to five of the greatest hotels in Europe.*

for individual masters; instead the masters came to them in their restaurants and hotels. At the Café Anglais in Paris, headed by chef Duglére of *sole Dugléré* fame, "one supped until midnight, the baccarat lasted until dawn and the Russian princes broke the house glasses with blows from the bottles of Champagne."

The achievements of Escoffier are hard to separate from those of César Ritz, the great hotelier whom

BIBLIOTHÈQUE PROFESSIONNELLE

# Le Guide Culinaire

*AIDE-MÉMOIRE DE CUISINE PRATIQUE*

**Par A. ESCOFFIER**

AVEC LA COLLABORATION

De MM. Philéas GILBERT — E. FÉTU
A. Suzanne, B. Reboul, Ch. Dietrich, A. Caillat, etc.

*Dessins de* Victor Morin

*Je place ce livre sous le patronage posthume de Urbain Dubois et Émile Bernard, en témoignage de mon admiration pour ceux qui, depuis Carême, ont porté le plus haut la gloire de l'Art Culinaire.*

A. E.

PARIS
1903

Tous droits de traduction et de reproduction réservés pour tous les pays, y compris la Suède, la Norvège et le Danemark.

Opposite:
*"Le Dîner" by Albert Guillaume evokes all the carefree gaiety of the* belle époque, *with its flowers, feathers, and deep décolletages. Escoffier, king of the kitchens of the time, once recalled the greatest mishap of his career—the day an inexperienced waiter tipped a dish of peas down a lady's dress. Losing his nerve completely and stammering in broken English, the poor man began frantically to retrieve the peas one by one, until he was knocked to the floor by her outraged husband.*

Escoffier met in 1880 at a providential moment in his career. Escoffier was thirty-four, with a thorough training behind him, but at the time of this meeting there seems to have been little hint of his special gifts. After a six-year apprenticeship at his uncle's restaurant in Nice (near Escoffier's home village of Villeneuve-Loubet), Escoffier had gone to Paris when he was nineteen, spending the next five years at the fashionable Le Petit Moulin. Later he admit-

ted how hard he found the work; a sensitive man, the conditions of a busy kitchen with its incessant din and vulgar behavior were hard to bear, and being small, Escoffier was forced to wear platform shoes to avoid suffocation by the burning heat of the stovetops. At the time of the siege of Paris in 1870 (famous for its culinary curiosities as the hungry population began to deplete the zoo), he was drafted as *chef de cuisine* at the headquarters of

the Rhine army in Metz. Metz too was put under siege. "Horsemeat," Escoffier later remarked, "is delicious when you are in the condition to appreciate it . . . and as to rat meat, it approaches in delicacy the taste of roast pig."

*La bonne cuisine est la base du véritable bonheur*

*A. Escoffier*

*Mai 1911*

*During the siege of Paris in 1870, cat, rat, and dog meat was sold openly and the animals at the zoo were slaughtered for food. On the battlefront in Metz, the young Escoffier was learning to make the most of these unpromising materials.*

Soon after this war ended Escoffier returned to Paris where he spent six years as head chef of Le Petit Moulin, followed by posts in several top restaurants. Then, at the height of the winter season at the Grand Hotel in Monte Carlo, César Ritz lost his chef Giroix to the rival Hotel de Paris. Escoffier was called in, and so began the great partnership. In the next six years Escoffier divided his time between Monte Carlo and Ritz's Grand National Hotel in

175

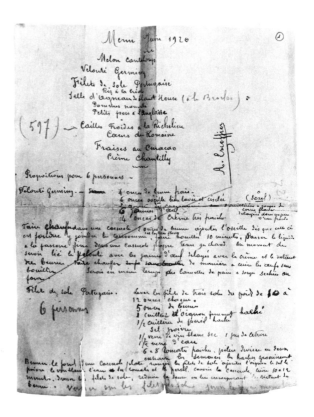

Lucerne, resorts frequented by such celebrities as the Emperor of Austria and the Prince of Wales, for whom Escoffier created his *poularde Derby*. Ritz was past master at attracting such a glittering clientele; his unerring chic was combined with a gift for making each guest personally welcome, to which Escoffier added the crowning touch with his superb cuisine.

Escoffier cut down on the cumbersome garnishes that had survived from the eighteenth century, substituting instead a few simply-cooked vegetables and a sprinkling of parsley, insisting that all must be edible. He gave up the ornamental *hâtelets* (skewers) impaled with truffles, cockscombs, and crayfish, and the elaborate *socles* on which food had been mounted so as to be more impressively displayed. Food, he believed, should look like food. He had an equal abhorrence of a profusion of flavors and aimed instead to achieve the perfect balance of a few superb ingredients. Typical was his *sole Alice*, where sole, poached in wine, is heated in a chafing dish in a sauce flavored with shallots and thyme, to which oysters are added at the last moment. Escoffier was quick to point out that such simplification marked a development, not a decline, in the art of cooking: "What already existed in the time of Carême, which still exists in our time, and which will continue as long as cooking itself," he declared, "is the *fonds* [foundation] of that cooking; because it is simplified on the surface, it does not lose its value; on the contrary. Tastes are constantly being refined and cooking is refined to satisfy them."

In 1889 the Ritz-Escoffier team took over the Savoy Hotel in London. By now their reputation was unrivaled, and they were followed at once by the Rothschilds, the Vanderbilts, the Morgans, the Crespis, and the rest of the *beau monde*. Escoffier was kept busy with his new dishes—*coupe Yvette*, *poularde Adelina Patti*, *consommé favori de Sarah Bernhardt*, and *salade Tosca* are just a few of the hundreds of creations of his fertile imagination. Ritz, with his inimitable style, had persuaded ladies to dine in public for the first time; professional beauties like Lily Langtry were often to be seen at the Savoy, and Nellie Melba lived there whenever she was singing across the way at Covent Garden. It was after her performance in *Lohengrin* that Escoffier served the first version of *pêches Melba*—poached peaches on a bed of vanilla ice cream set in a swan of ice, recalling the swan in the Wagnerian opera. (Not for several years did Escoffier add the

176

Escoffier's style of drafting recipes, with its complex series of cross-references, is hard to follow for anyone without considerable experience. The following selection of his simpler recipes is from *Ma Cuisine*; only the one for *tournedos chasseur* gives an idea of the technical nature of *Le Guide culinaire*, written for the professional chef.

## Purée Crécy

This carrot soup illustrates how even the simplest ingredients are accorded meticulous attention by Escoffier. A *tamis* is a strainer of linen or wire mesh used to give a velvety consistency to soups and sauces.

*Chop 5 or 6 carrots weighing 500 to 600 grams, put them in a pan in which 2 tablespoons of butter have been melted and add a chopped onion; season with a pinch of salt and a small pinch of sugar. Let stew a few minutes. Moisten with a liter of stock; add 125 grams of well-washed rice and cook gently. Strain through a fine tamis; thin the purée to just the right consistency with boiling stock and to finish, stir in 2 tablespoons butter.*
**Garnish:** *little croûtons fried in butter.*
**NOTA.** — *to make the purée into crème Crécy, just before serving add 2 deciliters of boiling cream per liter of purée.*
*The croûtons can be replaced, as you wish, with several spoons of rice or pearl tapioca cooked in consommé.*

22. Tamis pour purée (v. p. 17).

## CREAM OF CARROT SOUP

2 tablespoons (30g) butter
5-6 medium carrots (500-600g) chopped
1 medium onion, chopped
salt
small pinch of sugar
4-5 cups (1-1¼ l) beef or chicken stock
½ cup (125g) rice

TO FINISH:

¾ cup (2 dl) heavy cream
2 tablespoons (30g) butter

FOR CROÛTONS:

3 slices bread (crusts discarded), diced
¼ cup (60g) butter
¼ cup (7cl) oil

This quantity serves 6.

In a heavy-based pan melt the 2 tablespoons (30 grams) butter and add the carrots and onion with the salt and sugar. Cover the pan and cook over low heat 5–7 minutes until the butter is absorbed and the vegetables are soft. Add 4 cups (1 liter) of the stock and the rice, bring to a boil, cover, and simmer 25–30 minutes until the rice and carrots are very tender.

FOR THE CROÛTONS: Fry the bread in the butter and oil until golden brown, stirring so the bread browns evenly. Drain on paper towels and keep warm. When cooked, purée the soup in a blender or work it through a fine strainer. Return it to the pan, bring just to a boil, and add more stock if necessary to make it the consistency of thin cream. Add the cream, bring just back to a boil, and taste the soup for seasoning. Take from the heat, stir in the butter until melted, and serve with the croûtons in a separate bowl.

115. Bassin à blancs d'œufs avec son fouet (v. p. 14).

## Oeufs à la Lorraine

By the time of Escoffier, the traditions begun by Carême of serving certain dishes only at certain meals had hardened into rules which are still followed in classic menus. An egg dish like this one, for instance, should only be served at lunch, as should hors d'oeuvres (of the antipasti type) and substantial cold dishes such as roast beef or lobster salad. At dinner at least one soup is mandatory, and in the old days a cream soup might be followed by a consommé. The garnish à la Lorraine often refers to a combination of cheese and bacon, as in quiche Lorraine. In his measurement of salt to the nearest centigram, Escoffier seems to be carrying precision a little too far!

*General Principles: allow two eggs per person for this method of cooking. The normal amount of butter is 15 grams, of which half is spread in the dish and the rest melted and spooned over the egg yolks. The appropriate seasoning is 32 centigrams of salt for two eggs.*
*For eggs Lorraine: in the bottom of the dish place two slices of lean bacon, blanched and lightly broiled, with some thin slices of Gruyère cheese. Break the eggs on top; surround the yolks with a spoonful of cream and cook them as usual, with attention to the following points.*
*1. cook the white until it looks milky*
*2. the yolks should remain glistening*
*3. do not allow the eggs to catch on the bottom of the dish.*

(continued from previous page)

## BAKED EGGS LORRAINE

8 slices (125g) bacon
4 tablespoons (60g) butter
8 thin slices (125g) Gruyère cheese, halved
8 eggs
½ cup (1.25 dl) heavy cream
salt

4 shallow individual baking dishes or 1 large shallow baking dish

This quantity serves 4 as a light supper dish. For an appetizer, halve the quantities and bake the eggs in smaller dishes.

Set the oven at hot (400°F or 205°C). Broil the bacon, keeping it as flat as possible. Spread half the butter in the baking dishes, set the bacon in the bottom and add the cheese, overlapping it so it does not spread up the sides of the dishes. Carefully break in the eggs, spoon the cream around the edges of the yolks, and sprinkle with a little salt. Melt the remaining butter, sprinkle it on the yolks of the eggs and bake them in the heated oven for 12–15 minutes until the whites are milky; the eggs will continue to cook in the heat of the dishes. Serve them at once.

## *Sole Alice*

*Sole Alice*, one of the innumerable recipes Escoffier named for celebrities, honors Princess Alice of Athlone, a granddaughter of Queen Victoria. The cooking is completed in a chafing dish at the table.

*Have ready an excellent fish stock, concentrated and very pale.—Trim the sole; place it in a special heatproof earthenware dish, with the base buttered, and poach it gently. At the right moment send it to the dining room with a plate on which are arranged separately: a little finely chopped onion, a little ground thyme, 3 finely ground rusks and 6 raw oysters.*

*At the table, the maître d'hôtel sets the dish on a burner, lifts out the sole, then detaches the fillets and puts them between two hot plates. To the cooking liquid from the sole he adds the onion and cooks it a few moments; then the thyme and enough breadcrumbs to bind the liquid; at the last moment, he adds the oysters and 30 grams of butter, in small pieces. As soon as the oysters are firm, he replaces the sole fillets in the dish, bastes them generously with the sauce and serves them at once, very hot.*

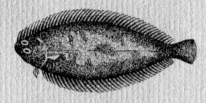

## SOLE ALICE

1 whole (about ¾ pound or 400g) Dover or lemon sole, flounder, or other flat white fish
2 tablespoons finely chopped onion
½ teaspoon powdered thyme
¼ cup (30g) very fine browned breadcrumbs
6 shucked oysters, drained
2 tablespoons (30g) butter, cut in small pieces
salt and pepper

### FOR THE FISH STOCK:

½ pound (250g) fish heads and bones
1½ cups (3.75 dl) water
¾ cup (2 dl) dry white wine
1 slice onion
sprig of parsley
5-6 peppercorns

Escoffier made this dish with Dover sole from the English Channel. Sometimes imported into the United States, it is the only small flat fish which can be skinned raw and left on the bone. With any other type of sole or flatfish, it is best to poach the fish in fillets so the skin can be removed before cooking. This recipe serves 1.

FOR THE FISH STOCK: Wash the fish heads and bones and put them in a pan with the water, white wine, onion, parsley, and peppercorns. Bring to a boil and simmer 20 minutes. Strain and boil until reduced to ¾ cup (2 deciliters). Pour the stock over the whole fish or fish fillets in a buttered flameproof dish, cover with buttered paper, and bake in a moderate oven (350°F or 177°C), allowing 10–12 minutes for fillets or 15–20 minutes for a whole fish or until the fish can almost be flaked; it can be cooked in advance.

To serve, take the fish in its dish to the table with the onion, thyme, breadcrumbs, oysters, and butter. Heat the fish over a table burner until very hot; lift it out, discard the bone if using Dover sole, and keep the fish fillets on a warm plate. Add the onion to the fish stock and simmer 1–2 minutes until soft. Stir in the thyme and breadcrumbs—the sauce should be the consistency of thin cream. Add the oysters and butter and cook just until the edges of the oysters curl, shaking the pan so the butter melts into the sauce. Taste for seasoning; replace the fish fillets, baste them thoroughly with sauce, and serve as soon as the fish is very hot.

The singer Nellie Melba (below, right) was one of Escoffier's favorite patrons, and he named several dishes for her. It was during one of her periodic slimming bouts that Melba toast received its title.

The original pêches Melba (left), an ice swan filled with vanilla ice cream and poached peaches, was more to her usual taste.

crowning touch of fresh raspberry sauce.) When Ritz opened his hotel in the Place Vendôme in 1896, the story was the same, and all Paris flocked to sample Escoffier's cuisine. Three years later he was on the move again, back to London and Ritz's new Carlton Hotel. Here at last he found time to assemble his recipes and ideas on cooking, published as *Le Guide culinaire* in 1902.

*Le Guide culinaire* is an astounding compendium of classic recipes and garnishes—over 5,000 in all—and Escoffier acknowledges the help of several other top chefs. Starting with the *fonds*—the basic sauces, stocks, and pastries—Escoffier builds them like bricks into the great dishes for which he and the chefs before him were so famous. "A tool rather than a book" was his stated aim, and behind its somewhat forbidding façade of technicality lie forty years of practical experience in making almost every dish. What it is not, is a guide for the private kitchen, and even a layman who can follow the recipes would still be hard pressed to reproduce them at home. For example, the recipe for one of Escoffier's specialities, *tournedos Rossini*, in the space of five

*Sarah Bernhardt* (left), one of Escoffier's most famous clients.

lines uses two technical terms (*sauter* and *déglacer*), two basic preparations (meat-glaze and demi-glace sauce) which take hours of advance cooking and which themselves demand other basic preparations, and an ingredient (fresh foie gras) which is a rarity even in Paris. To the professional chef, however, who knows cooking terms intimately and has all the basic sauces ready at hand, *Le Guide culinaire* is the perfect quick guide to thousands of recipes—it is indeed the "constant companion" that Escoffier hoped it would become.

Escoffier was not without his critics. "It would be difficult to serve these *suprêmes* in the way they were created," remarked a cookbook called *La grande cuisine illustrée*, referring to an Escoffier dish *suprêmes de volailles Otéro*. "Their only originality, hardly a recommendation, was to be placed on croûtons cut from truffles of which the smallest must have weighed a pound after peeling." The writers were two young chefs, Prosper Montagné and Prosper Salles, both trained under Giroix, Escoffier's rival in Monte Carlo. Their book shows even more clearly than *Le Guide culinaire* (which appeared two years later) how far cooking had developed from the fulsome *pièces montées* of mid-century, but it was a less comprehensive work than Escoffier's and never earned the same fame for its authors. It was more than thirty-five years before Prosper Montagné proved himself Escoffier's equal in influence and prestige as author of *Larousse gastronomique*, the outstanding encyclopedia of cookery to which Escoffier contributed a generous introduction just before his death.

Escoffier's greatest innovations were in menu-planning, which had already begun to change shortly after Carême's death in 1833. For hundreds of years, dinners had been served in the style called *à la française*, with a large number of different dishes set out on the table at once. The dishes might be changed twice or even three times to make three or four courses. The basic idea was to make an impressive show of luxury, with as great a variety of dishes as possible (a principle dating from medieval banquets). *Service à la russe*, which gradually replaced *service à la française*, is the practice we know today of serving dishes consecutively rather than simultaneously. It has two great advantages: food is served at once while at its best, and wastage is reduced because quantities can be estimated better. Carême had come across *service à la russe* during his time in Russia and it did not suit his love of show. "This manner of service is certainly beneficial to good cooking," he admitted, "but our service in France is much more elegant and of a far grander and more sumptuous style."

For this reason *service à la russe* was slow to spread and it was not until 1856, when Urbain Dubois, who had cooked for twenty years in Russia, produced his massive *La Cuisine classique* with Emile Bernard (both "men of genius" in Escoffier's eyes) that the method caught on. By the 1870s, when Escoffier appeared on the scene, *service à la russe* was universal, enabling him to drastically reduce the number of

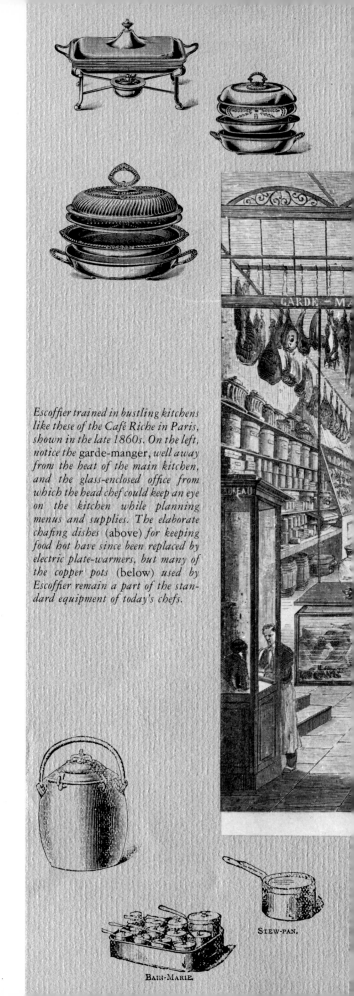

*Escoffier trained in bustling kitchens like these of the Café Riche in Paris, shown in the late 1860s. On the left, notice the* garde-manger, *well away from the heat of the main kitchen, and the glass-enclosed office from which the head chef could keep an eye on the kitchen while planning menus and supplies. The elaborate chafing dishes (above) for keeping food hot have since been replaced by electric plate-warmers, but many of the copper pots (below) used by Escoffier remain a part of the standard equipment of today's chefs.*

BAIN-MARIE.

STEW-PAN.

GRANDS RESTAURANTS DE PARIS. — Les nouvelles cuisines du café Riche, fondé en 1785, agrandi en 1865.

BOILING-POT.

BRAIZING PAN.

BLOCK TIN SAUCEPAN.

DOUBLE, OR MILK, SAUCEPAN.

STOCK-POT.

DINER SERVI A LA FRANÇAISE.

DINER SERVI A LA RUSSE.

dishes in his menus. In *Le Livre des menus*, published in 1912, he outlines the principles that should underlie a well-planned meal: it should be appropriate to the occasion and to the guests; the season should always be borne in mind; if time is limited, the menu should be as well, and in any case a superfluity of courses should be avoided. A typical winter dinner served at the Carlton Hotel consisted of: blini and caviar; consommé; sole in white wine sauce; partridge and noodles with foie gras; lamb *noisettes* with artichoke hearts and peas; champagne sherbet (all such menus were broken up by a tart wine or fruit sherbet to refresh the palate); turkey with truffles; endive and asparagus salad; and various desserts. Even allowing for smaller helpings, such a repast is lavish by our standards, but nonetheless it called for but a fraction of the dishes that Carême would have served for a comparable meal *à la française.*

Grey-haired and gentle of manner—according to Madame Ritz he "looked like a man of letters"—Escoffier would leave the kitchen rather than lose his temper with an erring subordinate. In this he was very different from the traditional loud-mouthed chef. At the beginning of his career, the profession had not been highly regarded, and with his own unhappy apprenticeship in mind, Escoffier was determined to improve it. He forbade the swearing and general brutality that had been the rule, insisting that a well-run kitchen should be calm. He himself never raised his voice and, symbolically, he changed the name of the *aboyeur* who barked out orders to *announceur*. About the appalling heat he could do little, but he saw to it that a

*Prosper Montagné (below), author of the* Larousse gastronomique, *was Escoffier's contemporary and a rival for fame.*

## Poulet grand-mère

This simple chicken dish from *Ma Cuisine* is bourgeois cooking at its best—an interesting contrast to the elegance of such recipes as *tournedos chasseur*. Grand-mère (grandmother-style) always means good home cooking.

*Stuff the chicken with the following mixture:*
*Lightly brown in butter a spoonful of finely chopped onion, mix in 60 grams of ground sausage meat, the chopped liver of the chicken, a pinch of parsley and 2 spoonsful bread-crumbs, all moderately seasoned with salt and pepper. Truss the chicken and put it in an earthenware cas-serole with 50 grams of lean bacon cut in very small dice, a spoonful of butter and 10 baby onions. Cover the casserole, and set it over low heat. As soon as the chicken and the onions are golden brown, add 300 grams of potatoes, cut in small cubes; continue cooking over low heat.*
*Serve the chicken in the same cas-serole.*

## CHICKEN GRAND-MÈRE

2½-pound (1¼-kg) whole chicken,
  with the liver
3 tablespoons (45g) butter
½ cup (2 ounces or 60g) diced
  Canadian or other lean
  bacon
10 baby onions, blanched
  and peeled
salt and pepper
2 medium potatoes

FOR THE STUFFING:

½ medium onion, finely
  chopped
1 tablespoon (15g) butter
¼ cup (2 ounces or 60g)
  sausage meat or 1
  country sausage, skinned
2 teaspoons chopped parsley
⅓ cup (30g) fresh white
  breadcrumbs
salt and pepper

Trussing needle and string

This recipe serves 2.

FOR THE STUFFING: Sauté the onion in the butter until lightly browned; add the sausage meat or skinned country sausage and stir to break up. Add the chicken liver, chopped, and cook until just brown. Take from the heat and stir in the parsley, breadcrumbs, and salt and pepper to taste. Let cool, fill the chicken with the stuffing, and truss it.

In a casserole melt the 3 table-spoons butter, add the chicken, bacon, and onions with salt and pepper to taste. Cover tightly and cook over very low heat, stirring and turning the chicken from time to time, for 20 minutes; the chick-en, onions, and bacon should be lightly browned. Peel the potatoes, cut them in ½-inch cubes, and add to the casserole. Cover and con-tinue cooking, stirring occasion-ally, for 20–25 minutes longer or until the chicken is very tender and the potatoes are browned. Remove the trussing strings from the chicken and serve it in the cas-serole.

## Pêches Melba

This most famous of all Escoffier's recipes is rarely made correctly; i.e., with fresh peaches, fresh raspberry purée, and homemade

vanilla ice cream. A timbale is a high-sided metal dish, often made of silver plate; the name comes from the Arabic *at-thobal*, the drum.

*Choose tender peaches with flesh that does not adhere to the pit; plunge them briefly in boiling water, lift them out quickly with a slotted spoon and put them in water with ice cubes; peel them, set them on a plate, sprinkle them with sugar and chill. Have ready a very creamy vanilla ice cream and a sweetened purée of the freshest possible raspberries.*
*Arrange the ice cream in a timbale or in a crystal bowl, set the peaches on the ice cream and coat with rasp-berry purée.*
*NOTA.—During the season for fresh almonds, finely slivered almonds may be sprinkled on the peaches if you like; never use dried almonds.*

## PEACH MELBA

6 ripe freestone peaches
1 lemon (for coating)
a little sugar (for sprinkling)
1½ pints (7.5 dl) vanilla ice
  cream, if possible
  homemade

FOR THE PURÉE:

1 quart (500g) fresh raspberries
  or 2 packages (500g) frozen
  raspberries
confectioners' sugar to taste

6 coupe or sherbet glasses

As with all simple recipes, peach Melba depends on the quality of the peaches, ice cream, and rasp-berries used to make it. This recipe serves 6.

Pour boiling water over the peaches, let stand a few seconds, and transfer to a bowl of ice water containing ice cubes; if very ripe, the skin will peel easily after 10 seconds' soaking in boiling water but longer may be necessary if they

*(continued from previous page)*

are less ripe. Rub the peaches with a cut lemon and sprinkle at once with sugar to prevent browning. Set them on a plate, cover tightly with plastic wrap, and chill. If this is done quickly, the peaches can be prepared 3–4 hours ahead and will not discolor.

FOR THE PURÉE: Work the raspberries in a blender with sugar to taste — the purée should be fairly tart and if frozen raspberries are used, extra sugar may not be needed. Strain the purée to remove the seeds and chill it. Chill the coupe glasses.

Just before serving, spread vanilla ice cream in the base of the coupe glasses. Set a peach on top, spoon the raspberry purée over the peaches, and serve at once.

## *Soufflé Rothschild*

Soufflé Rothschild is enriched with candied fruits macerated in Danziger goldwasser, a liqueur appropriately flecked with gold leaf. The recipe is scattered over several pages of *Ma Cuisine.* Starting with the *soufflé Rothschild* ingredients, one must turn back to the mixture for *soufflé à la crème,* and back yet again to the method of cooking.

*To the mixture for* **soufflé à la crème,** *add 80 grams of diced candied fruits macerated in a good Danziger goldwasser with plenty of gold flakes. Just before serving, surround the soufflé with a border of large fresh strawberries, or when they are out of season with preserved cherries.*
*Mixture for* **soufflé à la crème** *for four people: 1 deciliter milk; 35 grams sugar, a spoonful of flour; 10 grams of butter; 2 egg yolks; 3 egg whites, very stiffly beaten.*
*Bring the milk to a boil with the sugar, add the flour, mixed to a*

*smooth paste with a little cold milk and cook the mixture for 2 minutes; take from the heat and finish it with the butter, egg yolks and egg whites. Presentation and cooking of soufflés: Soufflés are served in a timbale or in a special mold buttered and sprinkled with sugar. They should be cooked in a fairly moderate oven so that the heat slowly penetrates the mixture. Two minutes before taking the soufflé from the oven, sprinkle the top with sugar so it caramelizes and glazes the surface.*
*The decoration of soufflés is a matter of choice but should always be simple.*

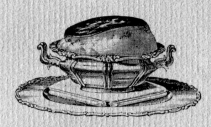

## SOUFFLÉ ROTHSCHILD

¾ cup (160g) chopped mixed candied fruit
¼ cup (7cl) Danziger goldwasser
confectioners' sugar (for sprinkling)
8–10 large fresh strawberries or 1 can (8 ounces or 250g) cherries in light syrup (for garnish)

### FOR THE SOUFFLÉ MIXTURE:

⅔ cup (1.75dl) milk
¼ cup (60g) sugar
2 tablespoons (20g) flour mixed to a paste with ¼ cup (7cl) milk
1 tablespoon (15g) butter
4 egg yolks
6 egg whites

Soufflé dish (1½-quart or 1½-liter capacity)

Escoffier's allowance of 2 eggs and 1 egg white to make a soufflé for 4 people seems rather optimistic; here the quantities have been doubled to serve 4. Kirsch can be substituted for the Danziger goldwasser.

Finely chop the candied fruit, add the liqueur, cover, and leave to macerate at least 1 hour. Butter the soufflé dish and sprinkle with sugar.

Heat the milk with the sugar until dissolved and stir in the paste of flour. Bring to a boil, stirring constantly until the mixture thickens, and simmer 2 minutes. Take from the heat, dot the top with the butter, and let cool until tepid. The butter will melt and prevent a skin from forming. This mixture can be prepared 2–3 hours ahead.

To finish the soufflé, preheat the oven to moderately hot (375°F or 190°C). Reheat the milk mixture to soften it. Beat in the egg yolks with the macerated fruit and liqueur, making sure the pieces of fruit do not stick together. Stiffly beat the egg whites and fold into the fruit mixture as lightly as possible. Spoon into the prepared soufflé dish and bake in the heated oven for 15–18 minutes or until the soufflé is puffed and brown—it should still be soft in the center when served. Sprinkle the top of the soufflé with confectioners' sugar and set it on a platter. Arrange the strawberries or cherries around the edge and serve at once.

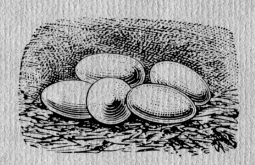

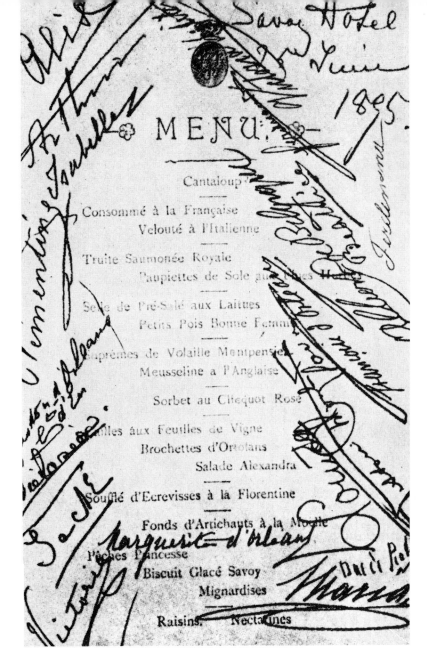

The signatures on this menu from the Savoy Hotel in 1895 include royalty from all over Europe. The occasion was the marriage of the Duke of Aosta and the Duchess of Orleans.

MENU

Cantaloup

Consommé à la Française
Velouté à l'Italienne

Truite Saumonée Royale
Paupiettes de Sole aux ...

Selle de Pré-Salé aux Laitues
Petits Pois Bonne Femme

Suprêmes de Volaille Montpensier
Mousseline a l'Anglaise

Sorbet au Clicquot Rosé

... aux Feuilles de Vigne
Brochettes d'Ortolans
Salade Alexandra

Soufflé d'Ecrevisses à la Florentine

Fonds d'Artichauts à la Moelle

Pêches Princesse
Biscuit Glacé Savoy
Mignardises

Raisins    Nectarines

caldron of barley water was always available for quenching thirst, thus cutting down on the consumption of beer and wine, the cook's habitual failing.

Even more important was Escoffier's revision of kitchen organization. Since medieval times, kitchen staff had been divided into sections, each of which was more or less independent. This meant that general preparations like sauces or pastry might be made several times by different sections—a wasteful duplication that also made quality hard to control. Escoffier reorganized his kitchens into five main sections, called *parties*, each dependent on the others. The *pâtissier* produced the pastry for every *partie*, the *garde-manger* supervised the cold dishes and supplies for the whole kitchen, while hot dishes came either from the *entremettier* (in charge of soups, vegetables, and desserts), or from the *rôtisseur* (roasts and broiled and fried dishes). Second in command under Escoffier, as befitted his importance, was the *saucier*. When a dish was ordered, not only could it be rapidly assembled by the appropriate *parties*, but Escoffier could more easily keep an eye on the finished result. A similar system is still followed in large kitchens today.

Though generally regarded as a great exponent of the *grande cuisine* found in restaurants, Escoffier was equally at ease in a private kitchen. His *Ma cuisine*, published in 1934, is an admirable survey of the *cuisine bourgeoise* that is so popular today—the *poulet sauté bourguignonne*, *brandade de morue*, and *pâté de veau et de jambon* that are the backbone of

French family cooking. The book is as comprehensive as *Le Guide culinaire* and infinitely more usable, with fewer cross-references and more explanation. In Escoffier's own words, "It is not a simple aide-memoire, but truly a cookbook with recipes that are practical and as clear as possible." Nonetheless Escoffier takes for granted considerable cooking knowledge—he gives some quantities but not in a systematic manner. He makes no mention of oven heats, cooking times, or number of servings.

Escoffier remained at the Ritz Carlton until the end of World War I, retiring to Monte Carlo to join his wife when he was seventy-three. He had spared little time for his family (he had three children) but he could look back on six decades of total commitment to cooking. He is remembered as the outstanding chef of the last hundred years and his *Guide culinaire* is still the primary book of reference for his profession. It is to Escoffier that we owe the familiar shape of modern menus which, though reduced since his time, still follow the same logical pattern, and it is he who created many of our favorite dishes. Above all, it is Escoffier who finally put an end to the medieval principle of luxuriant display; after 500 years, quantity had at last surrendered to quality, and gluttony to gourmandise.

186

## Tournedos chasseur

This is a good example of the step-by-step preparation of *haute cuisine*, resulting here in a deceptively simple steak with wine sauce. The recipe requires four basic preparations—stock, demi-glace sauce, meat glaze, and tomato sauce—for the final sauce. It is, moreover, one of Escoffier's easier recipes for tournedos, with no elaborate garnish. A dish with a chasseur (hunter's style) garnish includes either game or a chasseur sauce with mushrooms, shallots, and white wine.

*Sauté the tournedos and arrange them overlapping in a circle. Deglaze the pan with white wine; add the appropriate quantity of sauce chasseur; let simmer a few moments and pour over the tournedos.*

## Sauce chasseur

*Sauté in oil and butter 150 grams of finely chopped fresh mushrooms, letting them brown lightly. Add a spoonful of chopped shallot and almost at once drain off half the fat. Moisten the mixture with 2 deciliters of white wine, a Madeira glass of cognac and reduce by half. Finish with 4 deciliters of sauce demi-glace, 2 deciliters of tomato sauce and half a spoonful of meat glaze.*
*Let the sauce simmer 5 minutes and finish it with a small spoonful of chopped parsley.*

## Sauce demi-glace

*The sauce called "demi-glace" is espagnole sauce finished at the last moment with concentrated brown stock or a good meat glaze.*

## Sauce espagnole

*For a liter of espagnole sauce, prepare 100 grams of roux as described;*

as soon as it is ready, take the pan from the fire, let cool several seconds and stir in a liter of brown stock, using a whisk to obtain a smooth mixture without lumps; bring the sauce to a boil, stirring constantly with a whisk or spatula. Then keep it at the side of the fire, simmering slowly and evenly.

Add a mirepoix prepared thus: 30 grams of fat bacon cut in small cubes; 30 grams of onion, 50 grams of carrot, diced; a sprig of thyme, a small bay leaf and several stalks of parsley. Cook the bacon in a shallow saucepan with 30 grams of butter until the fat runs, add the vegetables and herbs; sauté them gently.

Continue the simmering for 3 hours, adding several deciliters of cold brown stock from time to time to help when skimming the sauce. This clarification will be all the more rapid if the stock is thoroughly flavored with the juices of the meat used to make it.

At the right moment, strain the sauce in a fine strainer set over a bowl, lightly pressing the mirepoix, and whisk the sauce until it is almost cold. Keep in reserve.

## Sauce tomato

For 1 liter of good tomato sauce, choose 3 kilos of fresh tomatoes; halve them; extract the seeds without crushing the tomatoes; chop them, put them in a pan with 75 grams of butter or, better still, 5 soupspoons of olive oil, 10 grams of salt, a pinch of pepper and a bouquet of parsley stalks wrapped around a clove of garlic. Cover the pan; cook for 30–35 minutes over a low fire. Work the sauce through a fine strainer; put the purée that results in a bowl; rub the surface with a piece of butter and set aside.

This method of preparing tomato sauce has the advantage of being quick and of preserving all the fresh flavor of the tomatoes.

## TOURNEDOS CHASSEUR

### FOR THE DEMI-GLACE SAUCE:

3 tablespoons (45g) butter
2 tablespoons (20g) flour
3½-4 cups (9-10dl) brown stock
1 tablespoon diced bacon
1 tablespoon diced onion
2 tablespoons diced carrot
pinch of thyme
small bay leaf
few stalks parsley
1 teaspoon meat glaze

### FOR THE TOMATO SAUCE:

1 pound (500g) fresh tomatoes, halved, seeded, and chopped, or 2 cups (500g) Italian-style canned plum tomatoes, drained and chopped
1 tablespoon (15g) butter or olive oil
few stems parsley wrapped around a peeled clove of garlic and tied
salt and pepper
1 tablespoon (15g) butter (to finish)

### FOR THE CHASSEUR SAUCE:

¼ pound (125g) mushrooms, finely chopped
2 tablespoons oil
2 tablespoons (30g) butter
2 shallots, finely chopped
¾ cup (2dl) white wine
3 tablespoons cognac
demi-glace sauce (ingredients above)
tomato sauce (ingredients above)
1 teaspoon meat glaze
2 teaspoons chopped parsley

### FOR THE TOURNEDOS:

6 tournedos steaks, cut 1½-2 inches (3.75-5cm) thick
1 tablespoon oil
1 tablespoon (15g) butter
salt and pepper
½ cup (1.25dl) white wine
chasseur sauce (ingredients above)
bunch of watercress (for garnish)

Meat glaze can be made by boiling 1½ cups (3.75 deciliters) brown stock until it is reduced to 2 teaspoons. This recipe serves 6.

TO MAKE THE DEMI-GLACE SAUCE: In a heavy-based pan melt 2 tablespoons (30 grams) of the butter, stir in the flour, and cook over moderate heat, stirring constantly, until the flour is nutbrown. Take from the heat, let cool ½ minute, then add 2 cups (5 deciliters) brown stock. Bring to a boil, stirring constantly, and simmer with the lid half on. Melt the remaining butter in a small pan, add the bacon, and cook until the fat runs. Add the onion, carrot, thyme, bay leaf, and parsley and sauté gently for 5–7 minutes or until the fat is absorbed and the vegetables are soft. Add this mirepoix to the sauce and continue simmering. From time to time, add ½ cup (1.25 deciliters) cold stock, bring the sauce back to a boil, and skim; this clarifies the sauce, making it glossy and semitransparent. After 2–3 hours of cooking, when all the stock is added and the sauce is the consistency of thin cream, strain it, pressing the vegetables to extract all the juice. There should be about 2 cups (5 deciliters) sauce. Add the meat glaze, bring to a boil, and taste the sauce for seasoning.

TO MAKE THE TOMATO SAUCE: Put the tomatoes in a heavy-based pan with the 1 tablespoon (15 grams) butter or oil, bunch of parsley, garlic, and a little salt and pep-

*(continued from previous page)*

per. Cover the pan and cook very gently for 30–40 minutes or until the tomatoes are very soft, stirring occasionally. Work the sauce through a fine strainer, reheat it, and simmer until it is thick enough to coat the back of a spoon. Taste the sauce for seasoning and rub the surface with the remaining 1 tablespoon (15 grams) of butter to prevent a skin from forming. There should be about ¾ cup (2 deciliters) sauce.

FOR THE CHASSEUR SAUCE: Sauté the mushrooms in the oil and butter over medium heat until slightly browned. Add the shallots, continue cooking 1 minute, and drain off as much fat as possible. Add the white wine and brandy and reduce the mixture by half. Add the demi-glace and tomato sauces with the meat glaze, bring the sauce to a boil, and simmer 5 minutes. Add the parsley, taste for seasoning, and keep hot.

TO COOK THE TOURNEDOS: In a heavy skillet, heat the oil and butter and sauté the steaks over fairly high heat, allowing 3–4 minutes on each side for rare steak. Sprinkle them with salt and pepper after browning and arrange them overlapping on a hot platter. Deglaze the skillet with the white wine, reduce well, add the chasseur sauce, and simmer a few minutes. Spoon a little of the sauce over the tournedos and serve the rest separately. Garnish the platter with watercress.

*Here Prosper Montagné (in white coat) entertains Escoffier (head of table, right, conversing with his collaborator Philéas Gilbert), Curnonsky (first left) and other members of the inter-war cooking establishment at his legendary Paris restaurant. The names and faces change, but French gastronomy is still ruled by a few influential men whose authority is virtually undisputed.*

# AFTERWORD

So what is happening to cooking now? Where do we go from here? Fannie Farmer would rejoice in the meticulous detail of modern recipes, but now that the battle for precision is won, has that spark of individuality which can make a good dish great been extinguished? Vatel would be relieved that deliveries of fish no longer depend on the vagaries of horse-drawn transport, but with the combustion engine have come standardization and supermarket shopping. Will cooking as an art survive?

Of course it will. Rarely has cooking been so fashionable a pastime or undergone such a revolution, thanks to new technology and the proliferation of ingredients. The cooks themselves have changed. The age-old gulf between the chef and the home cook has narrowed; the two traditions of cooking, represented on the one hand by the *grande cuisine* of Carême and Escoffier, and on the other by the household manuals of Hannah Glasse, Amelia Simmons, and Mrs. Beeton, are converging. Today a chef can make his mark in his profession without long years of menial apprenticeship, while more and more housewives are cooking the specialties of the great chefs in their own homes. The benefit is mutual: the public has a better understanding of what goes into the creation of a great meal, and chefs enjoy the challenge of a more discriminating clientèle.

The finest in cooking is no longer the monopoly of the grand tables. Restaurants are becoming smaller and more personal with the chef's presence often seen as well as felt. Modern life has done away with great *brigades* of cooks and with them the turn-of-the-century tomes that ordered their lives in the kitchen. But even though Escoffier is in eclipse, cooking will always remain inseparable from the master chefs of the past. The latest form of *nouvelle cuisine* has the same inspiration as that declared by Marin in 1742: "less trouble, fewer mixtures yet as much variety; a simpler, cleaner, and more knowledgeable kind of chemistry."

RECIPE INDEX

SELECT BIBLIOGRAPHY

PICTURE CREDITS

# RECIPE INDEX

Original recipes are in italics.

# SELECT BIBLIOGRAPHY

This bibliography covers about eighty books published before 1974, which were most frequently used in researching *Great Cooks and their Recipes*, but it excludes cookbooks already mentioned in the text unless they have been reprinted. For information about the original editions, one of the standard bibliographies listed below (Bitting, Lowenstein, Simon, Vicaire, or Westbury) should be consulted. Further references valuable for the researcher will be found in many of the books included here.

Specialist booksellers catering for the avid collector of antiquarian or out-of-print cookbooks include The Corner Book Shop, 102 4th Avenue, New York; Cookbooks Only, 1727 2nd Avenue, New York; Marian Gore, Box 433, San Gabriel, California; Librairie Salet, 5 Quai Voltaire, Paris; Librairie Morcrette, Box 26, 95270 Luzarches (just outside Paris); and in England, John Lyle, Harpford, Sidmouth, Devon, and Janet Clarke, Manor House, Hunsterson, Nantwich, Cheshire.

Academia Italiana della Cucina: *Atti.* Printed in Milan. First meeting, 1969; second meeting, 1971; third meeting, 1973; fourth meeting, 1974. This organization was founded to do serious research into the history of cooking in Italy. Its proceedings cover an interesting variety of topics, from the Venetian spice trade to the influence of French cooking in the Renaissance and of Italian cooking in England.

Acton, Eliza: *Modern Cookery*. London, 1845. Reprint. Elek Books, London, 1966.

Aebischer, Paul: "Un Manuscrit valaisan du *Viandier* attribué à Taillevent." *Vallesia*, Bulletin annuel de la Bibliothèque et des Archives cantonales du Valais, Suisse, no. 7, 1953. The author argues that this *Viandier* manuscript antedates Taillevent.

Ainsworth-Davies, J. R.: *Cooking through the Centuries*. Dent, London, 1931.

Alberini, Massimo: *Storia del pranzo all'italiana*. Rizzoli, Milan, 1966.

————:*4000 Anni a tavola*. Fabbri, Milan, 1972.

American Heritage Magazine: *The American Heritage Cookbook and Illustrated History of American Eating and Drinking*. American Heritage Publishing Co., New York, 1964.

Apicius: see Guégan, Bertrand.

Aylett, Mary and Olive Ordish: *First Catch Your Hare*. Macdonald, London, 1965.

Barber, Richard: *Cooking from Rome to the Renaissance*. Allen Lane, London, 1973.

Battiscombe, Georgina: *English Picnics*. Harvill Press, London, 1949.

Beeton, Isabella: *Beeton's Book of Household Management*. London, 1861. Reprint. Jonathan Cape, London, 1968.

Bitting, Katherine Golden: *Gastronomic Bibliography*. San Francisco, 1939. Reprint. Gryphon Books, Ann Arbor, Michigan, 1971.

Booth, Sally Smith: *Hung, Strung and Potted*. Potter, New York, 1971.

Burnet, Regula, ed.: *Ann Cook and Friend*. Oxford University Press, Oxford, 1936. This book recounts the bizarre tale of Ann Cook's attacks on Hannah Glasse.

Carême, Antonin: *Le Cuisinier parisien*. Second edition, Paris, 1828. Reprint. Daniel Morcrette, Luzarches, France, 1976.

Carson, Jane: *Colonial Virginia Cookery*. Colonial Williamsburg, 1968.

Castelot, André: *L'Histoire à table*. Plon, Paris, 1972.

Child, Lydia: *The American Frugal Housewife*. Boston, 1829. Reprint (12th edition, 1832). Ohio State University Library, 1971.

Clair, Colin: *Kitchen and Table*. Abelard-Schuman, London, 1964.

Cougnet, Alberto: *I Piaceri della tavola*. Bocca, Turin, 1903. This is a good history of banquets in France and Italy, although references and dates are sometimes vague.

Courtine, Robert: *La Gastronomie*. Presses Universitaires de France, Paris, 1970.

Dodds, Madeleine Hope: "The Rival Cooks: Hannah Glasse and Ann Cook." *Archeologia Aeliana*, Society of Antiquaries, Newcastle upon Tyne, ser. 4, vol. 15, 1938. It was in this authoritative article that Hannah Glasse's origins were first unveiled. I am grateful to Mr. L. G. Allgood, a direct descendant of Sir Lancelot Allgood (Hannah's half-brother) for providing me with additional information about Hannah taken from family letters (now in the keeping of Newcastle Public Library) which Mr. A. H. T. Robb-Smith summarized in some unpublished notes written in 1961.

Dombes, Prince de (attrib.): *Le Cuisinier gascon*. Amsterdam, 1740. Reprint. Daniel Morcrette, Luzarches, France, 1976.

Dumay, Raymond: *De la gastronomie française*. Stock, Paris, 1969.

Eluard-Valette, Cécile: *Les grandes heures de la cuisine française*. Librairies Associés, Paris, 1964.

Escoffier, Auguste: *Le Guide culinaire*. Paris, 1902. Reprinted frequently by Flammarion, Paris. Available in English as *A Guide to Modern Cookery*, Heinemann, London, 1957.

————: *Ma cuisine*. Paris, 1934. Reprinted frequently by Flammarion, Paris.

Faccioli, Emilio, ed.: *Arte della cucina*. 2 vols. Edizione il Polifilo, Milan, 1966. Contains full text of Martino ms. and extracts from other classical Italian cookbooks, including Scappi's *Opera* and Leonardi's *L'Apicio moderno*.

Farmer, Fannie: *The Boston Cooking-School Cook Book*. 1896. Reprint. Hugh Lauter Levin, New York, 1973.

————: *The Book of Good Dinners*. 1905. Reprint. Pyne Press, Princeton, 1972.

Fayot, F., ed.: *Les Classiques de la table*. Paris, 1843. Several different editions published over the years; most include an autobiographical fragment of Carême.

Francatelli, Charles E.: *The Modern Cook*. 1846. Reprint. Dover Publications, New York, 1976.

Franklin, Benjamin: *On the Art of Eating*. American Philosophical Society, Philadelphia, 1958.

Gault, Henri and Christian Millau: *Guide gourmand de la France*. Librairie Hachette, Paris, 1970. No country but France, surely, could fill a thousand pages of fine print with its gastronomic geography and history. A remarkable village-by-village account of French food.

Glasse, Hannah: *The Art of Cookery Made Plain and Easy*. London, 1747. Reprint of 1796 edition. S.R. Publishers, Wakefield, 1971.

Gottschalk, Alfred: *Histoire de l'alimentation et de la gastronomie*. 2 vols. Editions Hippocrate, Paris, 1948.

Guégan, Bertrand: *Les dix livres de cuisine d'Apicius*. René Bonnel, Paris, 1933.

————: *Le Cuisinier français*. Emile Paul Frères, Paris, 1934. The ninety-page introduction is one of the best historical surveys of French cooking.

Hampson, John: *The English at Table*. Collins, London, 1946.

Hartley, Dorothy: *Food in England*. Macdonald, London, 1954. A landmark in English culinary literature.

Hayward, A.: *The Art of Dining*. John Murray, London, 1883. A short classic.

Hazlitt, W. Carew: *Old Cookery Books and Ancient Cuisine*. New York, 1886. Reprint. Gale Research Co, Detroit, 1968. A standard if sometimes unreliable reference.

Herbert, A. Kenney: "The Literature of Cookery." *National Review*, 1895, pp. 676–684, 776–789.

Herbodeau, Eugène and Paul Thalamas: *Georges Auguste Escoffier*. Practical Press, London, 1955.

Horizon Magazine: *The Horizon Cookbook and Illustrated History of Eating and Drinking through the Ages*. American Heritage Publishing Co., New York, 1968.

Hyde, H. Montgomery: *Mr. & Mrs. Beeton*. Harrap, London, 1951.

Jeaffreson, John Cordy: *A Book about the Table*. 2 vols. Hurst and Blackett, London, 1875. A romantic but reliable commentary on food.

Lacroix, Paul: *Manners, Customs and Dress during the Middle Ages and during the Renaissance Period*. London, 1874.

Layard, A. H.: "Renaissance Cookery." *Murray's Magazine*, March, 1891.

Lotteringhi della Stufa, Maria Luisa: *Desinari e cene*. Olimpia, Florence, 1965.

————: *Pranzi e conviti*. Olimpia, Florence, 1965. Entertaining and very well documented histories of mainly Tuscan cooking through the centuries; contains a useful bibliography.

Lowenstein, Eleanor: *Bibliography of American Cookery Books 1742–1860*. Corner Book Shop, New York, 1972.

Mallock, M. M.: "Old English Cookery." *Quarterly Review*, January, 1894. An excellent short account.

Martino: see Faccioli, Emilio.

Messisbugo, Cristoforo da: *Banchetti*. Ferrara, 1549. Reprint. Neri Pozza, Venice, 1960, with notes by Fernando Bandini.

Montagné, Prosper: *Larousse gastronomique*. Revised edition by Robert J. Courtine, Librairie Hachette, Paris, 1960.

Morris, Helen: *Portrait of a Chef*. Cambridge University Press, Cambridge, 1938. This interesting account of Soyer's life draws considerably from a little-known work by F. Volant and J. R. Warren: *Memoirs of Alexis Soyer*. W. Kent, London, 1859.

Nicolardot, Louis: *Histoire de la table*. E. Dentu, Paris, 1868. One of the best of the nineteenth-century histories of French cooking.

Norman, Barbara: *Tales of the Table*. Prentice-Hall, Englewood Cliffs, New Jersey, 1972.

Pegge, Samuel, ed.: *The Forme of Cury*. J. Nichols, London, 1780.

Pennell, Elizabeth: *My Cookery Books*. Houghton Mifflin, Boston, 1903.

Pichon, Jérôme et Georges Vicaire, eds.: *Le Viandier de Guillaume Tirel dit Taillevent*. Paris, 1842. Reprint. Daniel Morcrette, Luzarches, France, 1976.

Pichon, Jérôme, ed.: *Le Menagier de Paris*. Paris, 1846. Reprint. Daniel Morcrette, Luzarches, France, 1963. Translated by Eileen Power as *The Goodman of Paris*. George Routledge, London, 1928.

Raffald, Elizabeth: *The Experienced English Housekeeper*. London, 1769. Reprint of 1782 edition. E & W Books, London, 1970. An interesting article about Mrs. Raffald appears in *Manchester Collectanea*, Proceedings of the Chetham Society, vol. 2, 1872.

Randolph, Mary: *The Virginia Housewife*. Washington, 1824. Reprint of 1860 edition. Avenel Books, New York.

Root, Waverley: *The Cooking of Italy*. Time-Life Books, New York, 1968.

————: *The Food of Italy*. Atheneum, New York, 1971. An authoritative and highly readable account of the cooking of the Italian regions.

Simmons, Amelia: *American Cookery*. Hartford, 1796. Reprint. Oxford University Press, New York, 1958, with an interesting introduction by Mary Tolford Wilson.

Simon, André: *Bibliotheca Gastronomica*. Wine and Food Society, London, 1953.

————: "From Esau to Escoffier: or the history of gastronomy." *Wine and Food*, no. 28, 1940. The early numbers of this magazine, edited by André Simon, contain several useful articles.

Smallzried, Kathleen Ann: *The Everlasting Pleasure*. Appleton Century, New York, 1956.

Smith, E.: *The Compleat Housewife*. London, 1727. Reprint of 1753 edition. Literary Services and Production Ltd., London, 1968.

Soyer, Alexis: *A Shilling Cookery for the People*. London, 1854. Reprint. David McKay, New York, 1959, as *Soyer's Cookery Book*.

Spain, Nancy: *Mrs. Beeton and her Husband*. Collins, London, 1948.

Stobart, Tom: *Herbs, Spices and Flavourings*. David and Charles, Devon, 1970.

Taillevent: see Pichon, Jérôme.

Varenne, La: *Le Cuisinier françois*, Paris, 1651. A later edition (Amsterdam, about 1696) which includes *Le Maître d'hôtel* and *Le grand Ecuyer-Tranchant* has now been reprinted (Daniel Morcrette, Luzarches, France, 1976).

———— (attrib.): *Le Pastissier françois*. Paris, 1653. The famous Elzevir edition of 1655 was reprinted by Librairie Dorbon Ainé, Paris, 1931, with an introduction by Maurice des Ombiaux.

Vehling, J. D.: "Martino and Platina, Exponents of Renaissance Cookery." *Hotel Bulletin and The Nation's Chefs*, vol. 49, no. 14, Chicago, 1932. Mr. Vehling was the finder of the Martino ms. now in the Library of Congress. Since this ms. is identical not only to the recipe sections in Platina's *De honesta voluptate et valetudine* (1474) but also to the cookbook *Epulario* (1516), Vehling's assumption that the ms. dates from about 1450 – i.e., was extant before Platina wrote his work – is questionable. An article by Agostino Cavalcabo ("Platina, maestro dell'arte culinaria," in *Cremona*, no. 7, 1935) and Vehling's subsequent monograph (*Platina and the Rebirth of Man*, Chicago, 1941) throw no further light on dating.

Vence, Céline and Robert Courtine: *Les grands maîtres de la cuisine française*. Bordas, Paris, 1972.

Vicaire, Georges: *Bibliographie gastronomique*. Paris, 1890. Reprint. Holland Press, London, 1954.

Warner, Richard: *Antiquitates Culinariae*. London, 1791. Not a Latin work, but one of the earliest English histories of gastronomy; still makes racy reading. Contains *The Forme of Cury*, in a more readable style than Samuel Pegge's original.

Westbury, Lord: *Handlist of Italian Cookery Books*. Leo S. Olschki, Florence, 1963. Includes an excellent introductory essay on Italian cookery.

Whitehall, Jane: *Food, Drink and Recipes of Early New England*. Old Sturbridge Village, Mass., 1963.

Wright, Thomas: *The Homes of Other Days*. London, 1871. Reprint. Singing Tree Press, Detroit, 1968.

# PICTURE CREDITS

## A

The Abby Aldrich Rockefeller Folk Art Collection: 116;

American Antiquarian Society: 119 (top); 121 (bottom); 126 (top);

The Art Institute of Chicago, Chicago: 122/123;

Author's Archives: 17; 33 (left and center, right and bottom, right); 39 (top); 41 (top); 44; 59 (top and center); 64/65 (bottom); 73 (top, right); 78; 87 (left); 89 (top); 90 (bottom); 93 (bottom); 117 (top, right); 126 (bottom); 129 (center, right); 140; 147 (center); 161 (center); 164; 165; 168; 169; 170; 171; 179 (top); 182 (top, left and right); 185;

## B

Bergamo-Collection, Lorenzelli B.: 106/107;

Biblioteca Estense, Modena: 25 (right; Photo Orlandini);

Bibliothèque de l'Arsenal, Paris: 51 (top; Photo J. Colomb-Gérard); 56 (left; Photo J. Colomb-Gérard);

Bibliothèque Nationale, Paris: 6; 9 (top, right); 12 (top); 21 (left); 28 (bottom); 31; 46; 47 (bottom, right); 82/83 (bottom); 86 (top); 134 (top, left and bottom);

The Boston Athenaeum, Boston: 118 (left; Photo Sam Masotta); 160;

British Museum, London: 9 (bottom, right); 10 (top and left); 12 (bottom); 16;

Bulloz, Paris: 13 (Musée du Petit Palais, Paris); 79 (top);

## C

Civica Raccolta Stampe Bertarelli, Milan: 110 (bottom); 114;

Collection Allgood: 96/97 (top; Photo Northumberland County Records Office);

Pa., Collection of Fred Wichmann: 125 (Photo Courtesy of the John Gordon Gallery, New York);

Collections of The Historical Society of York County, York: 127 (Photo Hayman Studio);

## E

Ermitage Museum, Leningrad: 71 (Giraudon, Photo Hanfstaengl);

## F

William A. Farnsworth Library and Art Museum, Rockland, Maine: 124;

J. Freeman, London: 64/65 (center); British Library, London 2/3; 10 (right); 11 (bottom, left); 18; 22; 23; 24 (top and right); 29; 33 (top, right); 34; 36; 37 (top and bottom); 38; 39 (left and center, right and bottom, right); 42; 51 (bottom); 54 (top); 55 (bottom); 56 (right); 60; 61; 62 (center and bottom); 63 (right); 64/65 (top); 76 (right); 77; 79 (bottom); 87 (right); 90 (top); 99 (top); 128; 129 (top and center, left); 130 (left); 131; 132/133; 135; 136 (left); 138; 141; 145; 150; 154 (bottom); 156; 158 (top); 176 (bottom); 177; British Museum, London: 58; 59 (bottom); 69; 82 (center); 93 (top); 98; Mary Evans Picture Library, London: 92;

## G

Giraudon, Paris: 8 (Musée Condé, Chantilly); 75; 100 (Museo Cà Rezzonico, Venice); 113 (bottom; Museo Cà Rezzonico, Venice);

## H

Hachette, Paris: 85;

Hotel Ritz, Paris: 173 (bottom);

## K

Kunsthistorisches Museum, Vienna: 43 (center, left);

## L

R. Lalance: 55 (top); 72; 73 (bottom, right); 129 (bottom); 130 (top); 134 (top, right); 172; 175 (center);

The Library of Congress, Washington: 21 (top, right);

## M

The Mansell Collection, London: 28 (top); 40 (Photo Alinari); 49; 66/67; 154 (top); 158 (bottom);

Manuel Frères: 188/189;

Mary Evans Picture Library, London: 54 (bottom); 62 (top); 68; 91 (bottom); 99 (bottom); 139; 147 (bottom); 148 (center and top); 155; 157 (bottom); 180/181 (top);

The Metropolitan Museum of Art, New York: 43 (right; Rogers Fund, 1947); 94/95;

Daniel Morcrette, Luzarches: 19; 101 (top); 102; 173 (center);

Musée de l'Art Culinaire, Villeneuve-Loubet: 175 (top); 176 (top; Photo Cl. Mille);

Musée de Strasbourg, Strasbourg: 52/53 (Cliché Franz);

Musée National du Louvre, Paris: 32 (Photo Agraci); 48 (Photo Agraci); 130 (right; Cabinet des Dessins; Photo Musées Nationaux);

Musées Nationaux, Paris: 80/81;

Musée Réattu, Arles: 82 (top);

Museo del Castello Sforzesco, Milan: 101 (bottom);

Museo Nazionale di S. Martino, Naples: 105;

Museo Storico degli Spaghetti, Pontedassio, Imperia (Collezione Agnesi): 30; 109; 115;

## N

National Portrait Gallery, London: 147 (top);